14⁹⁵

Donn J Nepute
426-3616

The Master of Sunnybank

The Master at his downstairs study desk

The Master
of Sunnybank

A BIOGRAPHY OF

Albert Payson Terhune

IRVING LITVAG

1817

HARPER & ROW, PUBLISHERS

New York, Hagerstown, San Francisco,
London

Excerpt on page 91, "His Mate," from *Lad: A Dog* by Albert Payson Terhune. Published by E. P. Dutton & Company. Reprinted by permission.

FIRST EDITION

Designed by Sidney Feinberg

Library of Congress Cataloging in Publication Data

Litvag, Irving.
    The master of Sunnybank, a biography of
Albert Payson Terhune.
    1. Terhune, Albert Payson, 1872–1942—
Biography. 2. Authors, American—20th century—
Biography. I. Title.
PS3539.E65Z75   813'.5'2 [B]   76–10071
ISBN 0–06–126350–8

77 78 79 80 10 9 8 7 6 5 4 3 2 1

For my dead father and mother

Contents

Illustrations follow page 118.

Acknowledgments

An obligation usually awaiting the writer of a biography is the statement of gratitude to all those who have helped him.

In my case, this is less an obligation than a necessity of conscience. I gladly make this public acknowledgment of my deep appreciation to all those who have assisted me with the extensive research for this book. The work extended over a seven-year period and there were many who contributed, to a greater or lesser degree. The following are those who were particularly kind, in interviews or in a few cases through correspondence, in sharing with me their memories or knowledge of Albert Payson and Anice Terhune or in helping me to locate those who could do so:

Beatrice Agazzi, Helen G. Anthony, Barbara Backer, Bruce Chapman, John Donovan, Phyllis B. Everett, Mrs. Gerrit Heemstra, Dale Hooper, G. C. Houman, Charles Kelly, Charles Kurzius, John Lafore, Mr. and Mrs. Hal LeRoy, William H. Mastbrook, Samuel Nochimson, Sheila Osmundsen, Norman Runnion, Mark Saxton, Claudia Schroder, Ab Sidewater, Marcia Sills, Fred Temby, Frederic F. Van de Water, Sr., Frederic F. Van de Water, Jr., Mrs. T. Durland Van Orden, Mr. and Mrs. Charles Vreeland, Ethel Vreeland, James Walsh, and Winthrop Watson.

I sincerely thank all these, along with others whose names I probably have overlooked (for which I apologize) and still others who requested that their names not be mentioned.

I spent hundreds of hours reading the works of Albert Payson Terhune and those of his wife and mother, as well as the great mass of material written about them in newspapers and magazines over the last hundred years. There also were many letters and other documents to be studied. In so doing, I was most grateful for the courtesy and assistance of staff members at: the St. Louis Public Library, Washington University Library, The Library of Congress, New York Public Library, Emanuel Einstein Free Public Library of Pompton Lakes, New Jersey, Columbia University Libraries, Barnard College Library, St. Louis County Library, the American Kennel Club Library, and the Van Riper-Hopper Museum, Wayne, New Jersey.

Finally, three very special notes of appreciation.

To Claire Leishman of Paramus, New Jersey. A devoted Terhune admirer, Claire almost single-handedly began a national campaign in the late 1960s to save Sunnybank, the Terhune home, from disappearing. She merits my gratitude on that score alone, but I owe her much more. She has made available to me her vast knowledge of the Terhunes and has given me full access to her fine collection of Terhune memorabilia. And she has even provided me with good food as I worked. My debt to Claire and her family for their help, encouragement, and hospitality is very great.

To Lawrence Freundlich and Joan Hitzig, for their faith in me and in my book; and to my editor at Harper & Row, Ruth Pollack, who took over the book in midstream and guided us safely home.

And, lastly, to my wife Ilene and our children Julie and Joe, whose love and laughter and occasional tears—the sounds of caring—enabled me to survive the dark nights of the soul that sometimes accompanied the writing of this book. Without them, it simply could not have been done.

IRVING LITVAG

St. Louis, Missouri
September, 1976

PART ONE

Beginnings

1

As his rental car swept slowly up the hill, The Visitor was flooded with an almost overwhelming sensation of homecoming. Each curving of the two-lane highway seemed to him familiar. His first glance, seconds before, of the dam and the tail end of the lake had startled him into the certainty that he was almost there.

On his right, as he drove up the long slope and filled his eyes with the scenes that were to him both old and new, was the entrance to a subdivision of suburban ranch-type homes. That must be new, couldn't have been here when —, he was thinking, and then he saw the name of the subdivision on a gatepost: "Sunnyridge." A blade of excitement ran through him, for he knew the significance of the name and it was further proof, if he needed it, that he was finally there.

He slowed the car a bit, so as not to miss seeing a thing along the stretch of road. Then, a short distance ahead and to the left, he saw the long, low stone wall and the entrance gate. He cut the car's speed down to a crawl for the last few yards so that he could linger at each changing angle of sight, so that he would remember later how it looked to him at first.

The Visitor pulled up opposite the entrance gate, then turned carefully into the entrance and stopped.

He climbed out of the car and, for a moment, felt unaccountably short of breath. He was neatly dressed in a suit and tie, hatless but burdened with a heavy blue overcoat. He was just on the near side of middle age and his brown hair was graying.

The Visitor walked a couple of paces away from the car. He stood in the

3

middle of the driveway and took the long, sweeping, encompassing look around him . . . the look that he had been thinking about and planning for ever since he first knew that he would come here.

Alongside him was an old, battered, yellow two-story house guarding the entrance gate. "My English superintendent, Robert Friend." The phrase came back to him automatically. This had been the house of Robert Friend.

He turned and looked backward across the highway on which he had arrived. He wanted to save the best for last like a little boy waiting to eat his chocolate cake so he could still look forward to it a bit longer. Across the road, there was still a tree-filled hillside. In those trees had been many of the delicious hikes, the wild adventures, the savage, rending fights in the snow. He marveled that it still was a wooded hillside after all these civilizing years.

He swung back slowly to his right and glanced down along the stone wall as it bordered the highway. Below the wall was a brush-covered hill, rough and unkempt.

He looked further. And there in front of him, just as he remembered it, was the famous driveway. It turned and twisted into the trees, moving down the hillside "for a furlong." It, like so many of the physical entities here, was almost like a living friend to him. He knew it well and it evoked so many memories.

And then he saw the house. Down there, below the oaks that filled the hillside on this cold, eminently clear December day, down there was the old, beloved house. He couldn't make it out clearly through the trees and bushes and high grass, but he saw its outline and knew it was there, where it should be. And, beyond it, the lake—the "fire-blue lake."

After so many years of dreaming about it, he finally had come home—home to his childhood, home to the friends of his boyhood dreams. Home to the sounds of barking collies, to heroic deeds, to twilight talks on a veranda overlooking quiet water. Home to a world he had longed to find and never could. He had come home to Sunnybank. And he had never been here before.

2

I was about, oh, twelve when I got my first glimpse of him. But even though I had never seen him until then, his name had long been like holy words to me.

Albert Payson Terhune.

The three words, for some unfathomable reason, used to make me silently shiver with awe. They still do.

My first sight of him was a small photograph that accompanied an article on dog care he had written for a pamphlet put out by the Sergeant Company, makers of all manner of dog medicines.

I hadn't a dog of my own but wanted one desperately, passionately. And, thanks to Terhune, it ought to be a collie (was there any other breed of worth?). I knew, of course, that a collie would be impossible in our small house with its small yard. So, though the longing never ceased for a giant gold-and-white descendant of Terhune's Lad, I pragmatically reduced my demand to "Just a dog, Dad, any kind of dog: Please?"

As part of my campaign to prove my worthiness to be a dog owner and trainer, I secured and read every available piece of literature on canines, their care and training. And among them was the Sergeant pamphlet.

As soon as I saw the article by Albert Payson Terhune, I knew that I had struck gold. And then I saw his picture: I still have a clear memory of that picture in the upper right-hand corner of that pamphlet page, over thirty years later. It was the face of a big and strong man, a firm, no-nonsense man, with a granite-like solidity. The face was dominated by a massive chin that looked like a promontory of Mount

Rushmore. The hair was rumpled and a few locks of it came down over his forehead.

I remember, too, when he died. Strange how some things, though they don't seem particularly consequential at the time, remain clearly etched in one's memory. It was a winter day. I was thirteen years old and home from school, reading the evening paper, the St. Louis *Post-Dispatch,* when I saw a one-paragraph story which said that Albert Payson Terhune, the famed writer of dog stories, was dead in Pompton Lakes, New Jersey, at the age of sixty-nine.

I didn't get very emotional about it. At thirteen one doesn't get teary over the death of a writer of kids' books. But I can still recall thinking that I'd never have the chance to meet him and talk to him and ask him questions about his great collies. I worried about his dogs and what might happen to them. And I strangely remember that my mother fixed sausage and eggs for dinner that night, a favorite of mine, and somehow I couldn't eat and she kept asking me if I was sick. I guess that I did grieve for him, in the only way that I could.

Terhune was one of the most popular writers in American literary history. He was unquestionably the most famous, the most productive, and the best-compensated writer of dog stories that ever lived. Exact sales figures for his many books are almost impossible to obtain but it has been reported that six, some say eight, of his books have sold over one million copies each. Most of those sales, it should be remembered, took place at a time when the country's population was considerably smaller than now and before the era of mass-market paperback books with their gigantic press runs. At one time he was earning $2,500 for a single dog story and magazine editors couldn't get enough of them. His income soared during the 1920s to almost $100,000 a year during a period when $5,000 was considered executive pay.

At the peak of his popularity, he received between 200 and 300 letters a week from his readers. He was besieged by people who wanted to come into his house, to walk in his steps, to touch him, to stare at him and his wife.

His stories and books were read and reread throughout the world and his name was instantly recognized wherever he traveled. To some he was cantankerous and rude, to others gentle and compassionate. He was a friend of the literary great, though he never claimed to be their equal.

He had three great loves: his wife, his dogs, and his home. He wrote about them over and over again. And though literary critics say he was a patently unimportant writer and they probably are right, he accomplished something that very few important writers are able to do: in some ineffable way he transmuted his great loves into the hearts of other people so that they loved them almost as intensely as he did. So that now, long after he has gone, along with his wife, and the dogs, the strange love still remains. A mysterious legacy, but there it is.

3

The December day in 1940 was grayly threatening and cold. And the coldness there, at the edge of New Jersey's Ramapo Mountains, had a stinging bite that they hadn't felt when they left Manhattan just a short time before. The distance from New York City was only a few miles, yet the cold in the Ramapos always was more savage, the snow a few inches deeper.

They arrived in their cars, one by one a few minutes apart, at the entrance to the lovely old lakeside estate, identified themselves to the elderly man guarding the big iron gates at the top of the hill, glanced at the sign demanding a 5 m.p.h. speed limit, then drove slowly down the winding driveway to the old gray house where they were awaited.

The visitors were newspapermen, and one or two of the younger ones grumbled to themselves as they approached the house and questioned, as they did at least once each working day, their editor's intelligence, sanity, and masculinity for selecting them for this assignment. It was just a few days before Christmas, the height of the office party season in Manhattan, a time for last-minute holiday errands—not a time to be sent 40 miles out in the country to interview a faded old writer.

A few in the group did not mind the assignment. They had known Bert Terhune for years, regarded him as a friend, one-time newsman himself, kindred drinker and poker player, and particularly fine host. They knew the pleasure these annual get-togethers with the press gave him and they rather enjoyed it themselves.

When the city editors of these veteran reporters had said, "I want you to go out to Bert Terhune's place at Pompton Lakes and get a short news feature. He's having his annual birthday press lunch today. Bert's always good for a few paragraphs," they probably smiled and winked at their bosses, as if to say, "Sure, be nice to see the old-timer again."

Two or three of the reporters arrived about the same time and were let in at the front door by a smiling black maid, who welcomed them in a soft voice gently laden with a French accent.

Then Bert Terhune walked up and said, in his customary half-bellow, "Welcome, boys! Glad to see you! Come in and join the party!" The voice was deep and rich, just right for his big frame, but after he had spoken for a few minutes it tended to become raspy and hoarse. Terhune was old now and he looked tired and sick. But his huge body still showed signs of power and strength and he shook the hand of each new arrival with vigor.

For the last few years he had been inviting the newsmen out to Sunnybank for a gathering on his December 21 birthday. He seemed to need the encouragement that his name still was known, that he still was good copy even though his health had deteriorated to the point that he could do little more writing.

He knew that the newsmen would not continue to come, no matter how bountiful his hospitality and how plentiful the liquor, unless he was good copy. So his annual birthday gathering was the occasion for his predictions of things to come. Terhune's fame had come from his writing, not his ability to prophesy. But he had believed for years that

he was able to predict major coming events and, for the newspapermen who came to celebrate his birthday each year, he would issue a
few more of his pronouncements. One paper noted that Terhune had
achieved "uncanny accuracy" with his predictions, going all the way
back to his prophecy in 1920 that President Harding would die, as he
did, in 1923.

But this was December, 1940; Terhune's predictions were cen-
tered on the war raging in Europe, and on Franklin Delano Roosevelt
and the fierce domestic quarrels between the "isolationists" and the
"interventionists."

The United States, he prophesied in his resonant, almost pompous
tones, would enter the war by April, 1941. "It is already too late to
awake America to keeping a level head and refraining from getting
into this war." He reminded them of his prediction a year earlier that
Roosevelt would seek election to a third term in 1940, and would win.
And he reminded them also and reasserted his earlier prediction that
the man who was elected to the presidency in November, 1940,
would die in office.

Terhune argued at length and with his usual strong conviction
that the United States should do everything possible to keep out
of the European war. He insisted that he was not anti-British and
wished them well in their fight against the Axis powers, but the
United States, he argued, was impregnable "unless we stick our
necks out."

Terhune walked to the door with the reporters as they left, giving
each one a hearty handshake. As the last newsman walked down the
veranda steps to his car, Terhune called after him, "Goodbye! Hope
to see you again next year!" Then he closed the door and went to join
his wife, who had remained discreetly away from the gathering so that
the men could feel free to start telling ribald old newspaper tales, as
they were wont to do.

It was the last time the deep-voiced old giant would have his
birthday gathering for the press. He would live for one more birthday, but would be too sick then for company. No more need to issue
prophecies. No more need to be good copy.

He had been a late arrival, born on his mother's forty-second birthday. She called him "the handsomest birthday gift I have ever received." He was the last of six children and when he was born it had been eight years since the arrival of the second youngest. One sister had died as a baby and his only brother, Edward, had died of diphtheria at the age of four, eleven years earlier. The birth of the new little boy was greeted joyfully by his three sisters, but only two of them—Christine and Virginia—would grow to adulthood with him. The other sister, Alice, died a little more than a year later at the age of ten.

From the beginning, writers and writing swirled about him. He was born into a writing family and its star was his mother. She came from Virginia and her real name was Mary Virginia Hawes Terhune.

At fourteen, Mary Virginia Hawes had begun contributing articles to a Richmond newspaper under various pseudonyms and then began trying, without much success, to sell fiction to major magazines. One of her stories, sent to the popular *Godey's Magazine,* was finally published three years later. It had fallen behind a drawer of the editor's desk. When rediscovered, it was published and later reprinted in England and France.

At sixteen, the young writer began work on a novel but she told no one, not even her family, what she was doing. Her efforts to sell her stories and articles to magazines were mostly unsuccessful until 1853, when she was twenty-three. *The Southern Era,* a popular literary weekly published by a temperance organization, announced a contest to pick the best temperance serial and offered a $50 prize. Mary Virginia, more interested in seeing her work in print than in the money, wrote a serial for the contest. Her pen names always had been distantly related in sound to her own name—for this contest she chose a new one that she thought had a nice ring to it: Marion Harland. By that name, she became famous.

Her serial won the contest and she continued submitting material to the weekly under the name of Marion Harland. Meanwhile, she took out her long-finished novel, which she called *Alone,* and began reading it to her brother and sister. Their reaction was so enthusiastic that she started to rewrite the book with the hope of submitting it for publication. After finishing her work on it, she took the manuscript to a friend of her father's who owned Richmond's largest bookstore and also occasionally published a book. He kept her manuscript of Southern plantation life for two months, then rejected it. Her father, certain by then that his daughter had considerable literary talent, announced that he would take the manuscript back to the bookstore owner and pay for its publication himself.

Alone was published when Marion Harland was twenty-four. It was an immediate success. Within a few months, the book had gone through two printings and a third was on the press. A year later, *Alone* was in its sixth printing; eventually, it was to have a total sale of over 100,000 copies. The ambitious young writer already had a second novel well under way and six leading publishers had expressed interest in it.

Marion Harland, on the strength of one novel, was becoming a literary name of note. She began receiving letters of tribute from well-known writers, including Henry Wadsworth Longfellow. *Alone* was the first of more than twenty-five novels, which were accompanied over the years by the publication of much short fiction in women's magazines. Her fiction, much of it set in the antebellum South, was described by one critic as "mild, pleasant . . . often with a marked moral or religious tone."

In September, 1854, Mary Virginia Hawes met Rev. Edward Payson Terhune, a young minister who had come to Richmond temporarily to fill a pulpit while the regular clergyman was in Europe. She was attracted to him and his feeling for her became quickly obvious. "Miss Hawes walks well," he primly announced to friends after a group of young people had taken a stroll together. But she had made up her mind she would never marry a clergyman. She wrote years later that she already had turned down marriage proposals from four other ministers and, even if the sole alternatives were remaining single or spending an indefinite period in Hades, "I would risk the terrors of both states sooner than take upon me the duties and liabilities of a minister's wife. Upon that I was determined."

Her determination was soon broken down by the dignified young minister with the deep, resonant voice. He took over a small church in Charlotte Court House, Virginia, but made frequent visits to Richmond to court the ever more receptive Miss Hawes. Finally she accepted his proposal and they made plans to marry on September 2, 1856.

When she took over the parsonage at Charlotte Court House, the young wife quickly discovered that she was far less able than she had thought as a cook and housekeeper. "I didn't know anything when I got married," she wrote later, "how to dust or make a bed. I washed the first steak."

With the help of friendly neighbors, she learned quickly and soon became an excellent cook and housekeeper. She found that cookbooks on the market were of little help to her. A friend urged her to begin keeping her own book of tried and tested recipes, written in easily understandable language. She did so, and these kitchen notes became the foundation of one of the most successful books in publishing history. "I had learned to my bitter woe," she wrote in her autobiography, "that there was no printed manual that would take the tyro by the hand and show her a plain path between pitfalls and morasses. I learned, by degrees, to regard housewifery as a profession that dignifies her who follows it, and contributes, more than any calling, to the mental, moral, and spiritual sanity of the human race. I received my call to this ministry in that cottage parsonage."

Late in 1858, Rev. Terhune was offered the pastorate of the First Reformed Church in Newark, New Jersey. His father had been asking him to consider moving back North to be closer to him. Mary Virginia Terhune, on the other hand, had been hoping her husband would take a pulpit in Richmond. She accepted his decision to take the Newark offer in good grace, though she knew she would be desperately homesick for Virginia. One of her daughters later commented that her mother would inevitably make the best of things—if she were consigned to the middle of the Sahara Desert for the rest of her life, she would within ten minutes begin to lecture on the many advantages of residence in a dry climate.

They moved to Newark, then a city of less than 75,000 people, in February, 1859, and bought a house at 476 High Street for what was to be an enjoyable, productive stay of eighteen years.

Along with her duties as the wife of a busy minister and the mother of a growing family, Mrs. Terhune continued to write her novels of the South, which were consistently good sellers. But she kept thinking of ways in which she could turn her collection of recipes and other housekeeping information into a useful volume that would assist bewildered young wives who had no other guide. She set to work on it around 1870, calling it *Common Sense in the Household: A Manual of Practical Housewifery.* Before the new book was published in 1872, her friends and even her husband warned her that she was making a mistake in getting away from her tried-and-true novels.

She had great difficulty in getting it published. Carleton, which published her novels, declined it; other publishers also turned it down. Finally, Charles Scribner, a friend of Mrs. Terhune and her husband, was asked to consider it. It took a great deal of persuasion and Scribner admitted later that he accepted the cookbook only with the hope that he would then be allowed to publish the next novel by Marion Harland.

Common Sense in the Household, described by one modern critic as "the first book to treat homemaking as a skilled and dignified profession," was an immediate success. It went through ten editions in ten months and continued to sell steadily for years. *The Ladies' Home Journal* noted in 1920 that the book had sold far over a million copies. An old friend and former publisher of Mrs. Terhune commented a couple of years after the cookbook's first publication that her royalties already had amounted to three times the salary of the Governor of New York State (then $10,000 a year).

When her husband once noted that she seemed to take more pride in the cookbook than anything else she had written, she replied, "It will do more good than all of them put together."

There is a strangely prescient quality about the effect of the famed cookbook on her life and about the way she was henceforth to be known as a writer on domestic topics. Her son, who many decades later would surpass his mother's great fame, was to become known almost exclusively as a writer of dog stories and eventually would come to cringe at the description, wishing that the public would take note of the considerable body of other work that he had produced, some of it—to his mind—of much greater literary import than his dog stories. But the public never heeded his wishes; he was literarily type-cast and he never could shed the role.

There is poignancy in the way Bert Terhune wrote understandingly about his mother's career years after her death. Of the too-successful cookbook, Terhune said:

It condemned its author to be known henceforth as a writer on domestic topics instead of a novelist; and to build her future fame on what had been a mere experiment.

"It isn't literature, this household stuff I write," she told me once, with a whimsical resignation. "I know that. But it is *influence.* And it helps people. Perhaps that is even more worth-while than to feel that my next novel is looked forward to by those same people."

Yet I knew it galled her, unspeakably, that a younger generation should look upon her as a kind of super-cook and not as a popular novelist.

Always the cheery, indomitable grande dame, Mrs. Terhune was up at daybreak and insisted that her family be at the breakfast table by seven. She had a great scorn for sleep. She was indefatigable with her writing and there is little question that it was from her that Bert got his capacity for hard, sustained work at the writing table and for turning out a diversity of literary products in an almost continuous flow.

When Mrs. Terhune was in her sixties, she was sent to Palestine by a religious publication for a series of articles. At almost seventy, while caring for Bert's motherless daughter, she took over a syndicated newspaper women's page. Under her editorship, additional newspapers around the country began running the page. Mail from her readers rose quickly to twenty letters a day. Four years later, more newspapers were carrying the page and the mail pull was up to 100 letters a day. In another two years, the mail for Marion Harland was running up to 1,000 letters a week. In her seventies, she broke her wrist, making further longhand composition impossible. So she learned to type. At almost eighty, she wrote her autobiography. *Marion Harland's Autobiography* was less a story of her life than a detailed reminiscence of her beloved old South of pre-Civil War years. Her memory was incredible. Writing of shopping trips sixty years before, she named the friends who had accompanied her and what they purchased. Although written in the flowery, rhetorical style of her period, the autobiography is today, almost seventy years after it was written, a fascinating read for the loving look it offers at the ambiance of an era long gone.

The energy of the aged woman was prodigious. In 1919, when she was eighty-nine years old, she accepted an invitation from *The Ladies' Home Journal* to write a new series of articles about her Southern childhood. At ninety she went blind, so she hired a secretary, taught herself to dictate, and thus wrote her final novel, *The Carringtons of High Hill,* along with numerous magazine articles that were published during the last eighteen months of her life.

Shortly after her eighty-ninth birthday, she was visited by her son. "I'm a little tired," she told him. "I was at my desk nine solid hours today. There was an article the editors wanted in a hurry. Yes, I'm really tired." There was a pause, and then she asked, worry in her voice, "Do you suppose it is a sign I'm getting old?"

After her death in June, 1922, at the age of ninety-one, one magazine, *The Outlook*, wrote of her: "It is probably correct to say . . . there was no American city, no crossroads village so remote, but the name of Marion Harland was as familiar there as if she had been President of the United States." The magazine hastened to add that she was famous, not because she was a great writer, but because of her interest in American home life.

The amazing total of this woman's labors during a writing career of some seventy years was: twenty-five novels, three volumes of short stories, twenty-five books on homemaking along with an almost infinite number of magazine and newspaper articles, and more than a dozen books of travel, biography, and Colonial history. Her work in the latter field prompted her election as the first woman member of the Virginia Historical Society.

Mary Virginia Hawes Terhune was a writer and proud of it—and she helped nurture the skill in all three of her surviving children. Each eventually collaborated with her. With her daughter Christine she wrote another cookbook, with her daughter Virginia a book of etiquette, and with her son Bert a novel, published when she was seventy.

Her eldest daughter, Christine, followed in her mother's path by developing a reputation as an authority on domestic matters; her writing appeared frequently in *Harper's Bazaar* and *The Ladies' Home Journal.* She also wrote several books on household affairs. Fair, blue-eyed, and always fighting a battle against excess weight, Christine anticipated the modern craze for diet books when, in 1917, she published—anonymously—a book called *Lose Weight and Be Well,* which included a very frank account of her own repeated efforts to take off weight.

Younger daughter Virginia Van de Water wrote several novels, many serials, and articles on marital problems. She was a contributor to many national magazines and also worked for a time as an editorial writer for the *New York American.*

The father of the family, Edward Payson Terhune, was a successful minister in the Dutch Reformed Church who also held pulpits in Presbyterian and Congregational churches during his career of more than forty years. Born in New Brunswick, New Jersey, in 1830— the same year as his wife—Rev. Terhune was the son of Judge John Terhune, a prosperous merchant whose establishment included a bookstore, printing press, book bindery, and sales area for wrapping paper and stationery. The firm furnished Rutgers College and surrounding local schools with books and other essentials.

The judge's son was named for Edward Payson, a friend of the elder Terhune and a leader in American church activities. After graduating from Rutgers in 1850, Edward Terhune studied medicine for two years, then decided to switch to the ministry. He graduated from New Brunswick Seminary and began his career in Virginia.

Rev. Terhune was deeply, fervently religious, but he also was a hearty, rugged, outdoor type, who loved animals and sports and fed this love to his son from birth. There always were dogs and cats around the Terhune house, and fast horses. He was an outstanding horseman who rode often and enjoyed hitching two speedy horses to a buggy and going out for a 20-mile windswept run. Once, taken to task by a deacon of his church for his helter-skelter buggy rides, Rev.

Terhune replied that he thought he would as surely get to heaven behind a fast horse as a slow one.

The Terhunes were descendants of a Huguenot who emigrated from Holland to Long Island in 1641 and then, in the 1670s, moved to New Jersey. The original Albert Terhune came from Hunen in Holland and adopted his last name after coming to the New World to indicate his place of origin—Ter Hunen meaning "from Hunen." Bert Terhune's great-grandfather, Abram Terhune, was a young lieutenant in the Colonial army during the Revolutionary War and fought with Washington at Valley Forge. One of the family's proudest traditions was that Abram had been amongst General Washington's personal guard and was in the boat with the General during the famous crossing of the Delaware. The family account was that Abram Terhune was the main source of information about the crossing for painter Emanuel Leutze and that he is depicted in the famous Leutze painting of the crossing.

On both sides, it was a family of quite distinguished ancestry. Mary Virginia Terhune's ancestors on her father's side had arrived in the Massachusetts Bay Colony from Plymouth, England, in 1630.

Into this family, Albert Payson Terhune was born on Saturday night, December 21, 1872, in Newark. Twenty miles away, to the north and west, was Sunnybank.

5

The Visitor left his car parked at the gate and walked slowly down the long drive. His pace was not even a slow walk, it was a stuttering, halting sort of gait. A step, then a pause or two, then another. He could not do it quickly. He wanted to lengthen this experience, to extend it in time. He wanted each new vista, as he moved a few feet further down the hill and his perspective

changed, to stay with him for a while, to linger.

The trees on either side of the roadway, he knew, were the same ones that had been here then. The gravel surface on which he walked was the one he had so often read about, on which so many of the adventures had taken place, on which they *all had walked.*

The hillside forest was thinner than he would have expected, but still it was well timbered, mostly with sturdy trunks of oak. And though it was midwinter and the trees were bare, the slope was crowded enough with the big butts that The Visitor still could not see through them to the bottom.

It was silent. The cold beat against his face in waves, although the wind temporarily was calm. It was sunlit, freezing, and eerily still. He was alone on the hillside. And he was glad to be there alone.

He rounded a gentle turn in the driveway and then he saw the house. The Visitor stopped and was still for several minutes. He wanted to study the famous old house from where he was and remember how it used to look to them as they came cheerily down the hill, back from a shopping trip in New York City.

The house was smaller than he had thought. He had expected, and he knew it was incongruous and silly, a palatial country manse set imposingly above a broad lawn. As he walked slowly closer, he saw that it was hardly palatial, just an old gray house. Sitting empty. Waiting.

Now The Visitor was halfway down the hill. The house loomed up in front of him, looking a bit larger than at first. And he could see that it was crumbling, that it was more shell than home now. Then he glanced out beyond the house and, for the first time, clearly saw the lake. The old phrase again bounced through his mind, "the fire-blue lake," and he smiled at the memory, for Terhune had used the words over and over again when describing his home, and to any loyal Terhune reader they would echo automatically on first view of the lake. And there were the Ramapo hills beyond, "brooding protectively over the lake and valley as though they loved them."

Now he had come to the level ground on which the house stood, the plateau hovering above the lake. He walked closer to the building, looked up and saw the broken glass in the upper windows and the wisteria vines piercing the roof. And he wondered if they could know of this and how it would hurt them to know.

He stood on the driveway just before it began its wide circling route around the front of the house. He stood there for a long while, staring up at the rotting old building. Then he turned and looked back up the hillside, at the proud, ancient trees, at the brush that clogged the slanted side of earth, at the meandering old roadway that he had walked with such careful joy. He took a deep breath, lifted his head, and smelled the air, pulling it all in, enveloping himself in it.

"Sunnybank," he said softly. "Sunnybank."

6

The Place had become part of the Terhune family in 1865. While living in Newark, they often visited the beautiful Ramapo Mountain country to the northwest. Rev. Terhune had a sister who lived in the village of Pompton with her clergyman husband, and for the past three years, the Terhune family had spent summers nearby as boarders at a farmhouse. As the family grew larger, the vacation quarters at the farmhouse became inadequate and the minister and his wife began to give some thought to buying or building a vacation retreat in the lovely Jersey hill and lake country. On a summer day in 1865, they had gone out in their buggy for a ride on the dirt road that ran along a hillside on the eastern edge of Pompton Lake, across from the village.

There was only an occasional farmhouse along that side of the lake. It was mostly woods and fields. As their horse trotted easily along the narrow road, they looked down the hillside toward the lake and saw a group of men at work chopping down some of the great oak trees. They were fascinated by the beauty of the scene. The heavily wooded hillside fell to a plateau halfway down the slope, then there was a broad green lawn with more trees extending down to the lake. At one point along the shore, the lake curved suddenly, leaving a small wooded shoulder of land extending into the water. It was bathed in bright sunlight.

Rev. Terhune was incensed at the wanton destruction of the giant oaks. He always had railed at the way man could destroy, in a half-hour with an ax, what God had taken two centuries to create.

On impulse the angry clergyman stopped his buggy and sought out the foreman of the chopping crew. He learned from him the name of the owner of the tract and then bribed the foreman to give his men a break from their work while he hunted down the owner. An hour or so later, after Rev. Terhune had emptied all the ready cash from his pockets and written a check to cover the remainder, he was the new owner of the land. (The size of the original Sunnybank tract is unknown, but it probably was about 15 acres.) He ordered that no more trees be cut but since he also was the owner of the already fallen timber, it eventually became the oaken skeleton of the house he built.

Mrs. Terhune could not forget the picture of the sun-struck curve of land shouldering its way out into the blue lake. She announced that their new retreat would be called "Sunnybank." (The name was an old favorite of hers. It had been the name of a plantation in her first novel *Alone* and she was presently at work on a new novel, which was to be called *Sunnybank*.)

In her autobiography, Mrs. Terhune wrote the following description of her first sight of Sunnybank—the forerunner of innumerable rhapsodic tributes to the beauty of The Place written over several decades by her son:

A lake, blue and tranquil as the heavens it mirrored; green slopes, running down to the water; wooded heights, bordering the thither banks, and around, as far as the eye could reach, mountains, benignant in outline and verdant to their summits, billowing, range beyond range, against the horizon —why had we never seen this before? It was like a section of the Delectable Mountains, gently lowered from Bunyan's Beulah Land, and set down within thirty miles of the biggest city in America.

It is country redolent of history. Sunnybank was part of a huge tract acquired by one Arent Schuyler in 1695. Before those early Dutch settlers there had been only Indians in this valley, a small tribe of the Lenni Lenape people. The Indians had called the little river at the bottom of the valley "Pompton" for its twisting ways.

The dirt road on which the minister's buggy had traveled and which today is a U.S. highway had been laid out by Robert Erskine on orders of General George Washington; so pleased was the General with Erskine's work on the road that he made him his cartographer.

During the winter of 1775–76, a regiment of Washington's troops had camped at Sunnybank. When the Terhunes bought the land, they found the grave of an officer of the regiment who had died there and was buried with full military honors.

Some years before the Revolution, the little river, which the white settlers named "Ramapo" after the nearby hills, was dammed up to form a small lake, called Long's Pond and Ryerson's Pond and eventually Pompton Lake, as it is today. A gigantic rock in the middle of the river was used as the central foundation for the dam and still anchors it, more than 200 years later. In 1847 the land at Sunnybank became a part of Wayne Township, named for "Mad Anthony" Wayne, who fought with Washington.

After the purchase of the land was completed, the Terhune family continued to reside in Newark, although it was understood by all that Sunnybank was to be considered not only as a vacation site, but as the family's permanent home. A few weeks after the land had been bought, workmen began cutting up the fallen oak trees to use as beams and joists and the building of an eleven-room house was begun on the plateau above the lake. As the house went up, Bert Terhune's maternal grandmother planted, at the edge of the veranda, the wisteria vines that were to become almost as famous as the house itself. Their lavender blooms would be the house's crowning glory during its happy years of life; later their tentacles would slowly, with quiet mercilessness, tear the house apart as it waited to die.

The house, a barn, other outbuildings, and a smaller house for a caretaker that was built at the entrance gate on the hillside above, all were painted a neat shade of gray. But the gray coat soon flaked off and what was left was the priming coat, described by Terhune as "a vivid wild-rose pink—a hell of a color for a house."

For the next nineteen years the buildings remained bathed in this pink glow. Why his parents never altered the awful color Terhune did not know, although he surmised that they just didn't want to spend the money for another paint job. Eventually, though, the house was painted a dull brown and finally, when Bert Terhune became owner of Sunnybank, it was stuccoed in gray.

From the very beginning, Sunnybank took hold of the Terhune family with almost mystical force. Though it was not for some years yet to be their full-time home, they spent as much time there as possible. To the south of the house, along the lake, Rev. Terhune had a meadow cleared of brush and planted an orchard. In the nearly 40 acres of rich green woods (surrounding acreage was added to Sunnybank as the years passed), the minister patiently taught his young son to ride and to shoot, and on the waters of the lake to fish and to row a boat. He taught him, as Bert Terhune later described it, "forestry and weather signs and the rotation of crops and the ways of wild animals and birds."

At Sunnybank, Bert was given a meaningful lesson, one which never had to be repeated. There were always dogs about The Place and once, when he was six and playing with some pointer pups, he picked one up and swung it by its ears. The puppy yelped with pain. Rev. Terhune walked up to him, said not a word but picked up his son by the ears, twice swinging him to and fro. In the midst of his tears and anger, Bert realized what the puppy had endured and the point of the lesson. "It taught me," he wrote later, "more than would a ten-hour lecture on . . . cruelty to the helpless." The incident stayed with him throughout his life and he recalled it often in his articles on dogs.

To the boy, Sunnybank became a kind of paradise. "As far back as I can remember," he once wrote, "The Place has had a grip on me that I can't explain. It is the only spot on earth where I want to live. Every tree, every foot of its rolling wooded acres is inexpressibly dear to me. So is the fire-blue lake at the bottom of the lawn, with the green miles of hills that encircle it."

"Outsiders, visiting Sunnybank, may smile at me," he wrote another time, "though I like to hope the smile will be more kindly than derisive, for my foolishly illogical love for The Place. I suppose Sunnybank really has little in common with the world's historically beautiful estates. To me it is all I want or ever have wanted or shall want, by way of a home. Everywhere else I am homesick."

It had a strangely powerful effect on many others as well. Terhune told in one of his books of a woman he described as "beautiful, brilliant, high-bred," who was near death from an incurable disease and who came to Sunnybank as often as she could. "There is a strange peace that comes over me the instant my car turns into your gateway and down the drive," she told Terhune and his wife. "It helps me to carry on for days afterwards. Won't you let me rest for an hour or so on your big living room couch and look out through the wisteria vines and listen to a little Chopin? If you will, the peace will stay longer with me. It will give me something to hold onto in the nights that are so endless."

7

From the time he began to speak, Bert Terhune displayed an old family trait: a talent and propensity for telling vivid, richly descriptive tall stories. A relative said recently, "All the Terhunes were really much better actors than writers. They had a deep-rooted love for the dramatic and were fascinating to listen to when they spun yarns."

The little boy had a faithful nurse, Rose O'Neill, who was referred to by Mrs. Terhune as "The Invaluable." She was driven to distraction by Bert's wild stories. After his first brief horseback ride with his father at Sunnybank, the child ran to tell his nurse that he had saddled the horse by himself and had ridden for almost 100 miles at a thunderous gallop. He also related to her during the next few years, as his knowledge and imagination grew together, how he, using the pseudonym of Horatio, had—with the aid of two staunch friends—defended the Tiber Bridge against the entire army of the Etruscans . . . that he remembered having been an armor-bearer for King Saul . . . that he had climbed a beanstalk and then fought and slain a giant . . . that he had found a bear under his crib and finished him off with a pin.

One time, the Terhunes had taken Bert on a visit to the house of friends; while wandering around, he pocketed two rings that had been lying on a table. When they got home, he presented them to Rose and told her he had bought them for her at Tiffany's. The child was whipped and given an angry lecture by his father on the abuse of hospitality and the dangers of stealing.

The lesson about stealing apparently had little effect. The next day, strolling alone down a street in downtown Newark, the boy passed a furniture store and took a shine to a small rocking chair on the sidewalk. He picked it up and carried it to the middle of a busy intersection. He put the rocking chair on the streetcar tracks, sat in it, and began singing "I Want to Be Like Jesus!" at the top of his lungs. After his rescue and return home, Bert was again brought before his father. This time, the minister doubled over with laughter when he heard the story and then went to the furniture store and bought the rocker for his son.

One of Bert's earliest tall stories came when he watched his mother and father walk through the Sunnybank rose garden at sunset. He told Rose O'Neill that he had seen God walking between them. She dutifully reported the story to Rev. Terhune, who reprimanded the small boy for the sacrilege. Bert explained, with great sincerity, that he had been told that God had walked with Adam and Eve in the Garden of Eden. He thought that Sunnybank was the Garden of Eden and that the adventures of Adam and Eve had taken place there only a short time previously. Surely, if God had walked there with Adam and Eve, it was not surprising that He had reappeared to walk with Bert's parents.

A few years later, Rose O'Neill received a small legacy from a relative in Ireland and retired from her job with the Terhunes. Within a short time, however, she lost all her money to a swindler. Bert Terhune declared later that her loss had brought on an illness that killed her. The incident made a deep impression on the sensitive boy. It was his first experience with poverty in old age, and it helped trigger in him a haunting fear that was to bedevil him throughout his life.

In the spring of 1874, Mrs. Terhune's lungs began to hemorrhage. The family spent four months in the clear air of the Adirondack Mountains, hoping for a cure, but the trip didn't help. They returned home and she resumed her normal, busy life, but her health continued to fail. Finally the doctors diagnosed tuberculosis and estimated that she had only three months to live—a forecast that missed its mark by forty-six years. Mrs. Terhune, usually a bundle of energetic optimism, lost hope and prepared to die. She was just drifting, she said later, turning loose of life. Her husband, desperately trying to get her to fight, challenged her to hold on, warning that without her Bert was sure to go to the devil. She wrote later: "I saw the motherless boy, sensitive and high-spirited, affectionate and clever, the butt of rude lads, and misinterpreted by brutish teachers; exposed to fiery temptations at school and in college, and yielding to them for the lack of a mother's training and the aegis of a mother's love."

Her husband's psychological tactic had its effect; and it was greatly helped along by Bert's attitude during his mother's illness. In one of her low moods, exasperated at her son's misbehavior, she told him that he soon would have a "lovely young stepmother with blue eyes and golden hair; who would let [him] sit up to all hours at night and who would give [him] all the candy and pastry [he] could gorge." Bert took the prediction quite literally, for his mother never lied to him, and he found the whole thing very pleasant to contemplate. He started looking forward to the arrival of his stepmother and became irritable when told his mother was feeling a bit better. Once he was sharply reprimanded for including his future stepmother in his prayers. His anticipation of her successor, his mother later told him, did more to make her resolve to get well than any medicine.

Mrs. Terhune announced that she was going to get out of bed and was going to get better. Her health began to improve, but her husband knew that her lungs couldn't take another hard winter. He decided to take his family to the south of Italy. The minister resigned his Newark pulpit over the protests of the congregation, which wanted to give him an indefinite leave of absence. When they sailed for Europe, in the late summer of 1876, they carried with them a bon voyage gift of $3,000 presented to them by tearful leaders of the congregation.

They traveled briefly to Paris and then to Florence, but the climate of both cities bothered Mrs. Terhune and they went on to Rome. There they found the sunny and dry weather they had been hoping for, and her vitality began to return. She said later that she owed her long life to the four wonderful, healing months in Rome. The family lived in a small apartment and Rev. Terhune was named chaplain of the American Chapel, ministering to American residents of Rome and to tourists.

Bert, meanwhile, was falling madly in love with Crown Princess Margharita whom he frequently saw riding past in her carriage. He would scream wildly and wave and she would smile at him and throw a kiss. Some twenty years later, Margharita was again riding in a carriage when a bomb was thrown in, the blast killing her husband, King Umberto. The man who threw the bomb was from Paterson, New Jersey, 9 miles from Sunnybank.

After Rome, the family toured Italy and then went on to Switzerland. Rev. Terhune was asked to replace temporarily the minister of the American Chapel in Paris. He did so for the next four months while his family stayed in Geneva, where the sparkling air further improved his wife's now robust health.

They spent eight months altogether in Geneva, then went to England for the summer, sailing for New York in September.

Mrs. Terhune later wrote of the trip: "... I came home well! More robust than ever before and a devout believer in will-power, open air, and the deep breathing which ... added two and a half inches to my chest measure."

After their two-year absence, the Terhunes returned to what was now their only home, Sunnybank, and began to make plans for the future. Rev. Terhune quickly received calls from several large churches and soon decided to accept the bid from the Old First Congregational Church in Springfield, Massachusetts. It was a historic old church, the oldest in Springfield and one of the oldest in the Connecticut Valley.

They moved to Springfield, lived briefly in a hotel while a house being built for them was finished, then moved into the residence on Maple Street where they were to stay for the next five years, returning in the summer months to their beloved Sunnybank. The adjustment to Springfield was hardest for Mrs. Terhune, who found the New Englanders to be very different from anyone she had known—reserved and sometimes demanding. But she quickly began to make friends and busied herself with a Bible class, while continuing as always with her writing.

Bert was always the biggest boy in his class. At six, he was wearing ten-year-old sizes; at twelve, he was wearing sixteen-year-old sizes. And like many another minister's son, he soon acquired a reputation as a scamp and a hell-raiser. His size made him an inviting target and fights became a common occurrence for him. His first fight, he was to recall later, was with a cousin when he was not yet four. The cousin was getting much the best of it when Rose O'Neill came along and broke up the scrap. She reprimanded the tiny Bert and demanded that he tell his cousin that he wanted to be friends. "Tell him you're pleased with him," she demanded. "Okay, I'm pleased with him," Bert responded, "but I hate him like hell!" His father, told of the fight, said only, "If you had kept your guard up and your head down, the way I've taught you, he couldn't have given you that bloody nose."

Once, while with his family in Richmond, Virginia, visiting his mother's relatives, he was compelled to wear a sailor suit bought by his mother in England and which he loathed. During a large dinner party being given for his parents, he sneaked outside and soon got into a fight with some neighborhood kids who teased him about the sailor suit. After the fight, in sheer disgust, Bert stripped off the hated suit, threw it into a garbage barrel, and then walked naked into the big dinner party.

"I got an ungodly thrashing," he wrote years later, "but the loss of the abominable blue suit and scarlet sash was beautifully worth it."

Bert's thrashings usually were administered by his mother. His father struck him only after the more serious escapades. After one such misadventure, his father used a riding whip belonging to his older sister Christine to administer the punishment. In the midst of the whipping, Christine rushed in and begged her father to stop. Bert felt a warm glow of gratitude toward her until she added, "It bends the poor whip all out of shape."

Bert's talent for histrionics soon was put to use during the visit to Richmond. Having decided to make some money, he went to the local newspaper office and bought two copies for 2 cents each, all the money he had. Then he took off his shoes and socks, rubbed dirt on his face, and went into the streets to sell papers. He wept profusely and—using what he intended to be an Italian accent—told passers-by that he had to sell his papers to keep his widowed mother from starving. His sales were brisk, but since he sold the papers for the same 2 cents he paid for them, he wound up the day with just 4 cents. The escapade ended with another spanking when his parents drove by and spotted him on the street corner going through his Italian urchin routine.

Another time, after the move to Springfield, Bert climbed into the church bell tower to explore and found the remains of several dead pigeons. He gathered them into a bag and took them to the meat market patronized by his parents. The proprietor, asking no questions about his source of supply, bought the pigeons from him, paying him 15 cents for each. The next evening, his parents had guests for dinner and squab was served. Bert detected something faintly familiar about the main course and suddenly lost his appetite. It took him a month to summon up the courage to tell his parents what he had done; they remembered with horror the several squab dinners they had enjoyed during the period.

Bert's childhood reading caused him to be so impressed with Falstaff, Prince Hal, and Robin Hood that he organized a group of boys from the neighborhood to perform similar feats. They pilfered clothes lines for use as lariats, clothes poles did duty as lances, and the Springfield outlaws set out on their missions, raiding an orchard here and there and occasionally heaving a rock through the window of the biggest, grandest residences they could find. The identity of the leader of the roving outlaw band soon became known and Rev. Terhune began receiving bills for broken windows and other damages.

Just before the family left Springfield, in October, 1884, when Bert was eleven, he was arrested on the complaint of an elderly neighbor that he and his friends had been throwing tomatoes and ink at the sheets hanging from his washline.

Long years later, Terhune well remembered that when his first book was published—he was twenty-three and had left Springfield eleven years earlier—a Springfield newspaper prefaced its review of the book by noting that: "Bert Terhune is remembered by the people of this city as the worst boy we ever had here. Now he has written a book."

Bert's formal education began in Springfield at the small, well-regarded private school run by Miss Gertrude Kimball. At six, he was the oldest boy in his class and—as usual—the biggest, in his size ten clothing.

One of his favorite playmates and classmates was a small, pretty girl about ten months younger than he was. Her name was Annie Stockton and her great-uncle and aunt, with whom she was living at the time, were close friends of his parents and members of his father's church. She always remembered Bert sitting in church during his father's sermons, chewing on the brim of his straw hat. His mother finally had to soak the hat in alum to keep the boy from chewing it to bits.

The boy's best time at school was Friday morning—when each child had to recite a memorized poem. Bert's favorite was one called "The Skeleton in Armor" and he gave it a dramatic, full-voiced recitation with fervent gestures. More than sixty years later, he still could recite the poem, as dramatically as ever.

Bert was Annie Stockton's special friend and she began to take special care of him. His mother sent him to school dressed in knickers with long red stockings. Often one or both of the stockings were inside out and Annie would nag him until he went into the teacher's office and fixed them. He obeyed her devotedly and without protest as he was always to do during their long life together. "There was an elfin charm and a queer loveliness and an honesty and a fearless spirit about Annie Stockton," he was to write many years later, "which used to make me by turns bragful and sheepish in her presence. She was not . . . in the very least like any one else I have known."

Once Rev. Terhune came to the Stockton home especially to see the little girl. He sat down with her, took her hands in his and said worriedly, "Annie, I have been told that Bertie swears. Complaints have come to me about it. Now think carefully . . . did you ever hear Bertie swear?"

The little girl who was to become Bert Terhune's beloved wife vigorously defended her playmate. "No! Oh, no!" she cried. "I never heard him swear!" Then she paused and added, "But he said Ed Smith was a damned fool. And he *is!*"

Many years later she still remembered the roar of laughter with which the stern minister reacted to her defense of Bert. In fact, Bert already was beginning to develop a profane vocabulary that was truly awesome in its virtuosity.

Bert rewarded Annie with his first gift to her: a small white china pitcher from a toy tea set of his. He tied a mussed bit of red ribbon to it before presenting it to her. She still had it among her possessions when she died, eighty-five years later.

After a couple of years with Miss Kimball, Bert was transferred to Blake's Military Institute where the headmaster, having read some of Bert's poetry, told him he never could hope to be a writer like his mother when he grew up.

In the fall of 1884, Rev. Terhune accepted a call from the First Reformed Church in Brooklyn. The family left Springfield; the house on Maple Street in which they had lived would years later become a small hotel named "Terhune Hall" in honor of the roguish boy who had lived there and was to become a world-famous writer.

The Terhunes' elder daughter Christine was left in Springfield where, a few months earlier, she had married James F. Herrick, a newspaperman with the Springfield *Republican.* The Herricks also moved to New York in 1886; seven years later, he died. Their other daughter, Virginia, would marry Frederic Van de Water in Brooklyn in 1889.

Rev. Terhune's new church was in deep trouble. He knew it, but accepted the call anyway, turning down other bids from larger and more prosperous New York congregations. The church occupied an enormous red brick structure at Bedford Avenue and Clymer Street, but its membership had fallen off drastically and those left were engaged in bitter factional disputes. The church was almost insolvent. Edward Payson Terhune was a robust, confident fifty-three years old and he looked forward to the challenge of rebuilding the congregation. He set out first to raise funds. When this was in hand, he began building up the church's membership list. Firmly but kindly, he resolved the members' arguments and began bringing them together.

He won the hard fight, but it was at the cost of his own health. When he left, six years later, the church's $80,000 debt had been paid off and its membership rolls were crowded. But his father, Bert wrote later, had aged by a quarter century. He was "broken in health and life; sick with the malady which later was to kill him: his buoyancy and athletic vigor forever gone. . . . He had finished his work. It had smashed him. But he had won."

The next five years were spent at another Brooklyn church, the Puritan Church at Marcy and Lafayette Avenues. But the minister's health continued to grow worse. Forty families from his previous church joined him at Puritan, insisting on following their beloved pastor though he begged them to remain where they were.

Rev. Terhune retired from the active ministry in 1895. He spent the rest of his life living in Manhattan and at Sunnybank, preaching at churches around the country when his health permitted, and filling in occasionally as a minister at churches which could not afford a full-time clergyman.

Bert, during those years in Brooklyn, was growing into a young giant. From the age of sixteen on, he never was able to wear ready-made clothes, except for underwear, shoes, and hats. He later wrote lamentingly (though unconvincingly, for he was very proud of his size and strength): "Perhaps you think it must be a fine thing to stand six-feet-two-and-a-half in one's bare feet, and to have a fifty-inch chest and piano mover shoulders, and to weigh two-hundred-and-twenty pounds and more? Well, it is not. Take that from me. It is NOT! It is as inconvenient, sartorially, as it would be to have a hump on one's back or only one arm."

His father needed all the help he could get at his difficult new assignment in Brooklyn, and he asked Bert to set a good example for the other young people in the congregation. The son obediently began attending morning and evening services on Sunday, along with the afternoon Sunday School, plus Christian Endeavor meetings on Monday night, Young People's Prayer Meeting on Tuesday night, and the regular church prayer meeting on Friday night. To his great surprise, he found the church gatherings rather pleasant and interesting. He began there a habit of fairly regular churchgoing that was to continue throughout his life.

But the old ways could not be completely eradicated. At least twice, Bert came to church with a glowing black eye as a trophy of his latest battle.

He always insisted that the fights were forced upon him and that, despite his size advantage, he usually got licked. He was growing so fast, he explained, that he had no strength and older, if smaller, kids found fighting with him irresistibly attractive.

Finally, though, the size began to be matched with an appropriate amount of strength. Bert started to win some of the fights, though more through bull-like rushes than any boxing finesse. At length his father took pity on the clumsy youth and sent him to an ex-fighter who had set up a boxing academy on Fulton Street in Brooklyn. The old pug billed himself as "Professor McDermott, The Daddy of Footwork." Terhune wrote about him years later, describing him as "squat and simian," but a master of footwork with a genius for teaching it. "His supreme expression of approval was a hiccoughing grunt." The minister's big son went for lessons three times a week for several years and turned rapidly into a skilled boxer who came to love the sport passionately. McDermott begged Bert to train for the professional prize ring. "God never built you so big and rugged just to push a damned pen all day long," he would say. Bert never agreed, though he was tempted. He kept up with boxing for years, frequently going into the gym ring to spar with established fighters of the day. He often wondered what would have happened if he had given in to Professor McDermott's entreaties that he turn pro.

When he moved to 479 Greene Avenue in Brooklyn, Bert keenly missed the open spaces he had enjoyed in Springfield, where woods and hills were only a short distance from his home. In Brooklyn the only green space was in small back yards and the streets became the playgrounds. It intensified his constant longing for Sunnybank and he waited eagerly for summer vacations and the annual stay on the shore of Pompton Lake.

8

During the years that his body was growing like a young tree, he also was stretching his mind, under the careful tutelage of his parents and also through his own love of reading. The boy spent hours in his father's well-stocked library; before he was ten years old, he claimed later, he had read "all of Shakespeare, all of Longfellow, seven of Scott's novels, Bryant's translation of The Iliad, Bayard Taylor's translation of Goethe's Faust, Percy's Reliques, much of Gibbon, more of Tennyson."

His parents loved the theater and liked to mingle with show people. He had been taken to see *Pinafore* in Springfield when he was six. As a child he would go to the attic and produce one-man dramas; if he could not think of an appropriate line, he would improvise something about Sunnybank, which even then occupied most of his thoughts. About that time, too, he was taken to see a production of *Richard III* and when the curtain fell in the midst of a noisy battle scene, Bert shouted, "Hey, put that curtain up! They're fighting like hell back there!"

Throughout his life, Bert Terhune was to maintain a passionate interest in the theater and remain a constant theatergoer. He could talk for hours about the great plays and performances he had seen and, typically, had vehement, unshakable opinions on the merits of the best-known actors. He became a great fan of the actor Edwin Booth and boasted of having seen almost every one of the great Booth roles. Walter Hampden, he would insist in later years, was the finest American actor of them all. For some reason, he would consistently belittle the great Sarah Bernhardt.

Mrs. Terhune often held Monday or Tuesday evening open

houses in Brooklyn which were attended by writers, musicians, and people of the New York theater. Her own fame as a writer brought the perceptive boy into contact with many of the major literary figures of the day at a time when such meetings were extremely influential on his developing interests.

If his mother aided his burgeoning literary inclinations, his father inspired in him a fervent religious faith which was to burn throughout his life. It was one of many character traits in Bert Terhune which may seem hopelessly outmoded and old-fashioned today: he was a man of old-time virtues, paramount among which was his passionate certainty about religious values. His numerous autobiographical writings assert the strength of his own faith, while readily admitting that his manner of living had not been exactly pious:

When I speak of my religious faith, it is not with any pietistic slant. My personal life has never been consistent with my faith; which makes that faith none the less strong. One may admire and believe in Joan of Arc and John Brown and Stephen the Martyr, without seeking to emulate their lives or wishing to incur their doom. With me, my faith is more than mere belief. It is a rock-strong *knowledge.* I do not seek to impose it on any one else, nor do I permit others to argue religion with me. Let it go at that, please.

Terhune was utterly sincere in such statements; they echoed, also, in his private life. When a new minister came to his church in Pompton Lakes in 1931, Terhune wrote him a long letter in which he candidly described his own character as he saw it. He did this, he explained, because "I want to have you know the truth before you consent to become my pastor." He added: "I have led a pleasantly regrettable life; and one which the all-tender Father will judge no more harshly than I would judge a foolish and naughty little child of my own. . . ."

Bert's schooling in Brooklyn continued at private schools, first the Adelphi Academy and later, for a year or so, the historic Brooklyn Latin School, which was run along the lines of English private schools.

Despite his voracious personal reading, Bert was an indifferent, erratic student—excelling in the courses that appealed to him, such as English literature, and loafing through the others. His parents began to fear that he would not be able to get into a good college; so, during the last of his high school years, they had him privately tutored to bring up his grades.

Bert had hoped and planned to attend Yale, but applied instead to Columbia at the request of his mother. All her life had been spent in the midst of big, closely knit families. She dreaded the thought of being alone. Now, with her two daughters married and living in their own homes and her husband often out of town, she would be on her own if her son went off to college in New Haven. She asked him, firmly, to attend Columbia. He wasn't happy about it: he considered Columbia a kind of day school, with no dormitories and negligible athletics and campus life. But he agreed, and in 1889 he was enrolled in the Columbia School of Arts. (When he began, the title was Columbia College; it became Columbia University before he graduated. Columbia then occupied a midtown block between 49th and 50th Streets and Madison and Park Avenues.)

In addition to paying his tuition, Bert's parents gave him a regular allowance for expenses which he supplemented by doing manual labor, including one summer spent working with a construction crew. He and two friends also operated a free-lance roulette wheel until one customer's run of good luck took away all their operating capital.

During the free summer afternoons at Sunnybank, Bert and other neighborhood youths would meet daily for competition in boxing, fencing, and swimming. Two of his closest friends were Cecil and William De Mille, whose father, Henry C. De Mille, had purchased land a quarter-mile or so south of Sunnybank and built a large house there. Henry De Mille died of typhoid early in 1893, during Bert's senior year in college; the minister's son felt deep sympathy for the two younger boys and spent as much time as he could with them. Cecil B. De Mille, of course, went on to become a famous film director and producer, known to millions of Americans also as a radio personality where he served for years as host on the "Lux Radio Theater" program.

Though great size didn't run in his family—his mother was 5 feet 4 inches tall and his father was under six feet—Bert, as he neared college age, had grown into an oak of a man. He was 6 feet 2 ½ inches tall, weighed about 220 pounds, and his chest measured 50 inches.

And he was rock-hard. He loved to box and wrestle and to go for long runs in the Ramapo Mountains above Sunnybank.

Bert's appetite at this time was commensurate with his huge physique. A typical breakfast would consist of fruit, cereal with cream, two big cups of coffee, hot bread, two or three chops, or liver and bacon. Lunch might include a 16-ounce rare steak, a heaping dish of potatoes, and a quart of beer. An equally satisfying dinner would be followed by a mile run through the woods to help him digest it. And before bedtime, when he was hungry again, there perhaps would be a Welsh rabbit and several bottles of beer.

Cecil De Mille's memories of the strapping Terhune always were fond ones. In his autobiography, published in 1959, the film maker wrote that Terhune "always had time to impart to the boys of the neighborhood the deep and virile knowledge and love of nature which was to make his name . . . famous among American writers. We boys all idolized Bert Terhune; and it was an idolatry well placed and well deserved. Whether he was teaching us how to defend ourselves with our fists or how to read the wonder of all living things in woods and field and lakes, Bert Terhune was more than a teacher or leader. He was the kind of friend every boy, especially every fatherless boy, ought to have."

Another resident of the area and friend of Terhune was a young girl named Phoebe Ann Moses, who amazed the youths with her target shooting ability. They would throw rocks or mud balls high in the air and the girl, who had learned to use a gun as a child, would rarely miss. She later adopted the stage name of Annie Oakley and became renowned for her trick shooting as a long-time star of Buffalo Bill Cody's touring Wild West extravaganza.

Some time after her husband's death, Mrs. De Mille, who had been a teacher prior to her marriage, decided to establish a private boarding school. She built a schoolhouse across the road from her residence and enlarged her home so that she could offer room and board to students from outside the immediate area.

Many of the students came from New York City as word began to get around of the high standards and lovely physical setting of the Henry C. De Mille Preparatory Boarding and Day School for Boys and Girls. Some of the students were attractive teen-age girls. With his granite jaw, unruly thatch of brown hair, clear blue eyes and stevedore's physique, Bert had been much on the minds of Pompton girls for quite a while, although his own thoughts had been fastened securely on athletics, reading, the theater, and dogs. But the ready accessibility of a group of pretty girls at the De Mille School, only a few steps down the road from his house, was fascinating, and he took full advantage of his friendship with the De Mille boys to spend as much time as possible hanging around the school. William or Cecil or their mother would formally introduce him to the girl students and he would mentally file away their names for future reference.

One of the students appealed to him particularly. Her name was Lorraine Bryson, she lived in New York City, and she was small, very bright, and terribly pretty. She was more serious than the other girls, a very purposeful student with a gift for foreign languages. Bert soon found that Lorraine shared his love for the outdoors and liked to hike and fish. He began including her in some of the activities of his neighborhood friends and occasionally they would get away together for a picnic or a walk through the woods.

Lorraine was then seventeen, three years younger than Bert. Her parents—Gilbert and Louise Bryson—were wealthy and had moved to New York City from Baltimore a few years before. Bert's parents liked the girl and approved of the relationship. Bert found himself thinking frequently about Lorraine and beginning to envision a future with her—though he knew it would have to wait until he established himself.

Bert, at that time, was considered one of the best athletes in the Pompton area. In the Terhune papers at the Library of Congress, there is a yellowed clipping about the Columbus Day track events at Butler, New Jersey, in 1892. Terhune was captain of the Pompton team and won the 100-yard dash in 10 2/5 seconds with "one of his famous rushes." The time was an area record for the event. The impressed reporter went on to write: "Mr. Terhune deserves especial praise for his judgement in running the hundred yard dash. Any person who observed his starting would think he was not in the race; but after he covered the first fifty yards he astonished everyone by the suddenness of his rush and made a grand finish. If Mr. Terhune continues making the progress in his second year that he has made in the first, he will make one of the crack athletes in this country." The story also reported that Terhune won the 75-yard dash and tied for first in the shot put.

During his senior year, the long-time pleas from his old mentor, the Daddy of Footwork, finally had some effect. Bert decided to capitalize on his boxing ability and also earn some spare money by secretly turning professional. He called himself Kid Dougherty and fought several pro bouts, claiming later that he won most of them. He was a club fighter and his friends at Columbia did not inhabit the small, smoke-filled gyms where he fought, so his brief fistic career was kept secret, though the bruised face that he often brought to class was the subject of much speculation.

His time at Columbia also introduced him to fencing and he became a fanatic about that sport as well. He took lessons five days a week for almost four years. With all the practice, Bert became a skilled fencer and remained active in the sport for about ten years.

Bert's matriculation at Columbia caused little change in his slovenly study habits. He spent a great deal more time enjoying sports and Manhattan's fine restaurants than in preparing for his courses. He would get frantic just before final exams and spend the entire night cramming and guzzling black coffee to keep awake. Those last-ditch efforts, along with a memory capable of almost total recall, were sufficient to get him through courses in which performance depended on rote memorization. But when it came to such courses as math, he was hopeless.

Among his papers there is a notice sent to him by the Dean after his freshman year, informing him that he was deficient in Greek and mathematics for the first term and in all studies for the second term. In his autobiography, Terhune declared that he never did pass freshman or sophomore mathematics or second-term junior Greek or senior Latin, and completed college with no less than six "conditions" on his record. He attributed his graduation to the fact that Columbia President Seth Low and two members of the college's board of trustees were close friends of his parents. Had he gone to Yale, he wrote, he would have been dropped by the end of his second year.

His professors were noted scholars. He studied psychology with

James Hyslop, later to become more widely known as a researcher of psychic phenomena and founder of the American Society for Psychical Research. One of his philosophy professors was Nicholas Murray Butler, who would be one of Columbia's most distinguished presidents.

Bert's respect for Professor Butler increased substantially after an incident in his class. The youth sometimes accompanied his customary gigantic lunch with too much wine. After one such lunch, he fell asleep in the back of Butler's philosophy class. He slept undisturbed until the droning of Butler's lecturing voice penetrated the mists of sleep and suddenly awakened him. Forgetting completely where he was, Bert shouted out, "How am I going to get a decent nap with your damn jabbering going on? Shut up, can't you?" The wild laughter of his classmates brought him to full consciousness as he sat in horror at what he had done. But Professor Butler made no comment about the outburst, simply continuing with his lecture.

All the boredom, the sense of time being wasted in unnecessary courses was forgotten, however, when Bert walked into the English classes taught by George E. Woodberry and Brander Matthews. He took every course offered by the two professors and was enthralled by them. Matthews had come to Columbia only a couple of years earlier and was yet to make his reputation as an outstanding teacher, although he was already well known as an author and playwright. Bert was one of the first students to take Matthews's famous playwriting course, which fascinated him. He said he learned then that he never would be a playwright, but the instruction he received in drama served him well years later when he wrote a number of movie scripts.

There is perhaps no tribute quite so sweet as that received from an old teacher. In April, 1924, Bert Terhune returned from a trip to Africa to find a letter from Brander Matthews. The man who had been so inspirational in the classroom more than thirty years before had written to tell Terhune how proud he was of his success as a writer and how much he had enjoyed reading his dog stories. In his reply, Terhune apologized for the delay in answering the letter and said he wanted " . . . to tell you how inordinately vain it has made me. As to my dog yarns—haec nihil esse novimus—but the fact that you should have written of them as you did makes me very happy. . . . Of old, I dreamed of becoming a worthwhile author and of writing a masterpiece whose dedication should announce grandiloquently that I owed all my literary incentive and basic training to your lectures. Then, when I found out what manner of writing man I had developed into, I forebore to play so cruel a joke on you. But the gratitude is there, just the same."

Whatever his academic problems, Bert began doing some writing at Columbia and getting recognition for it. His plan for several years past had been to become a lawyer, but the example of his mother's highly successful writing career and the influence of many conversations with her literary friends began to affect him and he devoted more and more thought to becoming a writer. At nineteen, he entered a competition for the best short story by a Columbia undergraduate and won the $10 first prize. "Mine was the only typed manuscript," he wrote later. "Always I have had a morbid belief that that was why it won the ten dollar award. For it was frightful drivel, even for a nineteen-year-old."

During that period he also sold a poem to *Lippincott's Magazine* for $20 and other poems to *Harper's Bazaar* for another $20. He began to have visions of turning out such poems by the ton, selling all of them and quickly acquiring great wealth. In fact, however, he sold nothing more for two years although he faithfully kept at his writing. Two of his teachers explained patiently, if unencouragingly, that his poetry was not selling simply because it was worthless.

As his college days drew to a close, Bert felt remarkably unprepared for any vocation. In later years he would deride the education he had received as utterly impractical in preparing anyone for life and described the A.B. degree he received as a "fetish for impressing those who did not have one." He was vacillating between law and writing; the one thing he was sure of was that he would be very glad to be finished with college.

His haste to leave school was a matter of concern to his parents. His doting mother was very involved with her children's lives. This had been especially true of Bert, her youngest and her only surviving son. She worshipped the boy and also tended to dominate him. She saw nothing improper in taking a hand, even if a somewhat shadowy one, in guiding his activities.

In November, 1892, a few months before Bert was to graduate from Columbia, his mother wrote to Brander Matthews, asking his help in what she termed "a delicate task." She explained that Bert had intended to study law—there had been many attorneys in the Terhune family—but that recently his friends had begun to talk him out of it.

He had been persuaded by these friends, Mrs. Terhune went on, of the importance of getting to work right after college in the American tradition. This false notion, she declared, "underlies two-thirds of the slovenly educations which disgrace our country." She said that her son had no need of "hasty, superficial work," and his parents wanted him at least to undertake a year of graduate study if he would not study law, as they wished him to. With the letter she enclosed a sample of Bert's verse, pointing out that he had a "naturally excellent mind" and had done extensive reading in his father's library since boyhood. His parents were not encouraging him to take up literature as a profession, she continued, but felt that a business career would be "a life of sordid slavery . . . to one of his tastes and education." She asked Professor Matthews to speak with Bert and emphasize to him that those who can should get a good education and not succumb to a mistaken impatience to pay their own ways in the world. She closed by inviting Matthews to one of her regular Tuesday evening open houses. And she beseeched Matthews not to mention her letter to Bert lest any advice he would agree to give the youth be discounted because of it.

Whether Matthews ever did speak to Bert is not known, but when the youth received his degree from Columbia in June, 1893, he had no firm plans for the future, though realizing, with an increasing sense of panic, that he would have to do something with his life. For neither the first time nor the last, he was rescued from his dilemma by his mother. Mrs. Terhune was sixty-three now, but still energetically active as a writer. About the time of Bert's graduation, she got a letter from the editor of a publication called the *Christian Herald*. He wanted her to write a serial that would run for six months and asked her to come in to discuss it. The serial, it turned out, was a ploy to get her into the office. The editor really wanted to propose to her a much more ambitious project: a trip to Palestine, then part of Syria, to investigate the conditions of women there and study their domestic life, as well as send back sketches of places prominent in Biblical history. He wanted her to write a weekly report; in return, he would pay her a handsome fee plus her travel expenses and those of her husband or other companion.

All her life Mrs. Terhune had wanted to visit the Holy Land. Now she could do it, earn a substantial amount of money, and probably come up with wonderful material for another book. She quickly accepted the offer after getting her husband's approval. Rev. Terhune was unable to make the trip with her. She could not go alone and the choice was an obvious one. Bert happily agreed to escort his mother and assist her with research.

Until they were ready to leave, he spent a delightful, anticipatory summer at Sunnybank. There were more picnics and long talks with Lorraine Bryson and once again he began thinking of marriage, although he was careful not to commit himself. She had now graduated from the De Mille school and told him that she had accepted an offer to stay on at the school as a French teacher. Bert was very pleased to know that she would still be close by.

Bert and his mother sailed from New York in September, 1893, on a seven-month trip. After two weeks in Paris, they continued to Syria, stopping briefly at Port Said and Beirut, then on to Jerusalem.

The three months they spent in Palestine and Syria was the first great adventure of Bert's life and he made the most of it, traveling by horse across much of Syria, swimming across the Jordan River, living for a time with a Bedouin tribe, and even visiting a leper colony, reportedly gaining entrance by posing as a touring physician.

Bert established then a pattern that was to become life-long: his amazingly retentive memory grasped and held every small incident of the trip. Everything was grist for his writer's mill. The trip itself was the raw material for his first book; various incidents would turn up years later in his articles and short stories. Even the colorful dialect of his dragoman or interpreter was not permitted to go to waste—Terhune used it years later in stories written about a character called "Najib."

In Bethlehem, on Christmas morning in 1893, Bert bought a mother-of-pearl crucifix and had it blessed by a priest at the Church of the Nativity. He wore it for several years, then gave it to Anice Terhune shortly after their wedding. She in turn wore it faithfully until her death in 1964.

The trip was not all pleasure for Bert. In Egypt he was laid low for a time with Asiatic cholera. Just before leaving Syria, he was kicked in the right side by the little Arabian stallion he had been riding, but dismissed the injury as not serious.

After leaving Syria, the mother and son went back to Egypt for a few days, then on to Greece, Italy, and finally back to Switzerland, where she looked forward to showing Bert the magnificent scenery amid which she had recovered her health some seventeen years before, when he had been too small to appreciate the mountains, lakes, and the cool, bright air that was medicinal in its healing power. As they made their way to Lucerne, Bert's side continued to hurt and finally he saw a doctor. The diagnosis was a mild case of appendicitis, apparently combined with peritonitis as a result of the horse's kick. The physician told him that surgery for the appendicitis was not necessary but he would have to remain in bed for a month in Lucerne before resuming the trip. After returning to the United States, he was to forego athletics or any other strenuous exercise for six months.

With the required month in a Lucerne hotel finally out of the way, the journey continued. The last stop was England and a visit to the home of the Brontë family, about whom Mrs. Terhune planned to write an article.

Then back to the United States and Sunnybank. Bert, restless and still without a job or plans for the future, decided to try writing again by putting together a book about his wanderings in the Holy Land called *Syria from the Saddle.* His wife said years later that the book had been started as a test of his memory. He had misplaced the notes of his trip and determined to see how much he could recall. Later, when the book was finished, he came across the notes and checked them against the completed manuscript. He had made only two minor mistakes.

Syria from the Saddle became Bert Terhune's first published book, but getting it published was not easy. It was rejected by eleven publishers before finally being accepted by a Boston firm, Silver, Burdett & Co. Terhune received a minuscule advance against royalties of $50. The book was not very successful, although it received generally good reviews. Terhune always claimed later that it was a commercial disaster and didn't sell enough copies to cover the tiny advance. But his wife, in writing of her husband's career beginnings, said the book was an instant success. His mother loyally called it "a remarkable book, coming, as it did, from the pen of a boy of twenty-one." Her own book about the trip, published as *The Home of the Bible*, far surpassed the other in sales, but that was not surprising: almost any book with Marion Harland's name on the jacket was assured of a very healthy sale.

Meanwhile, the ambitious young writer was having a few other, if small, successes. A sonnet written aboard ship and titled "Sea Gulls" was published in *Harper's Bazaar*, as was a short story and an article on Branwell Brontë, based on material gathered in England. The publication of his book at the age of just twenty-three, along with the acceptance of his work by a major magazine, helped convince him finally that he must devote his life to writing.

The decision did not make his parents happy. His father always had hoped the boy would eventually perceive a call to the ministry. His mother—despite her love of writing and her assurance that Bert had literary talent—had wanted him to be a lawyer. But it was now obvious that writing was the only thing he felt strongly about. Bert understood, however, that a writing career could not come quickly or easily, even with his mother's contacts. He estimated later that the few magazine sales he made during this period represented less than 1 percent of his total literary production during that time span.

10

In the cold December sunshine The Visitor walked over the earth of Sunnybank.

He had come around to the front of the house and stood there, on the circular drive, looking down to the lake. Before him was the front lawn so often described, the site of the famous "Garden from Everywhere." It looked very little like a garden, today. The exotic plants and shrubs were mostly gone now, long dead like those who had planted them there. Only a few brown, tattered remnants remained, scattered here and there across the grass. There were some trees of various types and sizes still living on the lawn, but it was a nondescript scene, a far cry from the lavishly planted and landscaped floral paradise that had been the pride of the estate in its prime.

A picture suddenly came to The Visitor. He had to think for a few minutes to remember where he had seen it, then his eyes brightened and he half-smiled as he thought of it.

It was the cover illustration of one of Bert Terhune's books in its late-1960s form, one of the many Terhune books then still in print. He had gone to a department store just before Christmas and purchased the entire set of fifteen books. They were for his own children, for he was determined that they would have the pleasure of reading Bert Terhune's dog stories even if the books were no longer for sale when they had grown old enough to enjoy them. He still remembered the look of surprise and confusion on the face of the elderly saleslady in the book department when he placed his order.

"You—you really want all of them?" she had stammered. "You want to buy all fifteen of the Terhune books?"

On the cover of one of those books was a drawing of two big collies charging lustily across the Sunnybank front lawn, the old house towering behind them.

Their thick white ruffs shone like snow and their mouths were open in expressions of unfettered joy.

And now here he stood, on that same fabled turf. He reached down, picked up a bit of the cold soil and let it sift through his fingers. Perhaps right on this spot, Lad and Wolf and—. Then another thought struck him as to what else Lad and Wolf might have been doing on this bit of ground and he grinned and hastily dropped the grains of sod and brushed his hands off. "The sacred and the profane," he muttered to himself, and continued his slow walk.

Just down the grassy slope were the sagging remains of the little summerhouse. It was a morose sight: the little house barely stood, thin and wasted in the lakeside wind. It looked like a frail old woman, standing there holding its breath for a few final, proud moments, knowing that if it relaxed it would collapse to the ground and all would end. Another of the random, miscellaneous parts of Sunnybank, it had inevitably found its way into one or another of the Terhune writings. And, like the house, the barn, the entrance gate, the little summerhouse had woven itself inextricably into the memories of thousands of Terhune's readers.

A thin slab of wood was nailed across the entrance to the summerhouse, making sure that no one would dare to enter the old structure, though The Visitor could see no reason why anyone would wish to. The inside was empty, except for a fragile wooden chair that faced out toward the lake. Perhaps someone had set it there as an illustration of the way the Terhunes and their friends had sat in the summerhouse on mild May evenings, enjoying the breeze off the lake and watching the sun settle behind the hills across the water. Or perhaps, The Visitor thought illogically, perhaps that actually is one of the Terhunes' chairs still sitting there, with no one having thought or cared to take it away.

Mawkish, ridiculous as it was, he could not help thinking of the chair as waiting faithfully for an owner who was forever gone. It was silly, he knew. Yet, there stood the chair, looking out at the lake, waiting endlessly in the crumbling old summerhouse and hearing only the silence, feeling nothing except the wind and sun and sleet.

The Visitor crossed down below the summerhouse and walked along the shore, listening to the small waves lap against the steep bank. Pieces of ice floated in the dark water. He walked south. The lake narrowed considerably there, to a width of just a few hundred feet, as it assumed more the proportions of a river and prepared to confront the dam a half-mile or so downstream.

Across the narrow stretch of water loomed another hillside and on it were houses. A string of wash flapped behind the nearest one and took the winter wind. The Visitor wondered whether the people living in those buildings had lived there during the glory days. What a ringside seat they had: They could look right down on Sunnybank and watch the golden collies dart around and see the great man walk among them and perhaps wave or shout a "halloo" across the blue lake. He remembered that even those houses across the water had been utilized by Terhune. There was one of the *Gray Dawn* stories, for instance, in which the giant gray collie had swum the narrow neck of lake and gone across to visit a pretty female collie neighbor, only to wind up in the usual crises that befell a Terhune collie, narrowly escaping being poisoned by the witchy owner of the female.

If people actually were living there across the lake at the time the *Gray Dawn* story was published, The Visitor thought, they probably were not enthralled by the way they had been portrayed.

He turned away from the lake again and looked back at this portion of Sunnybank. This was the southernmost part of the estate, the area that had been cleared by the Rev. Terhune more than 100 years earlier and turned into an orchard.

It looked now more like a giant vacant lot. It was open and uncluttered, as it always had been, but it wore a kind of absent-minded drabness. It was just a field now, not lushly overgrown, but unkempt with weeds and scrub trees.

At the foot of the orchard, he remembered from the old accounts of Sunnybank and from pictures, a line of weeping willow trees had stood near the lake bank and cast their overhanging leaves into the water. They had formed a tunnel of green at the edge of the blue lake. The willows were gone.

He looked back across the field and up the hill. Through the trees near the top of the slope he could see the next house, the nearest neighbor to the south. But it was some distance away and there was no sign of activity there. Again he felt the overpowering sense of quiet and aloneness. He felt once more as if he had stepped into a noiseless ancient world, full of haunting memories, echoing with the footsteps of people and animals who were just there up ahead . . . who had turned the corner just ahead of him, who couldn't quite be seen.

The Visitor studied the old orchard. There were more trees still standing across the big field than he had first realized. He recognized some elms and maples, a couple of hemlocks, and one or two dogwood trees. The chestnuts had disappeared, victims of a massive blight years before.

He was looking for a way back to the house without retracing his path when he caught sight of the vista and his breath stuck. You could really see it only from a particular spot along the lake shore—it was just chance that he was at that point when he happened to look back up the hill. Now it was only an ill-defined, ragged linear opening in the hillside brush. But he knew immediately that this was the impressive aisle down the magnificent rose garden that had led from the hillside near the house all the way to the water's edge. He had found the photograph in one of the old Terhune books along with others of Sunnybank; to him it always had typified the grandeur of the estate during the years that Bert Terhune had lived and written there.

The picture had been taken from the hillside, looking down toward the lake. On the right, the path was escorted lakeward by a neat row of narrowly spaced trees, perhaps elms. Equidistant on the left was another companion row of lower, broader trees, probably dogwood. And flanking the manicured pathway on either side were long rows of sumptuously blooming rose bushes.

Framing the scene perfectly, almost as if the photograph had been a painting, came a series of delicate trellises, roses clinging to their sides and tops, a chain of flowery gateways drawing one onward to the distant water. The trellis closest to the camera loomed directly in front like a giant entranceway, the others stretched out in the distance, seemingly to infinity.

The Visitor walked up the hill, along the weed-choked remains of that regal pathway. No trace remained of the walk; there was only a narrow space through the brush. The rose bushes had vanished; only the tree rows still stood on either side.

As he ascended the hill and approached the upper end of the old rose vista, he saw a rusted iron trellis hanging above him, still crossing the empty spaces that no longer bore the scent of rose. The trellis, like everything else at The Place, looked ready for collapse. But still it stood, hanging there above the weeds, the last rusted vestige of one corner of a beautiful world that once had been.

11

The planting had begun at Sunnybank soon after the minister and his wife had taken the afternoon buggy ride that made them owners of the country tract.

The willows at the edge of the water were the descendants of twigs brought from Devonshire in 1652, which had been planted at a Virginia plantation called Olney, birthplace of Mary Virginia Hawes Terhune. Twigs from the Virginia trees were carried to Sunnybank.

When Bert accompanied his mother to Europe in 1893, it was not their intention to undertake a floral talent hunt. But at Anne Hathaway's cottage at Shottery near Stratford-on-Avon, the caretaker gave them a sprig of rosemary from the garden. And when they visited the garden of William Cowper, another caretaker gave them a sprig of southernwood.

It was then that Mrs. Terhune decided to create a beautiful "from everywhere" garden at Sunnybank. She would bring back to her beloved home bits and pieces of flowers and plants from all over the world. It was hoped that they would take root and flourish in northern New Jersey, reflecting something of their original homes.

And so it was that the grounds of Sunnybank, and especially the flowing lawn running from the house down to the lake, boasted a spray of ivy from the Black Prince's Well and a tiny shrub from Charlotte Brontë's garden at Haworth. There was wild cyclamen from the hills above the Sea of Galilee, wallflowers from Kenilworth Castle, ivy from the Stoke Poges church and violets from the churchyard made famous by Gray's "Elegy Written in a Country Churchyard," deep-purpled, fragrant iris from a garden of the Medicis in Florence, sweet alyssum from Algeria's Atlas Mountains and from Pompeii,

Scottish broom from Virginia, and a rose bush from an old mission garden at Mackinac Island.

Bert Terhune wondered years later how his mother had managed to keep the slips and cuttings alive during the travel from Europe back to the United States. But she had a mystical communion with flowers. A gardener at Sunnybank once told him, "I don't know how much she loves flowers. But I *do* know how much they love her. Why, she can bring 'em back from dead, and she can do everything with 'em but make 'em talk."

Terhune's parents cared for the Garden from Everywhere and added to it as long as they lived at Sunnybank. It then became the great pride of Bert and Anice Terhune. From their own extensive travels, they brought to it arbutus from the Berkshires, a Bermuda "life-plant," poppies from the foothills of northern California, geraniums from San Juan Capistrano and roses from Santa Barbara, lupin and wild mustard from the Mohave Desert.

In Greece, Bert once asked his guide the name of a common weed near the Acropolis and was told it was acanthus. Knowing that the weed was often mentioned in the classics and described by many poets, he was determined to bring some home to Sunnybank. It did indeed flourish at Sunnybank, where he discovered for the first time that acanthus is merely the common dandelion. The dandelions that annoyed him by sprouting all over the carefully tended Sunnybank lawns were, he used to grumble, the descendants of the acanthus roots he had taken from the grounds of the Acropolis and brought with tender care all the way across the ocean to New Jersey.

Throughout his life, Bert Terhune continued to plant at Sunnybank. In 1934, he wrote:

This past year I have planted more than a hundred trees of various kinds; besides some dozens of shrubs.

Why in the name of all that is sensible did I do such a futile thing? I am sixty-one years old. The Mistress is only a bit younger.

What possible benefit can she and I hope to derive from the planting of trees which will take from twenty to seventy years to reach full maturity?

That is a rhetorical question. There is no answer to it. . . .

While we shall live, the Mistress and I shall plant. Not through any noble motive, but on the blind vital urge that makes a dying tree put forth a brave show of leaves in the spring of its last year of life.

12

Bert's trip was over, his book was published and the readers of America had taken little note of it. It was time for him to go to work. His one serious ambition was to write, preferably while living at Sunnybank. But he knew, having sold only a fractional part of his output, that building a writing career would take time. He would have to establish a name for himself. Until he did so, there was the need for a job. He probably could have continued to live with, and on, his parents while writing, but his pride wouldn't let him do that and he knew they would have been displeased with such an arrangement.

It seemed to him logical that, for a hopeful writer, a publishing job would be desirable. He could pick up valuable knowledge of the book business while making useful contacts.

Before leaving on the overseas trip, he had gone to see his mother's publisher, Charles Scribner, and had secured what he took to be a firm promise of a job with the prominent publishing firm after his return. When he came back to the United States, however, and contacted Scribner about a starting date for his job, the publisher kept putting him off and asking him to be patient, saying that things would be worked out shortly.

About the same time, when Terhune was wondering if Scribner was backing out of his commitment, a friend offered to get him a job as a cub reporter on the New York *Evening World.* The job would tide him over financially until the position with Scribner opened up, Terhune reflected, and the newspaper writing experience probably would help him in the publishing business.

So, on November 12, 1894, Terhune joined the news staff of the *Evening World,* fully intending to hold the job for just a few weeks. He remained with the newspaper for more than twenty-one years.

The *Evening World,* owned by Joseph Pulitzer, was one of more than a dozen New York City daily papers. It existed in a cutthroat journalistic world of fierce, no-holds-barred competition. The *Evening World* and its more prosperous sister paper, the *Morning World,* had separate editorial areas in the dingy, cluttered tower of the Pulitzer Building (or World Building as some called it) alongside the Brooklyn Bridge in the legendary newspaper area known as Park Row.

Terhune began newspaper work at a salary of $15 per week. The modest pay gave him, Terhune said later, "a feeling of wealth that never was mine before or since." His new-found affluence caused him to decide to leave his parents' home in Brooklyn and find a furnished room in Manhattan. He rented a tiny, airless cubicle on Gramercy Park and spent the next few years in various rented rooms in that area and in Greenwich Village. His parents hardly felt lonely after he left: Christine and her two sons had come back to live with them after the death of James Herrick a year earlier; and Virginia, her husband, and two sons were frequent visitors, as was Bert.

Bert Terhune was a rank beginner as a reporter, greener than grass. He never had covered so much as a dog fight. But his size and rather pugnacious expression made him look older than he was and the tailored suits he wore, purchased in England during the trip, impressed his editors. The fact that he had had a book published didn't hurt his reputation and a few of the more literary editors vaguely knew that his mother was some sort of big-name writer. So he stumbled through the first weeks without too much difficulty, learning how to write a news story and how a sheet of copy is set into type and then put into its proper place in the big forms in the composing room.

His years as a newspaperman were to provide Terhune with the base income that enabled him to develop his long-coveted writing career. And they brought him into contact with many prominent figures in the worlds of sports, entertainment, and politics, celebrities who left him with a mass of vignettes and anecdotes that were used later in his massive production of articles, stories, books, and radio scripts. Yet, despite all that, Terhune looked back on the newspaper part of his life with great disgust. He minced no words about it in his autobiography: "I did not like newspaper work. I loathed it. During my entire 21 ½ years on the *Evening World,* I never once ceased to detest my various jobs there and the newspaper game in general."

Another time, in an autobiographical magazine article, he referred to "twenty endless years of newspaper work, which I detested and of which I have not one pleasant memory." He expressed the same sentiments privately. In a letter to a business friend in 1932, he spoke of "the rotten old *Evening World* days."

Terhune's reasons for his hatred of newspaper work never were completely explained. He apparently got on well with his co-workers on the *Evening World* and some of them remained his lifelong friends. Like any reporter, he held some of his editors in contempt and spoke highly of others. The newspaper certainly made ample use of his talents and he wrote many popular special features.

One fact is that he blamed his newspaper service for ruining his writing style, from the standpoint of its literary value. The writing habits of his journalism days, he often said, had killed off any hopes he had for creating works of real artistic significance. He wrote years later: "Three years spent in various capacities on a big newspaper is grand training for any writer. It teaches him conciseness and concentration and a correct marshaling of his facts and to discard non-essentials. But every subsequent year at it renders him more and more unfit for anything else. At the last it tends to make his writing hurried and slovenly and without distinction. As it has made mine. (That is not false modesty by the ill-tasting truth. Nobody knows it better than I; and nobody can know or care, one-hundredth as much as do I, how doughtily and futilely I have tried to correct the incorrectable blemish.)"

One also can surmise that he found the restrictions of a regular newspaper job unduly confining and chafing. He was born to be a free-lance who writes only at his own instigation and only in a manner directed by his own creative impulses. To such a writer, whether his tastes lean to imagist poetry or confessions for the pulps, it is intolerable to have to write to someone else's order.

Three months after he joined the *Evening World,* Terhune's pay was raised to $20 a week. The raise was a result of his good work in covering the Brooklyn streetcar strike at the start of 1895. Until that assignment, his work had been mostly in the office and also covering routine news assignments. The paper's first edition hit the streets at noon. Terhune worked from 8:00 A.M. to 5:30 P.M. and his first three hours were spent taking stories from the *Morning World* and rewriting them for the noon edition.

The city editor sent the big, inexperienced cub to Brooklyn in a desperate effort to get better coverage of the violence-pocked street-car labor dispute. Soon after Terhune arrived on the scene, he was almost mobbed by a group of strikers who thought he was a Pinkerton man sent by the company to break the strike. When other newsmen vouched for his identity as a reporter, the strikers calmed down. They told him they wanted better coverage of their side of the strike and offered to feed him news tips if he would make sure their point of view was adequately presented. He agreed and remained in Brooklyn for three weeks, phoning in stories. He scored beat after beat, thanks to the strikers who kept their promise to inform him of every new development. The episode improved his standing at the *Evening World* and also made him feel that he finally was a real newspaperman, even if not a particularly good one.

Most of his newspaper career was spent in the office, writing features of various kinds, and he never really was a street reporter. But he did score one more major news beat in his career, thanks mainly to lucky proximity. On June 26, 1906, substituting for the paper's drama critic, Terhune was covering the opening of a musical comedy at the Madison Square Garden roof. There he witnessed the famous shooting of Stanford White by Harry Thaw. He raced to a telephone —forcibly took it away from a man talking to his girl friend—and phoned in a "flash" that made the next edition.

On his visits to Sunnybank, Bert always saw Lorraine Bryson. He was seriously interested in her, and she obviously felt the same way about him, but his financial situation was not yet stable enough even to begin thinking about marriage.

And then, shortly after starting at the newspaper, Terhune again met Annie Stockton, the pretty gamine who had been his playmate and advocate during their childhood in Springfield. She had displayed considerable talent as a musician, was studying composition, piano, and organ, and had ambitions to become a concert pianist. They had seen each other occasionally over the years, but this new meeting seemed to have more meaning than any before.

Annie Stockton had become Anice Stockton. Throughout her life as Bert Terhune's wife, she was always known by that name and was so listed in *Who's Who in America* and all other reference books, although it was not her given name. Her birth certificate read "Anna Olmstead Stockton" and her marriage license "Annie Morris Stockton." Somewhere during her adolescence, Annie—always very conscious of her distinguished family lineage—presumably decided that good old Annie was no longer a suitable name for a budding young concert artiste of notable breeding. And so she began calling herself Anice, a name probably taken from Annis Boudinot, who married one of her ancestors. She pronounced her new name Ann-iss, accented on the first syllable, in keeping with the way her ancestress had spelled and pronounced the name. New name or not, when they met again Bert called her Annie as before and would continue to call her that all his life.

Anice remembered years later that she was fascinated by his appearance. He had grown to his full height of 6 feet 3 ½ inches and, as a souvenir of his trip, affected a Van Dyke beard and turned-up mustache which she felt made him look like Mephistopheles. He seemed almost to have been carved out of rock—tall, thick, incredibly strong, and yet graceful when he boxed or fenced.

Both of them said later that they felt certain they were in love. But, through a series of misunderstandings, they again drifted apart. Once Bert called on her and was told she was ill. He came again a few days later, but she had gone to see a doctor and a maid forgot to tell her that he had come by. He thought she was avoiding him. There were other missed appointments and, as Anice wrote much later, "Everything went wrong. People came between us." Each felt that the other should have shown interest, each felt hurt in the way that only a young person in love can feel it. They did not see each other again for almost five years.

With Anice out of the picture once again, Bert began thinking of Lorraine Bryson. She in turn left her teaching job at the De Mille school and returned to New York City to live with her parents, possibly so she could see more of Bert Terhune. They began dating more frequently and more seriously. Bert was living rather well on his slowly increasing salary. His rented room was cheap and he spent almost everything else he made on his happy life as a young bachelor-about-town. A dollar went pretty far in those days. A big evening with Lorraine went something like this: two tickets to the theater at $1.50 each, a chartered buggy for the evening costing $3, a big bunch of violets for another $3, and a lavish after-theater supper at Delmonico's for $5 for two, including tip.

Food always played a big part in Bert Terhune's life and he reveled in Manhattan's array of fine restaurants. At good restaurants—The Black Cat, Morelli's, Maria's, or Duquesne's—a fine dinner plus a pint of wine could be had for 30 to 50 cents.

Right after payday, when money was no concern, Bert could go to Purssell's for an outstanding dinner with wine for only $1.25. But the favorite hangout for Terhune's newspaper friends was Jack's, where the proprietor, Jack Dunstan, provided a 16-ounce porterhouse steak, rolls and butter, a heaping dish of French or German potatoes, and a saucer of piccalilli—all for 50 cents. The newspaper gang, often including Bert, could be found there from 6:00 P.M. to 5:00 A.M. Just before payday, on the other hand, when money was low, one could always eat in the 24-hour-a-day restaurant on the fourteenth floor of the World Building, where one could get breakfast for 15 cents and lunch for a quarter and put the meals on the tab, with payment not due until Saturday.

During his first couple of years at the *Evening World,* Terhune was assigned to the city room staff and covered a variety of news assignments. In the fall of 1896, however, knowing that he would have Lorraine's expert assistance, he volunteered to review a French book which no one else on the staff could read. The managing editor noticed the review and Terhune was transferred to the editorial-and-magazine department, where he remained the rest of his years on the paper, except for occasional sports assignments and a few spot news jobs. Terhune was happy with the shift, which meant shorter working hours. His work ranged from supplying humorous photo captions to editing letters-to-the-editor to writing human-interest features and, occasionally, a minor editorial. For a time, he ran a book review section.

Then, to his delight, he was assigned to write some of the cheap fiction that adorned many of the newspapers of that era. At first, most of the fiction was rewritten from melodramatic play scripts sent to the newspaper by Broadway producers such as W. A. Brady and Charles Frohman. When the supply of scripts dwindled, Terhune was allowed to create his own stories.

"It was the kind of work one can do with one's eyes shut," he wrote later. "The formula was simple. . . . It was fun to write them. They were excessively terrible." The formula involved an exciting development taking place every thousand words through the story and a big climax at the end of each installment. Terhune persuaded his friends to write letters to the paper lauding his fiction in hopes that it would be continued.

It was then that Terhune discovered a device he used regularly for finding sufficient time to spend on his outside writing. He would write the 2,000-word installments of the current newspaper fiction during pauses in his regular morning's work. Meanwhile his editors thought the creation of the fiction required considerable effort and concentration and allowed him to take the afternoon off each time a new chapter was due, supposedly to work on it in the quiet of his home.

Terhune by that time had become one of the boys at the *Evening World*. He was good at his job, and he could drink and carouse and play poker with the best of them. The composing room crew had started calling him "Terry" and the nickname was picked up by some of the other writers.

One of the stranger concomitants of his friendship with the other newspapermen was the increasing frequency with which he was called upon to be a pallbearer when a member of the *Evening World* staff died. Terhune presumed that his popularity for this morose assignment was because he was big, maintained a rather solemn expression, and owned a frock coat and high hat. He estimated that he served fifteen times as a pallbearer during his more than twenty-one years with the paper.

As 1896 drew to an end, Terhune's salary continued slowly to increase. The improvement was due in part to his higher standing with his editors, but even more so to a newspaper hiring war. William Randolph Hearst had recently purchased the New York *Morning Journal* and was actively raiding the Pulitzer *World* staffs with offers of better pay. The result was a marked improvement in pay to *World* employees in an effort to counter the Hearst overtures. By 1898, Terhune's pay had reached $35 a week, more than doubling his starting salary, and equalling the amount received by the highest paid reporters when he had joined the staff.

His improving financial condition and the knowledge that his job was fairly secure finally gave Terhune courage to take the step he had been pondering for months. Around Christmas, 1896, he proposed to Lorraine Marguerite Bryson, was accepted, and gave her an engagement ring. No wedding date was set immediately, but long engagements were not uncommon then. Bert wanted to set aside some money to begin married life, and the likelihood is that they were thinking of a wedding some time in the summer of 1898.

The elder Terhunes were delighted at the news; they had become very fond of Lorraine and were relieved to learn that their youngest and last unmarried child had found a life partner.

It was a relaxed, happy time for Bert and Lorraine. His newspaper job provided him with plenty of passes to concerts and plays. After a concert at, say, the Madison Square Garden Music Hall, Bert could escort Lorraine to one of the summer roof gardens that had become so popular—places like Hammerstein's Olympia Roof or the Casino —where delightful entertainment could be enjoyed for a dollar.

The only thing marring Bert's happiness was his increasing concern over the failing health of his father. Rev. Terhune had undergone surgery shortly after resigning his last Brooklyn pulpit in 1895. He resumed an active life as a guest preacher at churches in Omaha, Chicago, and St. Louis, but the trips weakened him and when he returned to Sunnybank he was feeble and growing worse. He tried occasionally to ride horseback, but the pain caused him to return after only a few minutes. Doctors in Manhattan ordered another operation for what was diagnosed as a malignancy. He survived the surgery in reasonably good condition, but the ordeal triggered a flareup of his wife's lung condition and she was ordered south to Richmond for a rest with her relatives, leaving her husband in the care of his two daughters. When she came back to Manhattan, where they had taken an apartment, she discovered that her children had kept from her the news that Rev. Terhune's condition was much worse. He appeared to be dying.

In the late summer of 1897, Mrs. Terhune decided to make a last, desperate gamble. She remembered how her husband had saved her life by taking her to Europe in 1874 and she knew that nothing could be lost if she made the same effort for him. She announced to unbelieving family and friends that she would take Rev. Terhune to Europe in search of another miraculous cure. Her husband had agreed to the trip and no argument from anyone else could change her mind. It was decided that Virginia and her family would live at Sunnybank and that Christine and her two sons would accompany them to Europe.

When they sailed, virtually all of those who came to the dock to see them off were certain it was the last time they would see Rev. Terhune alive and most were in tears. Bert and Lorraine were there, and she later wrote Mrs. Terhune that the departure of the ship left him very depressed and despondent.

The miracle of twenty-three years before was repeated. Within a day or two, Rev. Terhune declared that the brisk salt air aboard ship made him feel very much invigorated, and soon he was striding the ship's decks with his old energy. The six-month trip was all that Mrs. Terhune had hoped: her husband grew increasingly stronger, his spirits rose dramatically, and the old pain was gone.

Some time after his parents sailed for Europe, Bert and Lorraine decided to elope. Why they made this decision is not known. Perhaps they had no taste for the big, lavish wedding they knew would be expected. Perhaps it was because Bert thought his father's death was imminent and it would be better to marry now, before it happened and plunged him into mourning.

Whatever the reason, Bert and Lorraine traveled to Cazenovia, New York, a small town southeast of Syracuse in central New York State, and were married there on January 10, 1898. He was twenty-five years old, she was twenty-two.

Returning to New York City after the ceremony, the newlyweds set up housekeeping at 53 Washington Square. Bert went back to his newspaper work and continued to steal as much time as he could for his own writing, which had become concentrated mainly on books. The previous year, the firm of G. W. Dillingham had published his *Columbia Stories,* a series of tales about undergraduate life at his alma mater, but the book had a poor sale. There is evidence that Terhune wrote several other books during the last years of the nineteenth century, but apparently could not get them published. The 1901–02 edition of *Who's Who in America* included Terhune's biography, although he was still under thirty years old, and the sketch listed him as the author of: *Paul Dufour, Bohemian* (1898), *The Deluge of '99* (1898), and *A Galahad of Park Row*, for which no date was listed. No publisher was indicated for these works, in contrast to three other books which had been published and for which publishers were listed. Within a few years, there was no mention of the above works in Terhune's sketch in *Who's Who* and they never were included in later Terhune bibliographies. He did not refer to them in his own autobiographical writings.

In the late spring of 1898, Terhune learned that he would be a father in December. He was exultant. Perhaps he would be fortunate enough to have the son he longed for. He always had enjoyed being with children; had relished teaching them about the outdoors and counseling them on their problems. He could hardly wait for the day when his own son would be old enough to walk by his side at Sunnybank, to tramp the desolate back woods of the Ramapos with him, to row and fish on the blue lake that he loved so much. He had decided, with Lorraine's approval, that if the baby were a boy, he would be named Edward, after his grandfather.

At the office, the work load increased steadily—partly as a result of the news pressures engendered by coverage of the Spanish-American War, and partly because of the bitter circulation war with Hearst's *Journal*. Hearst had greatly improved his position by his sensational demands for war against Spain during the preceding months. Pulitzer was urging his staff to make up the ground lost to Hearst.

In July, Bert's old problem with appendicitis returned; this time his doctors said immediate surgery would be necessary. The appendectomy was performed and Bert managed to get some time off from the *Evening World* so that he and Lorraine could go up to the Adirondacks where he recuperated for several weeks.

His parents had just returned from their trip. Bert was anxious to see them and get a first-hand look at his father's new lease on life that his mother had written about. Bert and Lorraine went from the Adirondacks to Sunnybank, where they spent another month relaxing with his parents.

They listened to long, gay accounts of the rejuvenating trip to Europe. Bert, now able to resume regular physical activity, went back on his beloved hikes through the woods and mountains, played with the hunting dogs on The Place, and took his father out on the lake to fish. Lorraine spent much time sitting on the veranda with her mother-in-law and excitedly discussing with the great purveyor of domestic expertise her own homemaking plans. She paused once during such a chat to tell Mrs. Terhune that she was almost frightened at her own happiness. After the month was over, she and Bert returned to their Washington Square apartment and he went back to work at the newspaper.

On October 5, 1898, Lorraine unexpectedly went into labor and soon delivered a baby girl, born two months prematurely. A telegram was sent to Sunnybank announcing the birth and reporting that mother and baby were fine. But shortly after the telegram was sent, the young mother developed an infection. Her condition grew steadily worse; four days later she was dead, at twenty-three. Lorraine was taken to Pompton Lakes and buried there in the Terhune family plot behind the Pompton Reformed Church.

After the funeral on October 12, Bert took his tiny daughter—who had been named Lorraine Virginia—and returned to his parents' home to live. He was staggered with grief, bewildered, and frightened when he wondered how he—a widower and father at age twenty-six—would bring up his daughter alone. And, though he hated himself for feeling it, there was a bitterness that kept rising in him toward the newborn baby who had cost the life of the pretty wife he loved so deeply. He could not help blaming the baby for the tragedy.

Mrs. Terhune had not had a baby living in her home—except for her grandchildren—in thirty years and she was now almost seventy. But with her usual ability to adjust cheerfully to any new situation, she took over the care of Lorraine Virginia. The child was to be left almost entirely to her care for the next eight years. Lorraine years later told friends that this was the happiest time of her life. Her grandmother was a firm disciplinarian, but very loving. The child needed love; her father paid little attention to her.

Partially in an effort to assist him out of his grief, Mrs. Terhune suggested to Bert that they write a novel together. They began their collaboration, writing in the evenings when Bert came home from work and the baby was asleep. *Dr. Dale—A Story Without a Moral* was published in 1900 by Dodd, Mead & Company, the first American novel ever written jointly by mother and son—and this was its main claim to distinction. It was a murder mystery set in an oil town in Pennsylvania. The young doctor-hero comes to the town and quickly is beloved by all. His wife, whom he has left, follows him to the town and threatens to ruin everything for him. He kills her and later commits suicide. A reviewer for *The Nation* said of the book: "this novel . . . is too much of a hodge-podge of mush, millinery, elementary aesthetics, misplaced tragedy, and occasional descents to vulgarity to take high rank." Other reviews were somewhat kinder, but the overall reaction to the book was very tepid.

Gradually the fierce edge of his grief began to dull and Bert once again could concentrate on his work without Lorraine's face constantly confronting him, without the memory of her happy anticipation of motherhood torturing him. Gradually his life began to return to normal. But old feelings of longing, forgotten somewhat during his joyous months with Lorraine, began to well up in him again. He never could really be content in New York City and he knew why. In his autobiography, writing about this period in his life, he said:

Not thirty miles away—yet as distant from me, just then, as the farthest of the blurry stars that shone through the murk of Manhattan smoke—was Sunnybank; with its peace and loveliness and gentle spaciousness and its lake and the coolness of its solemn summer nights; its limitless quantities of wonderful food, its quiet rooms, its jolly companionship, and the dogs that missed me and that I missed so keenly.

I knew then, once more, what the Israelites felt, during the Babylonian Captivity. . . . And I renewed a fervid oath which I had sworn on the name of Almighty God in my boyhood—an oath that one day I should own Sunnybank and live there. I had no idea how this was to be brought about. But never for an instant did I doubt that it would be.

13

About the time the new century began, Bert Terhune again called on Anice Stockton and the old attraction was quickly rekindled. The calls became more frequent, then there were dates, and soon the two began to make plans to be married.

From that time on, Terhune's tragic first marriage became something that both he and Anice wanted to forget and wanted others to forget. For him, it probably was the source of too much pain and he preferred not to think about it. For Anice, it was another matter: she was deeply, frantically in love with Bert. And the mere thought of his having been in love with another woman, much less having been married to her and having had a child with her, was enough to reduce her to tears. As far as she was concerned, Bert's love life began with their reunion and she wanted him and everyone else to think of it that way.

Whether Anice ever discussed her feelings about Bert's first marriage with her future mother-in-law is not known. But there is irony (and perhaps an attempt at persuasion directed at Anice) in an April, 1901, article by the elder Mrs. Terhune, which appeared in *The North American* as Bert and Anice looked forward to their coming marriage: "I think the popular idea that the second wife is jealous of the first is a fallacy. By a happy dispensation of nature and grace she is more likely to believe that her husband never really loved until he met her. It follows naturally that her stepchildren are taken to her heart as his offspring, with little thought of the pale shadow in the background of his past." The article was titled: "Marion Harland Defends Second Marriages and Says a Good Word for the Stepmother."

Terhune never mentioned his first marriage in his autobiography or in the many other autobiographical passages scattered through his writings. In her reminiscence of her husband, published shortly after his death, Anice said only this of the five years between their two meetings: "Through those years, both of us had our own experiences remote from each other. . . . Strange to say, very real sorrow came to each of us, in different ways, before the five years were up. But it does not belong in this story."

One wonders whether Bert Terhune turned to Anice Stockton mostly to assuage his loneliness and to provide a mother for his daughter. But the evidence throughout their more than forty years of married life was that Bert was deeply in love with her. He was thoroughly devoted to her and protected and rather babied her throughout their long life together.

In early June, Rev. and Mrs. Terhune gave a large reception for the engaged couple at Sunnybank. The place was in full flower and provided a gorgeous setting for the 300 guests. They were married on September 2, 1901, in Hampden, a town on the Scantic River in Massachusetts.

Bert had wanted to get married sooner, but Anice had obligations in connection with her musical studies. So they had a fairly lengthy engagement. Bert was working hard, having been temporarily as-signed to the "lobster trick," the night shift at the newspaper.

The village of Hampden was chosen for the ceremony because it was Anice's birthplace. Her mother's family had for 200 years owned a country home, known as "Seven Maples," and both Anice and her mother had been born in the house. Rev. Terhune co-officiated at the wedding with a local minister. Anice was fond of saying later that they had been married in a Methodist church by a Dutch Reformed clergy-man and a Congregational clergyman using the Episcopal marriage service. The wedding was followed by a small reception for family and close friends at "Seven Maples."

On the marriage certificate, Bert Terhune had checked the proper blank indicating that this was his second marriage. But the next ques-tion—asking "Widowed or Divorced?"—was left unanswered.

Anice was almost a year younger than Bert—he was twenty-eight and she was twenty-seven (although she fudged a bit and listed her age on the marriage license as twenty-five)—having been born on

October 27, 1873. Her parents were John and Elizabeth Stockton of New York City. Anice was one of seven children and her mother died when she was ten. Her father remarried and later sired five more children. He had been a medical student, then turned to law and became a prominent attorney in Jersey City. A cultured man, he was deeply interested in music and was the author of several books.

Anice was descended from families prominent in American history: the Stocktons, the Morrises, and the Olmsteads. One of her ancestors, Richard Stockton, was a signer of the Declaration of Independence and it was his wife, the former Annis Boudinot, whose name was adopted by Anice Stockton Terhune.

Like Bert's first wife, Anice was small and he towered over her. She had brown hair, big brown eyes, and a tiny button nose. Her interests were very cultural and artistic and she tended to speak in a slightly affected way, which Bert thought extremely "refined." She had greatly impressed him with her musical talent by taking a Syrian dirge from his book about his travels there and setting it to music— calling it "A Syrian Woman's Lament." It was accepted by the Schirmer music publishing firm.

After the wedding, the couple honeymooned at a small hotel in the White Mountains of New Hampshire, then spent some time with Bert's parents at Sunnybank before moving to a small fifth-floor walkup apartment at 167 West 80th Street in Manhattan. When they got to their new apartment, they waited in vain for the arrival of their four trunks, then finally were informed by the express company that the trunks, containing all their clothing as well as her furs and jewelry, had been stolen from the express wagon. The company, a small one, paid them a settlement for the loss but it was not nearly enough to cover the actual cost of the stolen items. Their ready cash amounted to only $18.

In spite of their near-poverty, they hired a woman to clean and cook. In part this was due to Anice's health, which was frail. But they also were quite certain they would soon be rich . . . an assurance that didn't miss its mark by too many years.

Lorraine, by this time three years old, continued to live with her grandparents. The ostensible reason was the fragile state of Anice's health. But the real reason was that Anice preferred not having Lor-

raine with them; it was difficult living the carefree life of newlyweds
—entertaining and being entertained—with a small child in the house.
And running like a deep bass chord beneath it all was the fact that
Anice could not bear to be reminded of Bert's first marriage. Bert's
mother had no objection to keeping the child with her—Lorraine's
presence made her feel almost young again. When she was occasionally out of town, Lorraine would live with the Van de Water family,
who had built a house, called "Kanesata," just to the south of Sunnybank.

Anice carefully, delicately made known her feelings about Lorraine to Bert. Though he must have felt some guilt at not having his
daughter with him, he did not protest. He was enchanted by Anice,
he did not want to do anything to make her unhappy. He reasoned
that Lorraine was being given the best of care by his parents and that
he would see her frequently.

Terhune was busily pounding out features for the *Evening World*
and also stealing bits of time during the day to do his own writing.
He was selling an occasional short story or article to a magazine, but
had comparatively little to show for the sales monetarily. His *Columbia
Stories* had been a financial failure and the novel written with his
mother, despite her large and loyal following, had only a modest sale.

Many of the co-workers on the newspaper, who had come to be
Terhune's good friends during his first five years on the staff, had
drifted away. A few had died, some had been fired or left New York,
some had given up newspaper work. The exodus was accelerated after
the Spanish-American War when Pulitzer brought Charles E. Chapin
from St. Louis to take over as city editor and Chapin drew other
associates with him. Chapin and Terhune quickly developed a mutual
dislike (though several years later this was dissipated) and Terhune
claimed later that Chapin tried several times to have him fired. One
result of this was that Terhune kept rather aloof from the new staff
members and didn't socialize with them as he had with the old crowd.
Anice didn't like the rough-and-tough newspaper crowd and preferred to spend time with more cultural and artistic friends.

Terhune was a nonstop worker—a fast, fluent, tireless writer—and
his editors took full advantage of his machine-like capacity for production. Beginning around 1897 he was the ghost writer for a number

of *Evening World* features, including a fiction serial ostensibly written by "Ten Beautiful Shopgirls" and a successor credited to "Ten Popular Actresses." He ghosted a serial under the name of Mrs. Leslie Carter and also wrote one under the byline—and apparently without the permission—of popular actress Lillian Russell, who wrote to the paper to proclaim publicly that "I am not in any way responsible for the incoherent drivel appearing in your pages under my name."

Later, having convinced his bosses of his knowledge of boxing, Terhune wrote a boxing serial under the byline of Jim Jeffries, a series of boxing tips supposedly written by Terry McGovern, and a muscle-building series credited to Jim Corbett . . . all leading fighters of the day.

A few years later he was asked by Dodd, Mead & Company to take a David Belasco play called *The Return of Peter Grimm* and turn it into a novel. However, the publisher said Belasco insisted that his name must appear on the novel as its author. Terhune agreed to the ghost job in return for some extra money in compensation for his anonymity. Three of the novel's chapters were written by Anice when her husband was ill with grippe and fearful that he wouldn't make the deadline. As revenge for the refusal to let him put his own name on the book, Terhune scattered through the novel the names of several residents of Pompton Lakes. He did so, he said later, to be able to prove, if he ever had to, that he was the real author of the book.

His salary at the newspaper had risen past $40 a week and he was adding to his base pay by writing additional stories and features and selling them to the *Evening World.* For a time—until his editor realized what he was doing—he averaged $20 a week by taking jokes from joke books, recreating them as colorful quotes and crediting them to well-known people in New York, most of whom were delighted by the publicity even if they couldn't quite remember having said what they were quoted as saying. He also wrote two- and three-line bits of editorial filler for 50 cents each.

One of the editorial crosses he had to bear was a sketch called "Up and Down with the Elevator Man," supposedly a monologue delivered by an elevator operator in the World Building. Terhune had written one as an experiment and Pulitzer took a liking to it and ordered that it be continued weekly. Terhune came to hate the sketch and found it unbearably difficult to write, but he was paid an additional $8 for it and continued to grind it out for almost a year.

His extra pay assignments became so numerous that the additional money sometimes surpassed his base pay. Always engraved in his memory was one week when he earned $63 in extra pay for a total of $103, all of which he lost in a poker game.

His editors became excessively fond of the number Fifty and he was assigned to write a seemingly endless series of features titled "Fifty Failures Who Made Good," "Fifty Blackguards of History," "Fifty 'Ifs' That Changed History," "Fifty Men Who Made Our Country." The research for these projects was a sort of mini-education for him and he uncovered much material that was to surface years later in one or another of his articles or books.

Being a physical giant and a writer of great resourcefulness, he was able to produce an immense amount of work. But sometimes even Terhune's incredible energy ran down, Anice recalled. One evening before their marriage when he came to call on her, he fell asleep on a couch and slept for two full hours.

The only part of his newspaper work that Terhune found really enjoyable involved his occasional duties in the "sporting department" as it was called then. Once in a while he filled in as a sports reporter, covering events ranging from championship fights to yacht races, which he called "pre-eminently stupid things to watch." He sometimes wrote sports features and took over for the sports editor when he went on vacation. The work brought him into close contact with professional athletes and he especially enjoyed the friendship of fighters.

Terhune still kept himself in good shape and boxed regularly. He spent some off-hours hanging around in the gyms inhabited by the New York boxing crowd and often would spar a round or two with a well-known fighter, usually managing to hold his own and at least giving the pro a bit of a workout. His amateur prowess as a boxer was known at the *Evening World* and led to an assignment that became one of Terhune's favorite anecdotes.

The managing editor of the *Evening World,* Nelson Hersh, was a big, gruff man, generally disliked by the paper's staff. He and Terhune had gotten along well, however, and one day he called in the big feature writer and asked him to take an unusual assignment. He was to perform what today would be considered a George Plimptonesque feat (Paul Gallico also undertook the same sort of assignment years before Plimpton): he was to box three rounds against each of six of the best heavyweights of the day and write about it for the newspaper. The six were Jim Corbett, Bob Fitzsimmons, Jim Jeffries, Kid McCoy, Gus Ruhlin, and Tom Sharkey. Terhune looked forward to the assignment with zest—he was confident of his boxing skill and he knew the fighters well and had sparred with them before. He anticipated some friendly trading of punches and an easy way of coming up with six good stories.

In the ring, however, the zest quickly vanished. Each of the big-name fighters attacked savagely, pounding the newspaperman around the ring without pity. "Never," Terhune declared later, "had I known them to display this vicious streak."

Terhune miraculously kept his feet and none of his six opponents was able to knock him down. But he took a considerable beating, suffering a broken left hand, losing two teeth along with much blood from facial cuts. "I used to limp back to the office in a deplorable condition," he commented later, "to write my daily tale of the carnage." As soon as he returned to his desk from the gym, Hersh would hurry over to get a first-hand account of the day's bloodletting.

No one had the courage to tell Terhune until a year later that Hersh had promised a special half-page feature story in the *Evening World* to the boxer who was the first to knock out the newspaperman. Each of the publicity-hungry fighters made a ferocious try for the grand prize, but none could achieve it. Corbett told Terhune after the exhibitions were completed that he regarded him as the best amateur boxer in the country.

Bert and Anice were enjoying their life thoroughly. His salary fluctuated greatly, depending on his ability to sell additional features. Some of the things he had been writing were eventually parceled out to other staff members and his salary dwindled back down to his base pay, which was up to $45 a week. The young married couple made little effort to save any money. Both of them were used to living well, eating well, and having a good time with their friends, and they were not about to change their mode of living. They spent almost every cent that he earned.

They began holding Sunday evening open houses for poets, artists, musicians, singers, a few newspapermen. Anice often would invite a small group for dinner, then others would come by until the crowd grew to thirty or thirty-five people. They would sit around and trade "yarns," as Bert always called them, and there would usually be some singing with Anice accompanying at the piano. Late at night, the women would cook a huge dish of Welsh rabbit while the men enjoyed cold beer.

Early in 1905, however, Bert was shocked into full awareness of his financial insecurity. Anice for several years had been troubled with a chest condition, which had been diagnosed as tuberculosis in a dormant, controlled state. Now she was stricken with pneumonia. The combination made for a very serious illness. Terhune took time off from work to care for her, but the doctor told them they must have a full-time nurse. Terhune didn't have the money to pay for it. He probably could have gone to his parents for help, but pride restrained him, along with the knowledge that his parents' financial condition was not as strong as it had been with the expenses of illness and the trips they had taken.

He hated to write humor, knew he had little talent for it, and certainly didn't feel humorous in the midst of this crisis. But he realized that the quickest way to earn some extra money at the paper was by writing jokes and comic fillers. In two nights, sitting at Anice's bedside, he wrote more than fifty jokes which he was able to sell, getting enough money to hire the needed nurse. That episode, Terhune said later, finished him forever as a writer of humor.

After Anice's recovery, her doctor recommended a move to Denver or a similar climate. Bert was quite willing to make the move, but Anice would not agree to it. She felt that Bert's writing career depended on his being in New York, the seat of editorial power, and she refused to ruin his career by making him move. The doctor said she must have fresh air and Anice answered that she would spend as much time as possible on the roof of the apartment building.

She asked for a year. Almost every day, for the next few months, she sat in a steamer chair on the roof—well bundled against the cold when necessary—while she sewed, read, wrote, and composed music. In the summers they spent Bert's vacation camping out in the fresh, cool mountain air of the Adirondacks.

In 1906, angered because their landlord would not fix a leaky roof, they moved to a third-floor apartment at 200 West 78th Street, where they were to live for the next ten years.

When the immediate crisis of Anice's illness was over, Bert had time to consider his financial situation. It appalled and frightened him. His work at the paper, including all the extra money he had earned for special features, didn't seem to be getting them anywhere from a financial standpoint.

In his autobiography, Terhune described his state of mind:

I had fooled myself into the idea that I was a moderately hard worker. But, after my joke-writing ordeal in January of 1905, I took account of stock and I realized I was a lazy failure. I must make a big change in my work and in my life itself, if ever I was to get anywhere. Especially if ever I was to get to Sunnybank.

I was thirty-two years old. I had not one hundred dollars in the world, above my weekly pay—which had been boosted from $45 to $47.50. I was several thousand dollars in debt. I had no reasonable hope of doing better along the lines I was following.

Once and again I had tried fiction writing. I had made barely enough by it to pay my typing bills. But I had been doing it only at odd times and when the spirit moved me. While youthful poverty may be amusing, there is no more humor in old-age poverty than in a malignant cancer. Fully a score of fellow-workers of my own age and even younger had died, leaving their wives penniless. I was not immortal. Also, a single long illness would wipe out not only my scant cash but my scantier credit; and might well leave me jobless.

That statement is probably one of the most revealing he ever made and depicted one of the most fundamental changes of his life. For at this point, some time in 1905, he made a momentous decision: he would write primarily to make money—as much money as possible. Whatever art he possessed, whatever claim he might feel he could make to literary greatness . . . all of this would have to give way to commercial objectives.

His deep-rooted fear was that he would be unable to care for his wife, that he might suddenly die and leave his wife and daughter completely penniless, or that he might find himself poverty-stricken in old age and shambling around to his old newspaper friends to ask for handouts. The last of those fears particularly haunted him.

Terhune cited a couple of the callers to whom he himself willingly gave handouts: a seventy-five-year-old man, once managing editor of a major New York daily paper, who supported a paralyzed wife and could not find a job even though he was a non-drinker, and an Englishman who had been a friend of Dickens and who had lost all his money when attempting to start a newspaper in this country. "To the few others on my unofficial and shifting payday list, I gave through no generosity or pity at all; but merely through a superstitious fear lest a refusal might come back upon me when, broke and old, I should make my own rounds of newspaper offices on paydays to cadge from former associates."

From that time on, and even after his writing had made him a rich man, Terhune worried incessantly about his income. Always there was the compulsion to write more and more and more. Always there was the burning necessity of earning as much as possible from it, and so the writing had to be as commercial, as marketable, as he could make it. It must be attractive and interesting to the buyers, the mass audience.

He never openly regretted the decision to become a commercial writer and sometimes vigorously defended the kind of writing he had chosen to do. Yet, there were also the poignant admissions which turn up here and there in his flood of writings, the sad little comments which say, in effect, "I wish things might have been different and I had been permitted to write . . . *really* write."

And, in addition to his fear of poverty, there was his eternal feverish desire to spend the rest of his life at Sunnybank. He wanted to be able to buy the estate from his parents eventually and he wanted to have the success as a writer that would enable him to escape the concrete mass of New York City and live permanently alongside the lake that he had loved since childhood. What Terhune called his "endless mortal craving" to live at Sunnybank was a major force in pushing him out of his continual semi-poverty.

Terhune resolved that he would write and sell fiction until his income from free-lancing allowed him to quit the *Evening World* and escape to Sunnybank. No longer would he wait for inspiration to strike before he wrote a short story or novel. Instead, he would set about his writing with the dogged energy and regular routine of any craftsman or artisan. He would set to work each day at a regular time and continue working a full schedule just like a plumber or pottery maker. Only in this way, he knew, could he produce the volume of saleable material necessary to achieve his objectives. It was a work routine he was to continue for the almost forty years of his active writing career.

Each night he would come home, after a nine-hour day at the newspaper, have a shower, eat dinner, and then sit down at his desk to begin writing. At that time, he composed everything in longhand. Five hours a night, five days a week, he sat and wrote.

"At first it was torment," he wrote later, "to attack fresh toil at the jaded end of a nine-hour work period. But, bit by bit, I got into my stride. The stuff I turned out was pretty bad, but presently I found a sale for it."

The nightly writing regimen continued for several years and gradually it began to pay off. He received $125 from *All-Story Magazine* for a serial called "The Secret of the Blue House." He had spent two months writing the 60,000-word serial and then skipped lunch for days and used the meal money to have the serial typed. He sold another 60,000-word serial to *Argosy* and got $180 for it. A second serial went to *Argosy* for $250 and eventually the payment from that magazine rose to $500 for a serial. He got $1,000 when one of his serials for *All-Story Magazine* was sold to the movies. Meanwhile, he was selling short stories to both magazines for small amounts ranging up to $50 each.

"I was working hard," Terhune said later, "for the first time in my life. And I was saving money. Not much money; but enough to keep me from lying awake half the night in futilely sweatful guessing at what would happen to my wife and daughter in case I should be laid by for a few months.

"It was a great sensation, this unprecedented freedom from penury. Fifty times over, it was worth the price in time and extra work which I was paying for it. The vow some day to own Sunnybank and to live there began to seem less fantastic than of old."

In 1906, Terhune had taken a moonlighting job doing promotional writing for a syndicator named Frank Lovell, who had been signing up big-name authors to write novels which he sold in serial form to newspapers in major cities. Lovell then would print the serials as cheap, paperbound books and sell them to department stores at discount prices. Lovell had persuaded some prominent authors to provide such novels for him and was anxious to add the novelist Winston Churchill to the list. Churchill had written a number of books with the letter "C" in the title and also had been writing some muckraking fiction about the financial methods of railroads. Lovell thought it might be easier to interest Churchill in the project if he could give him a ready-made story line tailored to the novelist's special interests. He asked Terhune to come up with such a plot. Terhune quickly put one together and called it "Caleb Conover, Railroader." It was presented to Churchill, who immediately turned it down. Lovell, in desperate need of another serial to market to newspapers, offered Terhune $1,500 if he would write the 60,000-word novel in thirty days.

Terhune, who never had earned such a large amount of money for a single writing job, eagerly accepted the assignment. "I was obsessed by a growing fear lest I might drop dead or break both legs before the book should be finished and the check in hand."

He began work immediately and finished the novel in twenty-one nights. Two of the chapters were written by his friend, humorist Irvin S. Cobb, because they involved politics and Terhune felt completely ignorant on the subject. Cobb would not accept any pay for his help. (Terhune and his writer friends—one of them was Sinclair Lewis—often helped each other out in this way; several chapters of Terhune's later *Dad* (1914) were written by Lewis.)

After it appeared in newspapers around the country, *Caleb Conover, Railroader* was published as a book by Lovell. It was Terhune's first book since his collaboration with his mother seven years earlier and he was extremely proud of it because he considered it to be "straight fiction" rather than a dime novel. The book managed to attract some critical attention. *The Independent* said: "This book is one of the strongest studies ever made of the American 'big boss' and from beginning to end is increasingly clever and interesting." Eventually it was made into a movie.

A year later, in 1908, Lovell decided to start a full-fledged publishing firm and asked Terhune to do another novel for him. The new book, published in 1909, was called *The Fighter* and its hero was a younger Caleb Conover. It was, wrote Terhune later, "the best thing I have done. It is almost the one book of mine of which I am proud. It is good, genuinely good. I admit that, myself. It is my nearest fictional approach to literature. I thought I was on the right road at last. . . ."

The book got generally good reviews and sold fairly well, being briefly on the best-seller list in a few cities. Paperback rights were bought by Grosset and Dunlap. Unfortunately, Lovell's publishing venture collapsed before he paid any royalties to Terhune, so the only money the author received was from Grosset and Dunlap, plus a small sum paid several years later for the movie rights.

It was as if Terhune had taken one last gamble as a serious writer and, with the financial failure of the publisher, had blown the try. He wrote in his autobiography: "So passed my one off-chance of rating as a fiction writer of quality. I fell back on the dime-novel serials."

Several of those serials were published in book form during these years, along with collections of the historical articles that he had written over a ten-year period for the *Evening World.* The titles included: *The World's Great Events* (1908), *The New Mayor* (1910), *The Woman,* based on a play by his childhood friend William C. De Mille (1912), *The Return of Peter Grimm,* credited to David Belasco (1912), *Dad* (1914), *Around the World in 30 Days* (1914), *Dollars and Cents* (1915), *The Years of the Locust* (1915), and *The Story of Damon and Pythias,* adapted from a film (1915).

He continued to punch out story after story, serial after serial, like a great drill-press. He was selling stories, novelettes, and serials to *Top Notch Magazine:* the stories brought him a cent a word up to 3,500 words and half a cent for each additional word. The novelettes of 8 to 10,000 words and the full-length serials brought him a half-cent a word.

Ainslee's Magazine hired him to write a series called "Super-women" (published in 1916 as a book) at $75, later $100 per installment. He began selling serials to the *Popular Magazine,* which paid better rates. Among the things he sold to the *Popular Magazine* were his "Najib" stories, featuring a character based on the dragoman who had escorted Terhune through Syria. The yarns were well received and reprinted in England. In 1925, when he was nearing the height of his popularity as a dog writer, the Najib stories were brought out in book form, but like most of his collie-less books they made little sales impact. By 1912, the ever-busy Terhune was getting $100 for most of the short stories he wrote and up to $1,400 for his serials. He was cranking out at least five serials and some twenty short stories a year. If too many deadlines piled up at the same time, Anice would help with some of the writing or part of the work was farmed out to his friends.

Around 1906, when she was about eight years old, Bert's daughter, Lorraine, came to live with them. Anice was not pleased and Bert hated to see his wife unhappy, but they agreed that they could not leave the little girl with her grandparents any longer. The health of Bert's father again was failing and it just didn't seem right to further burden the elderly couple with the task of raising the little girl.

Lorraine was enrolled in a proper private school and her father and stepmother simply made the best of the situation. During those years, whether explicitly or not, Anice Terhune made it quite clear to her husband that he must make a choice—between his wife and his daughter. She wanted him all to herself and she absolutely could not bear to share his affection with the child of another woman. Bert acquiesced. It was no contest, really. He worshipped Anice, could not deny her anything or make her unhappy. His daughter was something of a stranger to him, though he felt pride and some affection as he watched her grow.

Lorraine was well treated by her parents, there is little question of that, and when other people were around, the references to her and the gestures were reasonably affectionate. But the relationship never was a loving one and it grew cooler as the years went on.

On September 2, 1906, a golden wedding anniversary celebration was held at Sunnybank for Rev. and Mrs. Terhune. Their children and grandchildren presented them with a sundial made of Pompton granite for the Sunnybank lawn. Nine months later, on May 25, 1907, Rev. Terhune died.

For another couple of years, Bert's mother continued to spend her summers at Sunnybank and her winters in apartments on Manhattan's Upper West Side—on 94th, 95th, and 104th streets. She was dependent now on the financial support of her children. Although her family estimated that she had earned over $1 million from her writings, it was gone—spent on good living, lavish trips, and the accumulated expenses of years of illness. Her son had still another reinforcement for his always nagging fear of an old age of poverty. He resolved once again that this would not happen to him.

In 1909, thanks to increasing income from his outside writing, Bert satisfied the first part of his old dream: he bought Sunnybank from his mother. The transfer of The Place was not easily accomplished. In earlier years, when the elder Terhunes traveled, Sunnybank had been occupied by their daughter Virginia and her family. Mrs. Terhune assumed, therefore, that the Van de Waters would take over the place in time. But Bert would not hear of it. He felt that neither of his sisters loved Sunnybank as passionately as he did and it must be his. He pleaded, cajoled, and argued with his mother. Finally she agreed, citing an old Southern custom that the parents' real estate should go to the son of the family. And, she reasoned, Virginia and her family had the adjacent Kanesata and therefore could still enjoy the beauties of Pompton Lake and the Ramapos.

Her decision caused a serious rift between Bert and his sister Virginia, who also wanted Sunnybank. Her son Frederic remembered that, as a boy, he and the other Van de Water children were forbidden to visit Sunnybank or to speak to Bert and Anice. But the bitter feelings eventually were smoothed over and later Frederic, known to family and friends as "Fritz," became extremely close to Bert.

After the sale was completed, the elder Mrs. Terhune continued to spend the winters in Manhattan and the summers with Virginia at Kanesata.

Sunnybank badly needed repairs and money was required for its upkeep. Bert and Anice dug into their savings to add several rooms to the old house—the eleven rooms became sixteen—modernized the plumbing and made other changes. Meanwhile, the flood of mass-produced literary material kept coming and Terhune's income rose steadily. "The days of dead-brokenness were behind me," he wrote later. "I was working as never in the old times I had dreamed I could work. Again in quantity, not in quality." And then, in reminiscing about those years, came another of the sad little asides about what might have been:

> The stuff was less bad, by far, than had been the Lillian Russell and Leslie Carter and Ten Beautiful Shopgirls serials. But it was a billion miles from anything approaching literature. I knew that, better than did any one else; and I grieved bitterly at the knowledge. Yet the stuff was making money for me; not a fortune, but more money than ever I had had before. My office pay, too, had been increased to $80 a week.
>
> We were at Sunnybank at last—my wife and daughter and I. My early oath had been fulfilled . . . .

By about 1912 Terhune had made Sunnybank his permanent home, but for the six fall and winter months they remained in their Manhattan apartment. He continued with the *Evening World* because he did not feel certain yet that he could get by without the income from the newspaper job. During the months at Sunnybank, he would commute each day to the city.

Life at Sunnybank with his family was as glorious as he had anticipated. "Our life here . . . has been happier than I had believed any mortal lives could be," he wrote in 1930. "Reverently, fearfully, I have thanked God, a thousand times, for granting me not only my life-desire but the incredible and long-sustained happiness that has come with it. To many people, our glad daily and weekly and monthly routine here might seem monotonous. To my wife and myself it is an unceasing joy."

It no longer was necessary for Bert to spend many nights on his voluminous free-lance writing; he had discovered a much less tiring arrangement. He was given certain responsibilities at the *Evening World* and left alone to do them. He found that he could complete his newspaper work in about three hours and he spent the remaining six hours of the work day at his desk, intent on his outside writing chores. No one at the paper was aware of this. Terhune bore in smug silence his reputation as the *Evening World*'s hardest worker. One of his colleagues dubbed him "The Iron Man." A story attributed by Terhune to Irvin S. Cobb and by others to Thomas P. McVeigh, a *World* editor, told of McVeigh/Cobb coming out of the World Building and seeing a great pile of heavy chain in the street, each link weighing about 30 pounds. "Ha!" cried McVeigh/Cobb. "Terhune must be taking a day off!"

Terhune, who for several years had worked six nine-hour days a week at the newspaper and then gone home to write from 7:30 P.M. to 2:00 A.M., was quite aware of his reputation, enjoyed it, and poked some fun at it himself.

A few years after he left the *Evening World,* Terhune was interviewed by his old friend and co-worker Roy L. McCardell, who by then had moved over to the *Morning Telegraph.* In the feature story, Terhune compared his life as a free-lance writer to that of a prisoner released from a dungeon. Then he added: "From this time on, I shall loaf and invite my soul. I shall never do another tap of work as long as I live for anybody. That is, except a daily article for the *Evening World* and a big special or continued story for some paper from time to time when called upon. Then I shall write a few moving pictures a week, a story every month for the Red Book Magazine and, say, every week or so for the Saturday Evening Post, and one every issue for the Cosmopolitan Magazine, now that my friend Ray Long is editor."

The ethics involved in taking a full day's pay from the *World* for working just three hours a day never seemed to worry the highly ethical Terhune. The paper was satisfied with his work, he was efficiently doing everything assigned to him in three hours and felt that he had the right to spend the rest of the day on his own projects, even as other reporters sat around the city room and read or played cards during slack periods. He conceded, though, that had his bosses known of his work schedule, they would have reprimanded him, if not worse, and made sure that he was given more work. His free-lance writing was known to his bosses, of course, but they assumed that the writing was being done at home at night.

When John Jennings, editor of the *World*'s magazine section, fell ill, Terhune became acting editor, did Jennings's work as well as his own, and still had time for his outside writing. He got occasional job offers from other New York papers but turned them down because he knew he never could duplicate his ideal working conditions. When Jennings died, Terhune wanted his job desperately and got it. Though he hated editing he knew that a new editor quickly would doom his three-hour-a-day schedule.

The last five years he spent on the paper were much more pleasant than the preceding ones because he no longer needed the job so much. He wrote later: "No longer did I have to use up my sleep hours in wondering sweatingly what was to become of us if I should lose my job. No longer, on Thursdays, did I have to brace myself to get my office mail, lest the 'T' pigeonhole should contain a blue envelope . . . I do not think such job fear comes under the head of cowardice. No unmarried man need writhe at it."

Terhune was earning more than three times his $80 salary from free-lance writing and was expanding his list of buyers for fiction and articles. In 1913 Willard Huntington Wright—later to become known for detective stories written under the name of S. S. Van Dine, the creator of Philo Vance—became editor of the highly regarded *Smart Set* magazine. Wright liked a Terhune story narrated by a character named Aloysius Raegan, a philosophic small-time underworld character, and ordered a series of them. About fifteen of the stories were carried in *Smart Set*. Terhune was in good literary company: other writers getting about the same money for their stories in *Smart Set* included Theodore Dreiser, H. L. Mencken, Joseph Hergesheimer, and Witter Bynner.

One of the stories he had submitted to *Smart Set* was rejected by an assistant editor while Wright was out of town. Terhune decided to send it to Chicago, to Ray Long, editor of *Red Book*. Long did not know Terhune personally at that time but he knew his work and had admired some of the stories published in *Smart Set*. He bought the story, paid him $100, and offered more for future stories if they were acceptable. Long became a close friend of Terhune and bought many of his stories, serials, and articles for his three associated magazines— *Red Book, Green Book,* and *Blue Book*. A few years later, Long came to New York as editor-in-chief of the Hearst magazines and Terhune continued steadily to sell pieces to him.

It was Ray Long who changed Bert Terhune's life by casting him in a role that would make him rich and renowned and would envelope him until he died. It was Ray Long who made Terhune a writer of dog stories.

14

The Visitor had known that eventually he would come to the spot. When he did, he regretted that it happened so suddenly he had not prepared himself.

And then he thought, self-consciously, how silly it is to make such a fuss over just a place on the ground.

He had been walking slowly along the driveway that circled around the disintegrating old house, gazing up thoughtfully at the lonely wreck from time to time as if to get a new perspective on it, to see it as they had seen it, from a variety of angles and directions, during all those long, delicious years at The Place.

He was moving past the south end of the house, looking at what must have been the windows of the living room on the ground floor, when he turned his head to glance out toward the lake, and there it was. He angled across the gravel driveway, stood there, and looked down.

It was the grave of a collie dog and it lay in a little nook between trees just off the edge of the driveway, in a bit of hollow perhaps 18 inches below the level of the drive.

The dimensions of the burial place were partially marked by what remained of a stone border that mostly had been covered over with dirt. At the end of the small grave was a tidy little block of gray granite. It shone in the sunlight, as if someone recently had lovingly polished it. The Visitor knew the words engraved on the granite block, he had memorized them long years ago. But still he carefully read the inscription:

LAD
THOROUGHBRED IN BODY AND SOUL
1902–1918

The Visitor sat down in the cold December sunlight on the shelf formed by the edge of the driveway. He looked down again at Lad's grave and suddenly found himself crying.

Now you've done it, he thought to himself. Now you're really acting like a damned fool. But he couldn't stop and just sat there, alone in the desolate, sun-filled landscape, feeling the warm tears slide down his cheeks. He was relieved no one else was there to see him.

Why in the world would the grave of an animal have this effect on him? The tears abruptly ceased as he wondered about it. Was he crying for his lost childhood? Was he crying for his dead parents? Was he mourning for old heroes, long-lapsed fables, ancient dreams that disappeared as dreams always do?

Well, he thought, as he wiped his wet face on the sleeve of his overcoat, you're not the only maudlin character who has come to this grave and probably there have been more than a few who cried like you.

He knew that, while the Terhunes were alive, thousands of persons had come to Sunnybank and had expressly asked to see Lad's grave. Bert Terhune always had professed amazement that so many visitors would care to see a dog's grave.

Once Terhune stood at the grave with an Army general who had expressed the wish to see it. To Terhune's surprise and apparent embarrassment, the general bared his head. "But after all, he was only a dog," Terhune said. The general solemnly replied, "Sir, he was a brave soldier."

Terhune wrote: "Why folk should make pilgrimages to the grave of a dead dog is beyond my understanding. But come they do: and some of them bring sheaves of roses and others weep—this for an animal they never saw in life."

Yes, Terhune, you really did know why, you did understand, The Visitor thought as he sat there alongside the grave and stuffed his cold hands into his overcoat pockets. You gruff old bastard, with your fake toughness, you understood exactly why they came here and why I come here now and sit like a senile old lady and make a fool of myself, crying in the freezing weather for an animal I never saw. You knew why: Because you made him into some kind of saint, that's why. Because you took this collie dog and you told stories about his greatness and goodness and love and eternal loyalty, and with your storytelling skill, you made us—all the thousands or hundreds of thousands or millions of us—you made us actually fall in love with a damn dog! And he became the dog we always wanted to have and never did. Maybe even more than that—

maybe he became the friend we always waited to find, or even the brother, or the father. And this authentic-imaginary dog, whose only real interest in life probably was his next bowl of hamburger, this collie dog took hold of us and won't let go.

And you, Terhune, express wonder that people want to come see a dog's grave and you're probably having a hell of a laugh over it, wherever you are, watching me sit here and do my gray-haired weeping. Except that I know you wept, too.

You pretended not to understand why anyone would want to come visit the grave of an animal, but you made sure to bury him right there in that little sun-strewn hollow where he loved to lie when he lived . . . right there alongside the house, so he could keep watching over it and so you could glance out at him every now and again and smile a silent greeting.

You understand, you old fake. You know.

PART TWO

The Golden Time

15

Dogs had been a part of the life at Sunnybank ever since The Place had existed. Terhune's parents had loved dogs and always kept a few on hand, mostly bird dogs. One of them was the pointer pup which, with the help of his father's strong hands, had taught Bert Terhune as a small boy the misery that cruelty can bring to an animal, a lesson he never forgot.

Along the lake shore, in the trees a short distance north of the main buildings, was a little graveyard for dogs where the elder Terhunes would bury their pets when they died. Rough little markers were inserted at the graves, one of which dates back to 1876.

Bert was introduced to the more formal dog world in 1887—when he was fifteen and was taken to his first dog show, the Westminster Kennel Club show at the earliest Madison Square Garden.

Just when the first collie came to Sunnybank is not known. But Terhune wrote and told many times how he acquired his own first collie when he was thirteen. He had painfully amassed a savings of $9 and took it to the New York dog pound. There he bought a tricolored collie, which he named Argus.

"I devoted all my out-of-school hours to Argus's education," he wrote later. "He learned with bewildering ease, but I learned ten times as much from him as he ever learned from me."

It was Argus who made Terhune into a collie man—a strange, deep-rooted aberration afflicting collie owners by the score and, eventually, Terhune readers by the thousands. Its major symptom is the passionate, wholly illogical belief that one breed of dog rises regally far above the rest of the barking pack—and that the old Scottish sheep-herding breed whose very name, like its origins, is shrouded in mystery.

Though every breed has its equally impassioned adherents, collie people had the clear advantage, in Terhune, of a trumpet-like spokesman.

He was wont to write things like: "A dog is a dog, but a collie is —a collie." Or: ". . . the Sunnybank collies aren't merely dogs. They are super dogs!"

But much more than such extravagant claims about collies, it was the attributes given to the collies in his stories that had such a powerful effect on his readers. They were wise beyond belief, everlastingly gentle with those who merited such treatment (and the collies always knew), terrifyingly vengeful with those who didn't. And they were eternally loyal—so loyal that the word itself seems inadequate to describe their fealty.

Terhune also was apt to make sweepingly dramatic statements about the collie that would be impossible to prove:

"A collie is either the best dog or the worst dog on earth."

"A collie is always the easiest or else the most impossible breed of dog to raise."

"A collie has the brains of a man and the ways of a woman."

Some time in 1902, Terhune's parents acquired a collie puppy named Lad. It is difficult always to separate fact from fiction in Terhune's tales of his real-life dogs at Sunnybank, but he indicated in one of his Lad stories that the collie was purchased in order to have a watchdog on The Place. His parents' old pointer had died and there was a burglary scare as the result of a rash of thefts up and down the Ramapo Valley.

Just where Lad came from, Terhune never said. The dog apparently never was registered with the American Kennel Club, keeper of canine family trees and arbiter of pure breeding, but it seems quite certain, judging from pictures of him, that Lad was a purebred collie. It is possible that he was registered under another name by his original owners and the papers never were transferred to the Terhunes. But it was not at all uncommon for the owners of a purebred litter just not to take the trouble of registering the puppies with the AKC, particularly in rural areas where the dogs were bred as working animals rather than show dogs.

In his stories, Terhune claimed for Lad a lofty heritage. The puppy reached Sunnybank "preceded by a long envelope containing an intricate and imposing pedigree" . . . And "his pedigree shows a bunch of old-time champions" . . . And "with the mysterious foreknowledge of the best type of thoroughbred collie, Lad began to be aware that something unusual had crept into the atmosphere of The Place." In other Lad stories, Terhune declared that Lad had the names of twelve champion ancestors in his pedigree and described how the big collie won two blue ribbons at the famous Westminster Kennel Club show at Madison Square Garden, which was pure fiction.

Of noble blood or not, the real Lad came to The Place and was to become the beloved pet of the Terhune family and especially of Bert. Other collies came later—Lad's son Wolf, another big male named Bruce, and, eventually, his son Bobby. Figuring in some of the Lad stories was a nervous female named Lady who became Lad's mate and was killed by an automobile on the road above Sunnybank. Lady's life at Sunnybank was apparently rather short.

Whether Terhune gave any thought during the early years of the century, as he fought to establish himself as a writer, to making Lad a literary figure, we don't know. But he had been fervently interested in dogs since childhood, read everything he could find about them, and had begun to collect anecdotes about dogs in history as well as stories that sometimes appeared in the newspapers about modern dogs performing heroic or comic deeds.

He became a breeder of collies mainly so that there would be successors at Sunnybank to the loved dogs that were growing older. The breeding began in a very limited way, and as the puppies began to arrive it became necessary to sell most of them. The enterprise eventually became the famed Sunnybank Collie Kennels. It never was a huge operation, but Terhune sometimes had as many as forty collies in residence, a substantial population for a kennel operated only as a hobby. It probably was the best-known kennel that ever existed in the United States, thanks to the incredible reach of Terhune's pen, although many other collie breeders would angrily contend that the quality of the Sunnybank dogs—from a breeding and show standpoint —was inferior to a number of other, lesser-known collie breeders' stock.

Lad's rise to fame began late in 1914. The big collie was a senior citizen by then, twelve years old. Terhune's friend, Ray Long, the editor of *Red Book,* often stopped at Sunnybank on his trips to New York. Long was a tiny, quiet, kind man who was a masterful handler of temperamental writers. Sometimes he came to discuss story ideas with Terhune, sometimes he would just spend a few peaceful days resting at the beautiful Jersey estate. During these visits, Long took a liking to the old collie.

Lad apparently was an extremely reserved dog. Unlike the saccharine Lassie of television who licks everyone within tongue's reach, Lad wanted little to do with anyone except Terhune and his wife. The author turned this rather hostile reserve into a positive trait in his stories about the dog, describing him as "aloof" and "coldly civil" in a regal way.

Long had tried for a year to make friends with Lad, but to no avail. One day, finally, Lad surprised everyone by walking up to Long and resting his head on the editor's knee. "You'd have thought Ray had been knighted," laughed Terhune later.

Long, proud of his triumph in making friends with the solemn old collie, suggested to Terhune that he write a magazine story about Lad. The writer replied with great heat that he had been suggesting dog stories to editors for ten years but had been constantly turned down. All the editors insisted that the public wasn't interested in dog stories, so what was the use of writing one if it would be rejected everywhere?

"Write it," Long replied. "I'll print it."

It may have been Long's suggestion for a tale about Lad that first gave Terhune the idea of putting the real-life Sunnybank collies, along with The Place itself and his wife and himself in the role of the Mistress and the Master, into fictional stories. Or perhaps this was something that Terhune had in mind when suggesting dog stories to magazine editors during the past decade. Regardless of whose idea it was, Terhune quickly set to work on it.

The story was titled "His Mate" (a title used several other times by Terhune) and it was published in the January, 1915, issue of *Red Book*. A new canine hero was born and Albert Payson Terhune suddenly found his long-desired fame and fortune.

Here is that story:

HIS MATE

Lady was as much a part of Lad's everyday happiness as the sunshine itself. She seemed to him quite as perfect, and as gloriously indispensable. He could no more have imagined a Ladyless life than a sunless life. It had never occurred to him to suspect that Lady could be any less devoted than he—until Knave came to The Place.

Lad was an eighty-pound collie, thoroughbred in spirit as well as in blood. He had the benign dignity that was a heritage from endless generations of high-strain ancestors. He had, too, the gay courage of a d'Artagnan, and an uncanny wisdom. Also—who could doubt it, after a look into his mournful brown eyes—he had a Soul.

His shaggy coat, set off by the snowy ruff and chest, was like orange-flecked mahogany. His absurdly tiny forepaws—in which he took inordinate pride—were silver white.

Three years earlier, when Lad was in his first prime (before the mighty chest and shoulders had filled out and the tawny coat had waxed so shaggy), Lady had been brought to The Place. She had been brought in the Master's overcoat pocket, rolled up into a fuzzy gold-gray ball of softness no bigger than a half-grown kitten.

The Master had fished the month-old puppy out of the cavern of his pocket and set her down, asprawl and shivering and squealing, on the veranda floor. Lad had walked cautiously across the veranda, sniffed inquiry at the blinking pigmy who gallantly essayed to growl defiance up at the huge welcomer—and from that first moment he had taken her under his protection.

First it had been the natural impulse of the thoroughbred—brute or human—to guard the helpless. Then, as the shapeless yellow baby grew into a slenderly graceful collie, his guardianship changed to stark adoration. He was Lady's life slave.

And she bullied him unmercifully—bossed the gentle giant in a shameful manner, crowding him from the warmest spot by the fire, brazenly yet daintily snatching from between his jaws the choicest bone of their joint dinner, hectoring her dignified victim into lawn-romps in hot weather when he would far rather have drowsed under the lakeside trees.

Her vagaries, her teasing, her occasional little flurries of temper, were borne by Lad not meekly, but joyously. All she did was, in his eyes, perfect. And Lady graciously allowed herself to be idolized, for she was marvelously human in some ways. Lad, a thoroughbred descended from a hundred generations of thoroughbreds, was less human and more disinterested.

Life at The Place was wondrous pleasant for both the dogs. There were thick woods to roam in, side by side; there were squirrels to chase and rabbits to trail. (Yes, and if the squirrels had played fair and had not resorted to unsportsmanly tactics by climbing trees when close pressed, there would doubtless have been squirrels to catch as well as to chase. As for the rabbits, they were easier to overtake. And Lady got the lion's share of all such morsels.)

There was the ice-cool lake to plunge into for a swim or a wallow, after a run in the dust and July heat. There was a deliciously comfortable old rug in front of the living-room's open fire whereon to lie, shoulder to shoulder, on the nights when the wind screamed through bare trees and the snow scratched hungrily at the panes.

Best of all, to them both, there were the Master and the Mistress; especially the Mistress.

Any man with money to make the purchase may become a dog's *owner.* But no man—spend he ever so much coin and food and tact in the effort—may become a dog's *Master* without the consent of the dog. Do you get the difference? And he whom a dog once unreservedly accepts as Master is forever that dog's God.

To both Lad and Lady, from the first, the man who bought them was not the mere owner, but the absolute Master. To them he was the unquestioned lord of life and death, the hearer and answerer, the Eternal Law; his the voice that must be obeyed, whatever the command.

From earliest puppyhood, both Lad and Lady had been brought up within the Law. As far back as they could remember, they had known and obeyed The Place's simple code.

For example: All animals of the woods might lawfully be chased; but the Mistress' prize chickens and the other little folk of The Place must be ignored no matter how hungry or how playful a collie might chance to be. A human, walking openly or riding down the drive into The Place by daylight, must not be barked at except by way of friendly announcement. But anyone entering the grounds from other ingress than the drive, or anyone walking furtively or with a tramp slouch, must be attacked at sight.

Also, the interior of the house was sacrosanct. It was a place for perfect behavior. No rug must be scratched, nothing gnawed or played with. In fact,

Lady's one whipping had followed a puppy-frolic effort of hers to "worry" the huge stuffed bald eagle that stood on a papier-mache stump in the Master's study, just off the big living-room where the fireplace was.

That eagle, shot by himself as it raided the flock of prize chickens, was the delight of the Master's heart. And at Lady's attempt on it, he had taught her a lesson that made her cringe for weeks thereafter at bare sight of the dog-whip. To this day, she would never walk past the eagle without making the widest possible detour around it.

But that punishment had been suffered while she was still in the idiotic days of puppyhood. After she was grown, Lady would no more have thought of tampering with the eagle or with anything else in the house than it would occur to a human to stand on his head in church.

Then, early one spring, came Knave—a showy, magnificent collie; red-gold of coat save for a black "saddle," and with alert topaz eyes.

Knave did not belong to the Master, but to a man who, going to Europe for a month, asked him to care for the dog in his absence. The Master, glad to have so beautiful an ornament to The Place, had willingly consented. He was rewarded when, on the train from town, an admiring crowd of commuters flocked to the baggage-car to stare at the splendid-looking collie.

The only dissenting note in the praise-chorus was the grouchy old baggage-man's.

"Maybe he's a thoroughbred, like you say," drawled the old fellow to the Master, "but I never yet saw a yellow-eyed, prick-eared dog I'd give hell-room to."

Knave showed his scorn for such silly criticism by a cavernous yawn.

"Thoroughbred?" grunted the baggage-man. "With them streaks of pinkish-yeller on the roof of his mouth? Ever see a thoroughbred that didn't have a black mouth-roof?"

But the old man's slighting words were ignored with disdain by the crowd of volunteer dog-experts in the baggage-car. In time the Master alighted at his station, with Knave straining joyously at the leash. As the Master reached The Place and turned into the drive, both Lad and Lady, at sound of his far-off footsteps, came tearing around the side of the house to greet him.

On simultaneous sight and scent of the strange dog frisking along at his side, the two collies paused in their madly joyous onrush. Up went their ruffs. Down went their heads.

Lady flashed forward to do battle with the stranger who was monopolizing so much of the Master's attention. Knave, not at all averse to battle (especially with a smaller dog), braced himself and then moved forward, stiff-legged, fangs bare.

But of a sudden his head went up; his stiff-poised brush broke into swift wagging; his lips curled down. He had recognized that his prospective foe was not of his own sex. (And nowhere, except among humans, does a full-grown male ill-treat or even defend himself against the female of his species.)

Lady, noting the stranger's sudden friendliness, paused irresolute in her charge. And at that instant Lad darted past her. Full at Knave's throat he launched himself.

The Master rasped out:

"Down, Lad! *Down!*"

Almost in midair the collie arrested his onset—coming to earth bristling, furious and yet with no thought but to obey. Knave, seeing his foe was not going to fight, turned once more toward Lady.

"Lad," ordered the Master, pointing toward Knave and speaking with quiet intentness, "let him alone. Understand? Let him *alone.*"

And Lad understood—even as years of training and centuries of ancestry had taught him to understand every spoken wish of the Master's. He must give up his impulse to make war on this intruder whom at sight he hated. It was the Law; and from the Law there was no appeal.

With yearningly helpless rage he looked on while the newcomer was installed on The Place. With a wondering sorrow he found himself forced to share the Master's and Mistress' caresses with this interloper. With growing pain he submitted to Knave's gay attentions to Lady, and to Lady's evident relish of the guest's companionship. Gone were the peaceful old days of utter contentment.

Lady had always regarded Lad as her own special property—to tease and to boss and to despoil of choice food-bits. But her attitude toward Knave was far different. She coquetted, human-fashion, with the gold-and-black dog—at one moment affecting to scorn him, at another meeting his advances with a delighted friendliness.

She never presumed to boss him as she had always bossed Lad. He fascinated her. Without seeming to follow him about, she was forever at his heels. Lad, cut to the heart at her sudden indifference toward his loyal self, tried in every way his simple soul could devise to win back her interest. He essayed clumsily to romp with her as the lithely graceful Knave romped, to drive rabbits for her on their woodland rambles, to thrust himself, in a dozen gentle ways, upon her attention.

But it was no use. Lady scarcely noticed him. When his overtures of friendship chanced to annoy her, she rewarded them with a snap or with an impatient growl. And ever she turned to the all-conquering Knave in a keenness of attraction that was all but hypnotic.

As his divinity's total loss of interest in himself grew too apparent to be doubted, Lad's big heart broke. Being only a dog, and a Grail-knight in thought, he did not realize that Knave's newness and his difference from anything she had known, formed a large part of Lady's desire for the visitor's favor; nor did he understand that such interest must wane when the novelty should wear off.

All Lad knew was that he loved her, and that for the sake of a flashy stranger she was snubbing him.

As the Law forbade him to avenge himself in true dog-fashion by fighting for his Lady's love, Lad sadly withdrew from the unequal contest, too proud to compete for a fickle sweetheart. No longer did he try to join in the others' lawn-romps, but lay at a distance, his splendid head between his snowy little forepaws, his brown eyes sick with sorrow, watching their gambols.

Nor did he thrust his undesired presence on them during their woodland rambles. He took to moping, solitary, infinitely miserable. Perhaps there is on earth something unhappier than a bitterly aggrieved dog. But no one has ever discovered that elusive something.

Knave from the first had shown and felt for Lad a scornful indifference. Not understanding the Law, he had set down the older collie's refusal to fight as a sign of exemplary, if timorous prudence, and he looked down upon him accordingly. One day Knave came home from the morning run through the forest without Lady. Neither the Master's calls nor the ear-ripping blasts of his dog-whistle could bring her back to The Place. Whereat Lad arose heavily from his favorite resting-place under the living-room piano and cantered off to the woods. Nor did he return.

Several hours later the Master went to the woods to investigate, followed by the rollicking Knave. At the forest edge the Master shouted. A far-off bark from Lad answered. And the Master made his way through shoulder-deep underbrush in the direction of the sound.

In a clearing he found Lady, her left forepaw caught in the steel jaws of a fox-trap. Lad was standing protectingly above her, stooping now and then to lick her cruelly pinched foot or to whine consolation to her; then snarling in fierce hate at a score of crows that flapped hopefully in the tree-tops above the victim.

The Master set Lady free, and Knave frisked forward right joyously to greet his released inamorata. But Lady was in no condition to play—then nor for many a day thereafter. Her fore-foot was so lacerated and swollen that she was fain to hobble awkwardly on three legs for the next fortnight.

It was on one pantingly hot August morning, a little later, that Lady limped into the house in search of a cool spot where she might lie and lick her throbbing fore-foot. Lad was lying, as usual, under the piano in the living-room. His tail thumped shy welcome on the hardwood floor as she passed, but she would not stay or so much as notice him.

On she limped, into the Master's study, where an open window sent a faint breeze through the house. Giving the stuffed eagle a wide berth, Lady hobbled to the window and made as though to lie down just beneath it. As she did so, two things happened: she leaned too much weight on the sore foot, and the pressure wrung from her an involuntary yelp of pain; at the same moment a cross-current of air from the other side of the house swept through the living-room and blew shut the door of the adjoining study. Lady was a prisoner.

Ordinarily this would have caused her no ill-ease, for the open window was only thirty inches above the floor, and the drop to the veranda outside was a bare three feet. It would have been the simplest matter in the world for her to jump out, had she wearied of her chance captivity.

But to undertake the jump with the prospect of landing her full weight and impetus on a forepaw that was horribly sensitive to the lightest touch—this was an exploit beyond the sufferer's will-power. So Lady resigned herself to imprisonment. She curled herself up on the floor as far as possible from the eagle, moaned softly and lay still.

At sound of her first yelp, Lad had run forward, whining eager sympathy. But the closed door blocked his way. He crouched, wretched and anxious, before it, helpless to go to his loved one's assistance.

Knave, too, loping back from a solitary prowl of the woods, seeking Lady, heard the yelp. His prick-ears located the sound at once. Along the veranda he trotted, to the open study window. With a bound he had cleared the sill and alighted inside the room.

It chanced to be his first visit to the study. The door was usually kept shut, that drafts might not blow the Master's desk-papers about. And Knave felt, at best, little interest in exploring the interior of houses. He was an outdoor dog, by choice.

He advanced now toward Lady, his tail a-wag, his head on one side, with his most irresistible air. Then, as he came forward into the room, he saw the eagle. He halted in wonder at sight of the enormous white-crested bird with its six-foot sweep of pinion. It was a wholly novel spectacle to Knave; and he greeted it with a gruff bark, half of fear, half of bravado. Quickly, however, his sense of smell told him that this wide-winged apparition was no living thing. And ashamed of his momentary cowardice, he went over to investigate it.

As he went, Knave cast over his shoulder a look of invitation to Lady to join him in his inspection. She understood the invitation, but memory of that puppyhood beating made her recoil from accepting it. Knave saw her shrink back, and he realized with a thrill that she was actually afraid of this lifeless thing which could harm no one. With due pride in showing off his own heroism before her, and with the scamp-dog's innate craving to destroy, he sprang growling upon the eagle.

Down tumbled the papier-mache stump. Down crashed the huge stuffed bird with it; Knave's white teeth buried deep in the soft feathers of its breast.

Lady, horror-struck at this sacrilege, whimpered in terror. But her plaint served only to increase Knave's zest for destruction.

He hurled the bird to the floor, pinned it down with his feet and at one jerk tore the right wing from the body. Coughing out the mouthful of dusty pinions, he dug his teeth into the eagle's throat. Again bracing himself with his forelegs on the carcass, he gave a sharp tug. Head and neck came away in his mouth. And then before he could drop the mouthful and return to the work of demolition, he heard the Master's step.

All at once, now, Knave proved he was less ignorant of the Law—or, at least, of its penalties—than might have been supposed from his act of vandalism. In sudden panic he bolted for the window, the silvery head of the eagle still, unheeded, between his jaws. With a vaulting spring, he shot out through the open casement, in his reckless eagerness to escape, knocking against Lady's injured leg as he passed.

He did not pause at Lady's scream of pain, nor did he stop until he reached the chicken-house. Crawling under this, he deposited the incriminating eagle-head in the dark recess. Finding no pursuer, he emerged and jogged innocently back toward the veranda.

The Master, entering the house and walking across the living-room toward the stairs, heard Lady's cry. He looked around for her, recognizing from the sound that she must be in distress. His eye fell on Lad, crouching tense and eager in front of the shut study door.

The Master opened the door and went into the study.

At the first step inside the room he stopped, aghast. There lay the chewed and battered fragments of his beloved eagle. And there, in one corner, frightened, with guilt writ plain all over her, cowered Lady. Men have been "legally" done to death on far lighter evidence than encompassed her.

The Master was thunderstruck. For more than two years Lady had had the free run of the house. And this was her first sin—at that, a sin unworthy of any well-bred dog that has graduated from puppyhood and from milk-teeth. He would not have believed it. He *could* not have believed it. Yet here was the hideous evidence, scattered all over the floor.

The door was shut, but the window stood wide. Through the window, doubtless, she had gotten into the room. And he had surprised her at her vandal-work before she could escape by the same opening.

The Master was a just man—as humans go; but this was a crime the most maudlin dog-spoiler could not have condoned. The eagle, moreover, had been the pride of his heart—as perhaps I have said. Without a word, he walked to the wall and took down a braided dog-whip, dust-covered from long disuse.

Lady knew what was coming. Being a thoroughbred, she did not try to run, nor did she roll for mercy. She cowered, moveless, nose to floor, awaiting her doom.

Back swished the lash. Down it came, whistling as a man whistles whose teeth are broken. Across Lady's slender flanks it smote, with the full force of a strong driving-arm. Lady quivered all over. But she made no sound. She who would whimper at a chance touch to her sore foot, was mute under human punishment.

But Lad was not mute. As the Master's arm swung back for a second blow, he heard, just behind, a low, throaty growl that held all the menace of ten thousand wordy threats.

He wheeled about. Lad was close at his heels, fangs bared, eyes red, head lowered, tawny body taut in every sinew.

The Master blinked at him, incredulous. Here was something infinitely more unbelievable than Lady's supposed destruction of the eagle. The Impossible had come to pass.

For, know well, a dog does not growl at its Master. At its owner, perhaps; at its Master, never. As soon would a devout priest blaspheme his deity.

Nor does a dog approach anything or anybody, growling and with lowered head, unless intent on battle. Have no fear when a dog barks or even growls at you, so long as his head is erect. But when he growls and lowers his head—then look out. It means but one thing.

The Master had been the Master—the sublime, blindly revered and worshiped Master—for all the blameless years of Lad's life. And now, growling, head down, the dog was threatening him.

It was the supreme misery, the crowning hell, of Lad's career. For the first time, two overpowering loves fought with each other in his Galahad soul. And the love for poor, unjustly blamed, Lady hurled down the superlove for the Master.

In baring teeth upon his lord, the collie well knew what he was incurring. But he did not flinch. Understanding that swift death might well be his portion, he stood his ground.

(Is there greater love? Humans—sighing swains, vow-laden suitors—can any of *you* match it? I think not. Not even the much-lauded Antonys. They throw away only the mere world of earthly credit, for love.)

The Master's jaw set. He was well-nigh as unhappy as the dog. For he grasped the situation, and he was man enough to honor Lad's proffered sacrifice. Yet it must be punished, and punished instantly—as any dog-master will testify. Let a dog once growl or show his teeth in menace at his Master, and if the rebellion is not put down in drastic fashion, the Master ceases forever to be Master and degenerates to mere owner. His mysterious power over his dog is gone for all time.

Turning his back on Lady, the Master whirled his dog-whip in the air. Lad saw the lash coming down. He did not flinch. He did not cower. The growl ceased. The orange-tawny collie stood erect. Down came the braided whip-lash on Lad's shoulders—again over his loins, and yet again and again.

Without moving—head up, dark tender eyes unwinking—the hero-dog took the scourging. When it was over, he waited only to see the Master throw the dog-whip fiercely into a corner of the study. Then, knowing Lady was safe, Lad walked majestically back to his "cave" under the piano, and with a long, quivering sigh he lay down.

His spirit was sick and crushed within him. For the first time in his thoroughbred life he had been struck. For he was one of those not wholly rare dogs to whom a sharp word of reproof is more effective than a beating —to whom a blow is not a pain, but a damning and overwhelming ignominy. Had a human, other than the Master, presumed to strike him, the assailant must have fought for life.

Through the numbness of Lad's grief, bit by bit, began to smolder and glow a deathless hate for Knave, the cause of Lady's humiliation. Lad had known what passed behind that closed study door as well as though he had seen. For ears and scent serve a true collie quite as usefully as do mere eyes.

The Master was little happier than was his favorite dog. For he loved Lad as he would have loved a human son. Though Lad did not realize it, the Master had "let off" Lady from the rest of her beating, in order not to increase her champion's grief. He simply ordered her out of the study.

And as she limped away, the Master tried to rekindle his own indignation and deaden his sense of remorse by gathering together the strewn fragments of the eagle. It occurred to him that though the bird was destroyed, he might yet have its fierce-eyed silvery head mounted on a board, as a minor trophy.

But he could not find the head.

Search the study as he would, he could not find it. He remembered distinctly that Lady had been panting as she slunk out of the room. And dogs that are carrying things in their mouths cannot pant. She had not taken the head away with her. The absence of the head only deepened the whole annoying domestic mystery. He gave up trying to solve any of the puzzle— from Lady's incredible vandalism to this newest turn of the affair.

Not until two days later could Lad bring himself to risk a meeting with Lady, the cause and the witness of his beating. Then, yearning for a sight of her and for even her grudged recognition of his presence, after his forty-eight hours of isolation, he sallied forth from the house in search of her.

He traced her to the cool shade of a lilac clump near the outbuildings. There, having with one paw dug a little pit in the cool earth, she was curled up asleep under the bushes. Stretched out beside her was Knave.

Lad's spine bristled at sight of his foe. But ignoring him, he moved over to Lady and touched her nose with his own in timid caress. She opened one eye, blinked drowsily and went to sleep again.

But Lad's coming had awakened Knave. Much refreshed by his nap, he woke in playful mood. He tried to induce Lady to romp with him, but she preferred to doze. So, casting about in his shallow mind for something to play with, Knave chanced to remember the prize he had hidden beneath the chicken-house.

Away he ambled, returning presently with the eagle's head between his teeth. As he ran, he tossed it aloft, catching it as it fell—a pretty trick he had long since learned with a tennis-ball.

Lad, who had lain down as near to sleepily scornful Lady as he dared, looked up and saw him approach. He saw, too, with what Knave was playing; and as he saw, he went quite mad. Here was the thing that had caused Lady's interrupted punishment and his own black disgrace. Knave was exploiting it with manifest and brazen delight.

For the second time in his life—and for the second time in three days— Lad broke the Law. He forgot, in a trice, the command "Let him alone!" And noiseless, terrible, he flew at the gamboling Knave.

Knave was aware of the attack, barely in time to drop the eagle's head and spring forward to meet his antagonist. He was three years Lad's junior and was perhaps five pounds heavier. Moreover, constant exercise had kept him in steel-and-whalebone condition; while lonely brooding at home had begun of late to soften Lad's tough sinews.

Knave was mildly surprised that the dog he had looked on as a dullard and a poltroon should have developed a flash of spirit. But he was not at all unwilling to wage a combat whose victory must make him shine with redoubled glory in Lady's eyes.

Like two furry whirlwinds the collies spun forward toward each other. They met, upreared and snarled, slashing wolf-like for the throat, clawing madly to retain balance. Then down they went, rolling in a right unloving embrace, snapping, tearing, growling.

Lad drove straight for the throat. A half-handful of Knave's golden ruff came away in his jaws. For except at the exact center, a collie's throat is protected by a tangle of hair as effective against assault as were Andrew Jackson's cotton-bale breastworks at New Orleans. And Lad had missed the exact center.

Over and over they rolled. They regained their footing and reared again. Lad's saber-shaped tusk ripped a furrow in Knave's satiny forehead; and Knave's half deflected slash in return set bleeding the big vein at the top of Lad's left ear.

Lady was wide awake long before this. Standing immovable, yet wildly excited—after the age-old fashion of the female brute for whom males battle and who knows she is to be the winner's prize—she watched every turn of the fight.

Up once more, the dogs clashed, chest to chest. Knave, with an instinctive throwback to his wolf forebears of five hundred years earlier, dived for Lad's forelegs with the hope of breaking one of them between his foaming jaws.

He missed the hold by a fraction of an inch. The skin alone was torn. And down over the little white forepaw—one of the forepaws that Lad was wont to lick for an hour a day to keep them snowy—ran a trickle of blood.

That miss was a costly error for Knave. For Lad's teeth sought and found his left shoulder, and sank deep therein. Knave twisted and wheeled with lightning speed and with all his strength. Yet had not his gold-hued ruff choked Lad and pressed stranglingly against his nostrils, all the heavier dog's struggles would not have set him free.

As it was, Lad, gasping for breath enough to fill his lungs, relaxed his grip ever so slightly. And in that fraction of a second Knave tore free, leaving a mouthful of hair and skin in his enemy's jaws.

In the same wrench that liberated him—and as the relieved tension sent Lad stumbling forward—Knave instinctively saw his chance and took it. Again heredity came to his aid, for he tried a maneuver known only to wolves and to collies. Flashing above his stumbling foe's head, Knave seized Lad from behind, just below the base of the skull. And holding him thus helpless, he proceeded to grit and grind his tight-clenched teeth in the slow, relentless motion that must soon or late eat down to and sever the spinal cord.

Lad, even as he thrashed frantically about, felt there was no escape. He was well-nigh as powerless against a strong opponent in this position as is a puppy that is held up by the scruff of the neck.

Without a sound, but still struggling as best he might, he awaited his fate. No longer was he growling or snarling.

His patient, bloodshot eyes sought wistfully for Lady. And they did not find her.

For even as they sought her, a novel element entered into the battle. Lady, hitherto awaiting with true feminine meekness the outcome of the scrimmage, saw her old flame's terrible plight, under the grinding jaws. And, proving herself false to all canons of ancestry—moved by some impulse she did not try to resist—she jumped forward. Forgetting the pain in her swollen foot, she nipped Knave sharply in the hind leg. Then, as if abashed by her unfeminine behavior, she drew back, in shame.

But the work was done.

Through the red war lust Knave dimly realized that he was attacked from behind—perhaps that his new opponent stood an excellent chance of gaining upon him such a death-hold as he himself now held.

He loosed his grip and whizzed about, frothing and snapping, to face the danger. Before Knave had half completed his lightning whirl, Lad had him by the side of the throat.

It was no death-grip, this. Yet it was not only acutely painful, but it held its victim quite as powerless as he had just now held Lad. Bearing down with all his weight and setting his white little front teeth and his yellowing tusks firmly in their hold, Lad gradually shoved Knave's head sideways to the ground and held it there.

The result on Knave's activities was much the same as is obtained by sitting on the head of a kicking horse that has fallen. Unable to wrench loose, helpless to counter, in keen agony from the pinching of the tender throat-skin beneath the masses of ruff, Knave lost his nerve. And he forthwith justified those yellowish streaks in his mouth-roof whereof the baggage-man had spoken.

He made the air vibrate with his abject howls of pain and fear. He was caught. He could not get away. Lad was hurting him horribly. Wherefore he ki-yi-ed as might any gutter cur whose tail is stepped upon.

Presently, beyond the fight haze, Lad saw a shadow in front of him—a shadow that resolved itself in the settling dust, as the Master. And Lad came to himself.

He loosed his hold on Knave's throat, and stood up, groggily. Knave, still yelping, tucked his tail between his legs and fled for his life—out of The Place, out of your story.

Slowly, stumblingly, but without a waver of hesitation, Lad went up to the Master. He was gasping for breath, and he was weak from fearful exertion and from loss of blood. Up to the Master he went—straight up to him.

And not until he was a scant two yards away did he see that the Master held something in his hand—that abominable, mischief-making eagle's head, which he had just picked up! Probably the dog-whip was in the other hand. It did not matter much. Lad was ready for this final degradation. He would not try to dodge it, he the double breaker of laws.

Then—the Master was kneeling beside him. The kind hand was caressing the dog's dizzy head, the dear voice—a queer break in it—was saying remorsefully:

"Oh Lad! Laddie! I'm so sorry. So sorry! You're—you're more of a man than I am, old friend. I'll make it up to you, somehow!"

And now besides the loved hand, there was another touch, even more precious—a warmly caressing little pink tongue that licked his bleeding foreleg.

Lady—timidly, adoringly—was trying to stanch her hero's wounds.

"Lady, I apologize to you too," went on the foolish Master. "I'm sorry, girl."

Lady was too busy soothing the hurts of her newly discovered mate to understand. But Lad understood. Lad always understood.

Sunnybank Lad was introduced to the world.

The story contained many of the elements that were persistently to characterize Terhune's most successful dog fiction. The main character was a collie of noble, almost saintly character, yet who was fully capable in battle and expert at dispensing vengeance to a villainous enemy. The hero-collie was possessed of infinite intelligence and loyalty and was almost human in his ability to understand his beloved Master and Mistress, but also to reason out the consequences of his own actions. The appearance of the story brought down upon Terhune the first examples of the criticism that was constantly to recur: that he had anthropomorphized the dogs to an appalling degree. Terhune himself, in writing later about that first Lad story, insisted that "I made no effort to humanize any of the dogs. I wrote of them as they were. The plot was simple: the actions and motives of the canine characters were normal." He was fully qualified to describe the dogs' motivation for their actions, he often would argue, because he had long and carefully studied the collies at Sunnybank and the other dogs that had preceded them.

The story contained other features that became Terhune trademarks: the periodic inserts of nuggets of information, always given in a tone of positive, unarguable authority ("Nor does a dog approach anything or anybody, growling and with lowered head, unless intent on battle") . . . the occasional asides to the reader ("Do you get the difference?") . . . the graphically described, usually at great length, fight in which the miserable villain gets his proper thrashing . . . the characterization of himself (the Master) as a just, strict, well-intentioned but often rather bumbling man (in later stories the Mistress would supply the needed counterbalance—she always was wise, calm, and patient) . . . the loving descriptions of Sunnybank (The Place) . . . and the strong strain of sentimentality typified by the final lines of "His Mate" in which the Master almost tearfully apologizes to his wronged collies.

It certainly was not great literature. Neither Terhune himself nor probably anyone else ever tried to argue that it was. But the writing somehow possessed a magic. Readers everywhere, adults and children, found themselves fascinated by it and deeply moved.

And whatever its other characteristics, the story most of all had Lad. Whether or not his was a valid portrayal of canine reasoning and emotions, whether or not he was a sentimentalized, idealized dog as Terhune's critics would loudly complain, it is incontestable that Lad was a rarely effective fictional being. Propelled by Terhune's vivid imagination and colorful writing skill, the big Sunnybank collie was on his way to becoming one of the most celebrated and beloved characters—human or animal—in twentieth-century American literature.

The reaction to the story, when it appeared in *Red Book,* was immediate. Readers flooded Ray Long with mail asking for more stories about the great collie. He urged Terhune to come up with more Lad adventures at Sunnybank. Within a few months, editors of four other magazines also contacted Terhune about doing dog stories.

Terhune was paid $200 by Long for "His Mate." Nine years later, the same magazine paid him $2,000 for a dog story of the same length; other magazines went as high as $2,500 for a dog story.

One of the Lad stories that followed, called "In the Day of Battle," was listed by Long in 1932 as one of the twenty best short stories that had appeared under his aegis during his many years as a top magazine editor.

The success of his Lad stories was a major step forward in Terhune's drive to attain a sufficient income at free-lance writing to quit, at long last, his hated newspaper job. He continued to scrawl serials, mystery stories, and articles by the pound and was able to sell almost all of them. He continued to write to a basic formula: the hero of his serial must be of medium height or under, while the villain was more than 6 feet tall and strongly built. This was because most men were of medium height or less and would identify more easily with the hero. The serial almost always brought a fight between the two men with the hero winning. "This of course," Terhune wrote later, "is the veriest hokum. In real life, such a villain would punch the head off the smaller hero or throw him out of the nearest window."

The heroine of each of his serials, Terhune admitted, was "a sweet young stuffed figure—no more human than the equally pretty and adorable dolls my daughter used to play with." The weaknesses of his serials, which he kept writing during most of his career and many of which were later published as books, were readily admitted by Terhune, who constantly deprecated his own work. "Folks may smile at the crudities and rather obvious tricks," he said. "But, at least, they won't go to sleep."

Between 1910 and 1915 he also had eight books published, but they were innocuous efforts which earned him little attention and only modest money. Yet as a result of his monumental production of magazine pieces, during these five years his income rose from $12,-000 to almost $30,000 a year, a princely sum in those times, and only about $4,000 of this came from the *Evening World*.

Bert and Anice were still spending the six warmer months of the year at Sunnybank, the other six months in their apartment on Manhattan's West 78th Street. Only the necessity of reporting to work at the paper and the difficulty of commuting in the winter forced them to spend that much time in the city. They were planning to extend their time at Sunnybank to eight months a year and they always dreamed of the day they could move permanently to The Place.

Life was good and getting better. Bert had been accepted as a charter member of the Adventurers Club and hobnobbed with such as explorers Vilhjalmur Stefansson and Bob Bartlett, General Leonard Wood, Theodore Roosevelt, and Sinclair Lewis. He later joined the Explorers Club and became active in the Authors Club. As the years went on he became a member of the two old theatrical clubs, the Lambs and the Players, and of the Dutch Treat Club, whose weekly luncheons he attended for many years when he was in town.

By early 1914, Terhune felt that his income had risen to the point where he was secure enough to quit the newspaper. But with the outbreak of the world war, he decided to postpone the resignation. Always extremely cautious where finances were concerned, he decided to wait a while and see what effect the war might have on American magazines and their market for his fiction.

In 1915, with the demand for his dog stories at a high level, Terhune again began to consider resigning from the *Evening World*. He also had come into another lucrative writing assignment: an agent hired him to turn scripts for movie serials into novels which were sent free to newspapers by the motion picture companies as promotion. Terhune, after paying the agent his commission, netted $3,200 for each novel and was able to write them with little effort. He could complete a 3,000-word chapter during the six hours of a work day after he had finished his newspaper duties.

Terhune found it exceedingly difficult to make the decision to quit his job. He went from friend to friend, asking advice. One of them was William Gerard Chapman. Terhune sat down with him, brought out his notebooks, and carefully went over the details of his income before asking Chapman whether he thought the time was ripe to quit. Chapman urged him to go ahead and make the break. Years later, when Chapman ran a syndicated news service and bought material from Terhune, he used to remind Terhune of his old advice and said that he should share the credit for the writer's success.

Terhune always argued that his excessive caution stemmed from the example of many other newspapermen who had quit the business, then been forced to come back to the only type of work they could do. "The fate of these men made me afraid," he wrote. "How could I hope to win where they had gone to smash? Wherefore, I stayed on until there should be no faintest shadow of doubt that I could succeed elsewhere."

He was haunted for years after he left the paper by a recurring nightmare: he was back at his *Evening World* job and knew that he must remain until he died. He failed to make a living after quitting the job and was forced by poverty to go crawling back. The dream always depressed him for hours. When he came to breakfast with a long face, Anice would comment, "You must have had your *Evening World* dream again last night."

Finally, in May, 1916, Terhune made the long-awaited break and left the *Evening World.* Now, at last, he could devote all his time to writing and to Sunnybank. He had won his victory; but if there was perhaps a small sense of hollowness to it, it was because Terhune knew quite well what he had given to achieve it. As he wrote years later in his autobiography:

"I found I could make much more money as a scrawler of second-and-third rate stuff. While it is a noble thing to starve in a garret and to leave to posterity a few precious volumes which all folk praise and few read, yet to me there was something better worth while in grinding out work which brought me plenty of cash, if no high repute. . . ."

He had taken this commercial road "deliberately, happily," Terhune claimed. Yet, just a few pages earlier in that autobiography, he referred to himself scornfully as "the Apostle of the Obvious and a writer for the Very Young."

Eight to ten months of the year now were spent at Sunnybank, with Terhune placidly, steadily turning out his fiction, Anice composing songs and piano music, writing occasional book reviews and articles, practicing the piano, and beginning a collection of ancient parchment music manuscripts.

Two months or so during the winter were spent in an apartment at 126 Riverside Drive to which they had moved in 1916. With money coming in ever-greater amounts, Bert and Anice indulged their mutual love for travel, spending parts of each winter in Charleston, Bermuda, Nassau, or Cuba.

Terhune had always written in longhand, as did most other veteran newspapermen. (He recalled that when he first joined the *Evening World,* there was only one typewriter in the entire city room.) Shortly after he quit the paper, however, he was forced to begin using a typewriter. His right hand gave out on him. Terhune, never one to understate his own masculinity to his public, explained it this way: "Long before, I had broken it in a fight. Also a knife slash had done things to some of its muscles. So had a bullet graze." Friends were given to understand that, at some undetermined time, Terhune had been using a knife that slipped and wounded his hand. There is, however, a much more intriguing story about the source of the bad hand: Terhune and his nephew, Fritz Van de Water, were out on the town together one night and both had been doing considerable drinking. They went to the men's room at a Manhattan hotel and Fritz was impressed by the ornate water faucets on the wash basins. "You like those?" asked Terhune. "You want to take one home with you?" And with that, the giant of a man reached down, took hold of one of the fancy faucets, and ripped it right out of its mounting, badly tearing up his hand in the process.

Whatever the real source of the injury, Terhune never again could write longhand with ease; he could not readily bend a couple of fingers on his right hand and was forced to keep them extended when he signed his autograph or otherwise wrote with a pen. So, he bought a typewriter and slowly began learning to use it. After a few days of frustrating mistakes, he lost his temper and slammed his fist into the typewriter, smashing it to bits. Another machine was procured and the slow learning process went on.

For the rest of his life, Terhune had a love-hate relationship with his typewriters. He was a hunt-and-peck typist who used only his forefingers. He seemed convinced that the harder he typed the faster the machine would go. His hammering quickly put a typewriter out of commission. He wound up keeping five typewriters on hand; after four of them had been banged out of service by his fearsome pounding, he would summon a repair man to Sunnybank to put them all back into working shape. He finally managed to bring his typing speed up to 1,200 words an hour, about the same pace he had managed in longhand. A month after he began learning to type, he slowly, painfully punched out the rough draft of a 7,000-word short story. It took him a week to type the first draft, then another two weeks to rewrite and smooth the story, then it went to a professional typist for preparation of the final manuscript. The story became the first in a series he sold to *The Saturday Evening Post* about the adventures of a West Virginia mountain man.

Terhune was forty-four years old when the United States entered World War I in 1917, yet there is some evidence that he tried to enlist in the armed forces. He apparently had had some trouble with his heart and this, along with his age, kept him out of the service. His prodigious output of writing continued, seemingly unabated, during the two years of American involvement in the war; and yet there is at least one claim that he performed some rather varied services for the government during those years.

In the 1930s, when Terhune was doing a network radio program, a writer for the sponsor's advertising agency included the following paragraph in a biographical sketch:

His one real disappointment in life was that because of a bad heart and bad feet, the government wouldn't let him fight overseas during the war. Because he didn't get the chance to actually shoot and get shot at, he doesn't think that he even did his bit. However, any man that gives up his work, his pleasure, his very life, to work for the government twenty-four hours a day, raising money, recruiting men, keeping them happy, going abroad as the special agent of the USA, all the while trying to get into active service either for the United States or for Canada, is not my idea of a slacker.

Whether the laudatory paragraph was an exaggeration of the truth or whether it offended Terhune with its rather gushing prose, one doesn't know; but on the draft of the biographical sketch that was found among Terhune's papers, that paragraph was crossed out with the notation: "Kill this. A.P.T."

In 1917, Terhune made one final try at writing a novel that was more literary in style and subject matter. He had done so earlier with *The Fighter* and felt this was proof that he was capable of producing fiction of substantial quality. But the concern about money, the constant psychological need to balance further his financial reserves, had caused him quickly to revert to the hack writing of the cheap serials and mysteries.

Now, in 1917, he took care and great pain in writing an ambitious new novel called *Dead Broke.* It was accepted by the publishing firm of Doubleday, Page, but only on condition that Terhune change the last quarter of the novel and give it what the author called "a slimily happy ending." Symbolizing the change in the outcome of the story, the publisher also insisted that the title be changed from *Dead Broke* to *Fortune.*

Terhune agreed. Apparently his desire for literary recognition and a financial return from the new book overpowered his integrity as a writer. Even though he was proud of the book in its original form and felt it was one of the best things he had done in his career, he submitted to the changes rather than jeopardize its publication. Ironically, the book in its new form was not successful and sold fewer than 6,000 copies. Terhune always regretted that he had permitted the "syrupy substituted ending."

During these years in the second decade of the twentieth century there were increasing changes in the countryside around Sunnybank which irritated Terhune.

The Place always had been in the country—the house was one of the few buildings on the east side of Pompton Lake. There were only the thick, sweet woods, the hills, the fields, and the blue lake. Across the water was a tiny village and behind it the Ramapo Mountains. That was all.

But Sunnybank was not too far from New York City and even closer to Paterson and Jersey City. And things were changing. Terhune watched resignedly, but with unconcealed foreboding, as people began to congregate around him.

"The gracious frontier vanished," he wrote.

A village and mills sprang up overnight in the woods and meadows across our lake where I had shot quail. But on the Sunnybank side of the lake, a very few of us have been able to keep two miles or more of the pleasant country as it was. . . .

Of course, it is only a matter of time until our hard-held barriers must crash. Only for a pitiably short while can the past hope to hold the present. But during that space, Sunnybank remains Sunnybank. And two miles or so of eastern lake front are as they used to be.

On the friendly green banks of the lake, opposite us and less than a mile away, roadhouses have been opened, with fleets of livery boats and a swimming beach as added attractions. Hordes of motorists are drawn to them; and thence out into the lake either to fish or for a swim. . . .

They strip foliage and leave the once-bright greensward of the lake's verge an expanse of hard-trodden clay . . . their mirthful howls and songs smash the soft silences of the lake almost as distressingly as do the two roaring and sputtering livery motor speed boats which circle the waters on Sunday and on holidays.

And on and on and on. It is the familiar cry of protest and pain of the old settler who sees the newcomers moving in around him and must watch miserably as inevitable change occurs. The story is repeated endlessly, all across the country. But it was particularly difficult for Terhune, who idealized Sunnybank and the countryside around it as a kind of paradise on earth. Gradually it began to be a paradise lost, dissolving from countryside to suburb.

Terhune's protest over this slow transformation became a sort of melancholy litany in his works for the rest of his life. The interlopers were the villains—whether transient bums who trespass at Sunnybank, laughing, empty-headed "motor tourists" who picnic alongside the roads and rip up flowers, or nouveau riche businessmen from New York City who buy expensive homes and seek respectability. The invasion of his beloved country by hordes of outsiders was protested by Terhune in almost everything he wrote. He knew that he could not stop it, that no one could; but never could he forget the country as it used to be, and never would he cease to mourn for it.

In September, 1918, Lad, the Terhunes' beloved collie, died at the age of sixteen and was buried in the little nook to the south of the house.

Partly as a memorial to Lad and partly because the response to the Lad stories in magazines had proved the popularity of fiction about dogs, Terhune decided to bring together the dozen stories he had written about the big collie and have them published as a book.

Book publishers, however, apparently weren't paying much attention to reader response to magazine stories. To Terhune's monumental disappointment, the reaction to his proposal for a book of Lad stories was as discouraging as the rejections he had encountered years earlier when he sought to interest magazine editors in dog stories. The publishers insisted that fiction about dogs did not appeal to book buyers and could not hope to succeed commercially. Such books had been published occasionally, they declared, but had not sold well.

Doubleday, Page, which had published *Fortune* earlier in 1918, held an option on Terhune's next book, but the firm had no interest in the Lad stories. Harry Maule, an executive of the publishing firm, was a good friend of Terhune's and he warned him, "Don't send it to me. I don't want to be in the certain position of having to reject it. Rather than that, we will release you from your agreement."

Maule persuaded Doubleday, Page to relinquish its option and Terhune was free to seek a new publisher. Other companies also told him that dog books would not sell and they refused to read his manuscript.

The eventual publisher of the book that was to become one of the most durable sellers in American publishing history was found as the result of a Terhune hunch. Or perhaps he was just grasping at a straw.

Although he never had been published by E. P. Dutton & Company, he knew that the firm's president, John Macrae, was of Scottish descent and was fiercely proud of his heritage. Terhune reasoned that, since the collie originated in Scotland, perhaps Macrae would show more perception about Lad than the other publishers who had turned him down. The manuscript was submitted to Macrae.

A few days later, Terhune was asked to come to Macrae's office. He went, expecting to be handed back his manuscript. Instead, Macrae told him that Dutton would publish the collection of stories, although with considerable misgiving.

"This book will not sell," Macrae told Terhune with complete assurance. "But sometimes we publish a book that we know will not sell. I like the book. The dog is Scots and so am I. I'll bring it out in a limited edition."

The book was titled simply *Lad: A Dog.* It sold for $2 and went into the book stores for the first time in April, 1919.

The first critical reaction to the new book was good, although it gave little indication of the excitement that the stories would engender among readers.

The New York Times said: "They are delightfully written; so much better done indeed than any other of Mr. Terhune's work which has come to our attention that comparison is quite out of the question."

And the Springfield *Republican* in Terhune's Massachusetts boyhood home: "Mr. Terhune has told these stories so delightfully that the reader doesn't give a thought to the author, so entrancing is the narrative. Afterward one has time to reflect that this is what every artist tries to achieve whether with pen or brush."

A few weeks after publication, Terhune got a letter from John Macrae which began: "Lad is on the rampage. He can't be stopped."

The book went into a second printing in June, 1919, two months after the original publication, and then into a third printing in July. Book stores all over the country were demanding more copies to sell. The dead collie had taken the hearts of postwar America and become a new national hero.

In August of 1919, seven additional printings of *Lad: A Dog* were ordered by the publisher to meet the incredible demand, bringing the total number of editions to ten in the first five months after publication. By 1922, the book had gone through nineteen printings; and by 1930, more than a decade after its original appearance, the number of printings had passed forty. By 1940, it had gone through more than seventy printings. It never has been out of print since its original publication in 1919, and in 1975 was in its eighty-second printing.

More than fifteen years after initial publication, the book had sold over 250,000 copies and still was selling steadily at the rate of some 7,000 copies a year.

The book begins with "His Mate," the story about Lad, his mate Lady, and the rival collie that came between them—the story that began it all in *Red Book* in 1915. The eleven stories that follow run the gamut of wild, heroic adventure. Lad rescues the Mistress from the lake after a canoe mishap . . . remains quietly on guard outside her door, refusing to eat, while she recovers from a critical bout with pneumonia (this actually happened in October, 1912) . . . routs a burglar . . . saves a child from an angry snap by Lady . . . rescues the same child from an attacking copperhead (the snake bites Lad, who recovers, and the shock causes the previously paralyzed child to walk again) . . . educates his mischievous little son Wolf . . . rescues Wolf from the lake . . . wins two blue ribbons at the great Westminster Kennel Club show in Madison Square Garden . . . gets lost in Manhattan, but finds his way back to Sunnybank (a little feat that included swimming the Hudson River) . . . saves a flock of prize sheep from attack by another dog . . . wins a huge gold trophy with an amazing display of obedience to the Mistress's commands at a working sheepdog competition . . . rescues an unworthy man from a mad bull . . . catches a sheep thief (after Lad had been unjustly accused of killing the missing sheep and threatened with execution) . . . and finally— at the age of thirteen—valiantly defends himself against a combined blood-lust attack by a mongrel dog who lives at The Place and his own son Wolf.

It was an outrageously unbelievable list of adventures and feats, yet Terhune somehow made it all believable. What would have seemed outright nonsense and pulp-quality fantasy in the hands of another writer was transformed by Terhune's skill into a series of stories that captivated his readers. Terhune never claimed that the real Lad had all, or even several, of these adventures. For that matter, he rarely contended that the literary exploits of any of his dogs had actually happened to them. But he did insist always, despite the skepticism of many people in the dog world, that he only described canine feats of heroism, intelligence, or physical prowess that had actually been performed by a dog somewhere and recorded in newspapers or history books.

For hundreds of thousands, perhaps millions, of readers since the publication of *Lad: A Dog* in 1919, the big collie has become a literary figure so finely, so intensely stamped in their memories that he has assumed the proportions of a close family friend or well-loved relative. Silly as this may sound to the uninitiated, it is a fact. Terhune readers can ply you with details of the famed dog's life and some can recite from memory the oft-used descriptive phrases.

"Lad was an eighty-pound collie, thoroughbred in spirit as well as in blood" . . . "the gay courage of a d'Artagnan, and an uncanny wisdom" . . . "His absurdly tiny forepaws" . . . "His shaggy coat . . . was like orange-flecked mahogany" . . . "his wavy fur was like spun silk in texture; and it stood out all over him like the hair of a Circassian beauty in a dime museum. The white chest and forepaws were like snow. And his sides and broad back and mighty shoulders shone like dark bronze" . . . "the deep chest, the mighty forequarters, the tiny white paws, the incredible wealth of outer and under-coat, the brush, the grand head, and the soul in the eyes."

Lad's favorite hangout, as every faithful Terhune reader knows, was his "cave," a cool spot under Mrs. Terhune's piano in that section of the big L-shaped living room that was designated as the music room. Then there was an old rug in front of the fireplace, a rug Terhune called "deliciously comfortable," on which Lad liked to lie. At mealtimes, Lad could be found on the dining room floor, sprawled by the Master's left leg. He was the only one of the several collies then at Sunnybank who was permitted to be present at meals. On summer days Lad apparently took a daily swim, although Terhune notes in some stories that collies are not overly fond of water sports.

One culinary peculiarity of the real-life Lad was his hatred for potatoes. According to Terhune, if Lad found a bit of potato mixed in his dinner, he would not eat the food and would eat nothing for the rest of the day, apparently showing his disgust. On discovering the potato, he would trot over to Terhune, growling softly and shaking his head, and insist that his master accompany him to the food dish. Then he would walk away. Terhune claimed that Lad did this many times, whenever some potato was mistakenly put into his food, and always pushed the offending potato out of the dish with his nose before coming in search of Terhune.

Lad's disposition depends entirely on one's perspective. To the Terhunes, he was a "hero-dog," but they admitted that Lad didn't like strangers and remained coolly reserved in the face of friendly greetings from visitors. The Lad of the stories was a rigidly obedient dog, almost always faithful to what Terhune labeled the Law.

Now, the Law had its various articles. And first and foremost of these was the dictum that the Master's command was Godlike. He was "the unquestioned lord of life and death, the hearer and answerer, the Eternal Law; his the voice that must be obeyed, whatever the command." And if Lad did rarely disobey, it was only because—as in "His Mate"—he had a sensible reason to do so, as the Master always eventually discovered.

The collies were permitted to chase and hunt rabbits and squirrels, but the Law decreed that the domestic animals of Sunnybank must be left alone. Visitors walking or riding down the drive might be announced by barking, but otherwise not harmed. Interlopers coming in through the woods or from the lake shore were free game for attack, as was "anyone walking furtively or with a tramp slouch." A visitor to Sunnybank was well advised, apparently, to walk with a stiff backbone lest he be subject to assault by an 80-pound collie.

Inside the house, the Law demanded perfect behavior. None of the household possessions must even be damaged, much less destroyed. The Sunnybank collies (at least those which figured in the stories) were usually not restrained and had the run of The Place. According to the Law, however, they must know very well the boundaries of Sunnybank and must not stray beyond them. This was a part of the Law that apparently was not too rigidly enforced, because many of the Terhune stories involved adventures down the road from Sunnybank or even across the lake in the village.

Then there was the Guest Law: "Civilly, he would endure the pettings of these visiting outlanders. Gravely, he would shake hands with them, on request. He would even permit them to paw him or haul him about, if they were of the obnoxious, dog-mauling breed. But the moment politeness would permit, he always withdrew, very quietly, from their reach and, if possible from their sight as well."

In the stories, the Law was taught to Sunnybank collies from puppyhood and the speed with which they learned would vary greatly from animal to animal. But with Lad, it had been easy: "Lad himself had been one of those rare puppies to whom the Law is taught with bewildering ease. A single command or prohibition had ever been enough to fix a rule in his almost uncannily human brain."

Lad always displayed a courtly concern for creatures smaller than himself and was especially fond of children. "The big heart that ever went out to the weak and defenseless," was the way that Terhune described it. The Master and the Mistress were constantly having to defend the big collie against ignorant people who accused him of various things, always on circumstantial evidence: " 'He's not snarling,' the Mistress indignantly declared, 'he's smiling. That's Lad's way. Why, he'd let himself be cut up into squares sooner than hurt a child.' "

Terhune always took great delight in writing scenes of battle, and his dog heroes acquitted themselves well in such fights, whether their opponents were other dogs, wild animals, or human villains. Typically, Lad was both a brave and savage fighter. He knew no fear, Terhune wrote, with just two exceptions: mad dogs and poisonous snakes. As to his fighting skill:

"With ridiculous ease the collie eluded the mongrel's awkward counter-attacks, and ever kept boring in. To the quivering bone his short front teeth sank. Deep and bloodily his curved tusks slashed— as the wolf and the collie alone can slash."

Lad was forever being attacked by savage mongrels and usually dispatched them with alacrity, except for those occasions where he was slightly handicapped, such as wearing a muzzle or having his forepaws tied together, when the defeat of his opponent took a bit longer.

Lad's most courageous fight came in the final tale of *Lad: A Dog,* when he withstood a vicious double attack by a mongrel and his own son Wolf in a snow-choked Sunnybank forest by cannily fighting a rearguard action that gradually brought him nearer and nearer the house and help: "The old dog's wind was gone; his once-superb strength was going, but he fought on with blazing fury—the fury of a dying king who *will* not be deposed."

Adept as he was on the field of battle, the great collie had the sensitive spirit of a poet. He would, Terhune wrote, "rather have been whipped than laughed at." In describing one incident in which Lad had been rebuked for showing anger to a visitor, the Master noted that his "tone of fierce disapproval cut the sensitive dog more pain- fully than any scourge could have cut his body."

Lad would forsake his cool dignity only in the presence of the Master and the Mistress, who were to him as gods. In the story called "Quiet," in which the Mistress recovers from the grave bout with pneumonia, Terhune writes charmingly of Lad's madcap reversion to puppyhood after he becomes aware that the Mistress has survived the crisis. The regal collie, who has spent days standing guard outside the sickroom door and has refused to eat, suddenly goes on a wild spree, chases the family cat up a tree, overturns a bunch of milk cans, steals a leg of mutton from a refrigerator, thrashes a neighbor dog, and gets into every other variety of deviltry that he can conceive as a gigantic celebration for the end of the ordeal.

And when he triumphs at a dog show and the Mistress is happy over his win:

"Forgetful of the crowd, he licked at her caressing hands in puppy- like ecstasy; then he rolled in front of her; growling ferociously and catching one of her little feet in his mighty jaws, as though to crush it. This foot-seizing game was Lad's favorite romp with the Mistress. With no one else would he condescend to play it, and the terrible white teeth never exerted the pressure of a tenth of an ounce on the slipper they gripped."

In a brief epilogue to *Lad: A Dog,* Terhune movingly described the death of the famed collie (the following excerpt also includes a few additional lines from a second collection of Lad stories):

Then, on a warm September morning in 1918, he stretched himself to sleep in the coolest and shadiest corner of the veranda. And, while he slept, his great heart very quietly stopped beating. He had no pain, no illness, none of the distressing features of extreme age. He had lived out a full span of sixteen years—years rich in life and happiness and love. . . .

Over a magnificent lifeless body on the veranda bent the two who had loved Lad best and whom he had served so worshipfully for sixteen years. The Mistress's face was wet with tears she did not try to check. In the Master's throat was a lump that made speech painful. For the tenth time he leaned down and laid his fingers above the still heart of the dog; seeking vainly for sign of fluttering.

"No use!" he said, thickly, harking back by instinct to a half-remembered phrase. "The engine has broken down."

"No," quoted the sobbing Mistress, wiser than he. "The engineer has left it."

Yes, of course, it was rankly sentimental writing; maudlin, if you prefer to use that term. And it is rather old-fashioned to the contemporary ear. And yet, to anyone who came to know and love Lad, to anyone who was caught up in the fascinating web of Terhune's tales, the scene was a deeply moving one.

Was it all real, one wonders? Were these honest emotions, honestly reported by Terhune, or was this a cardboard scene, carpentered for the readers' emotions, jerry-built for tear-jerking? Was it a contrived ending, manufactured by a hack writer with an eye for money, or did it honestly portray the great love of a man and a woman for a faithful animal and their very real sorrow at his loss?

Perhaps this will help to answer the question:

In the Library of Congress, there is a collection of Albert Payson Terhune papers. An old scrapbook which includes items dating back to the early years of the century contains a small envelope turned

The approach to Sunnybank

Sunnybank House in the early 1930s

Bert and Anice Terhune on the veranda of Sunnybank House with Bruce, Bobby, and Wolf

The Barn and the "Winter Kennel"

Bruce, Lad, Wolf and the Master

Beth, Girl, Chips and Sandy with the Master

Anice with Tippy, the Persian cat, and Wolf

The Master in the puppy yard holding Sandy (left)

1923: Lorraine marries Dr. Franklin Stevens

Lorraine Terhune Stevens

Anice Terhune aboard
ocean liner to Europe

"The Cave" in the music room
at Sunnybank

Grave marker at the Reformed Church cemetery in Pompton Lakes, New Jersey. The Master: "I have fought a good fight." Anice: "I have kept the faith."

Monument erected and dedicated in 1972 (Terhune's 100th birthday year) by the Terhune Sunnybank Memorial Fund

yellowish-brown with age. On it is written in a small, neat, feminine hand: "Lad's hair. September, 1918." The envelope contains a small clump of collie hair, brown and gray and golden.

That scrapbook had been added to for many years after 1918. It is obvious that the Terhunes continued frequently to come across the little envelope for many years after Lad's death. It never was thrown away, but was kept tenderly with the other cherished mementos.

When the Mistress died, in 1964, the little clump of hair had been kept at Sunnybank for forty-six years. It had been cherished by a man and a woman who obviously remembered an old, long-gone collie with infinite love.

16

The Visitor half-expected to hear the trumpeting sound of collie barking. But there was just the frozen, sunlit silence.

The aching loneliness that permeated Sunnybank on this winter day was perhaps most typified by the quiet. The December wind occasionally picked up for a moment and riffled the empty tree limbs into a muted rustling. And, every now and again, there came the grinding of a car engine fighting off frigid slumber on the roadway across the lake or the brief roar of a truck working noisily up the highway on the hillside. But mostly there was a vacuum of silence.

Here, where the raucous, lilting sounds of collie throats had been engraved into the hillside rock over the years, only the freezing stillness reigned now. The Visitor found himself listening intently, though, expecting almost at any moment to hear the frantic greetings of legions of golden dogs, charging forth to challenge and to welcome him. He waited long minutes for the barking song that never came.

Behind the old house, he found the sagging, fragmented remains of a dog pen. The broken strands of chicken wire hung crazily from a wooden post that stood sturdily, loyally straight. It once had been one side of the gate to the pen. This had been the puppy yard that Terhune had so often mentioned, where the collie puppies were kept after being weaned, to romp and fight in joyous splendor.

Somewhere near this spot, The Visitor knew, had been the kennels where most of the famed Sunnybank dogs were housed, except for the favored few designated by the Terhunes as their house dogs. Now there was no remnant of the kennel left. On the weed-choked stretch of lawn behind the house, there was only space—and the torn piece of fencing against which generations of tiny dogs had wistfully pressed in greeting. The spacious kennels, like the living creatures which had slept and ate and loved in them, had vanished.

To get to his destination up on the hillside behind the house, The Visitor passed the little concrete lily and goldfish pool which, like almost every other physical feature of Sunnybank, had been incorporated into the stories. It was the lily pool in which lived Jack, a frog the Terhunes came to know through his tameness and unusual markings. They became fond of the little creature and would look for him each spring as he ended his hibernation at the bottom of the pool. He became as tame as a dog, they claimed, and Mrs. Terhune fed insects to him and scratched his back. For twenty years, according to Terhune, Jack was a resident of Sunnybank. One day they found his body up on the road outside the gates, where he had been crushed by a car. He had never wandered more than a few feet from the little pool in the trees where he made his home. He had been the victim, Terhune was certain, of one of the hated "motor tourists" who invaded Sunnybank and who had taken the little frog as a joke, then tired of the game and dropped him on the highway as they left The Place.

And this lily pool was unendingly fascinating to Bruce, another of the fabled collies, when he had been a small, clumsy puppy. He was constantly falling into the water, then yelping for help until fished out. The Master finally built a wooden ramplike contrivance leading into the water so that the puppy could use it to climb out to safety. But Bruce only used the ramp to facilitate his reckless plunges into the pool. After nine falls into the water in a single week, Terhune finally was forced to spread a wire cover over the pool to save the bumptious puppy from drowning.

The Visitor didn't linger at the pool. The water in it was brackishly dark green, covered with slime. A timber slanted into the bilious bottom of the pool, leaning against the cracked concrete side, where someone had left it after apparently stirring up the rotting water. The pool still was there, but it was moribund and gangrenous from lack of care or concern. It did not ask callers to stop and rest in peace for a moment as it once had.

As The Visitor walked further up the hillside, 100 feet or so behind the old house the same, strange amalgam of thrill and sorrow passed across him. He saw the big rock up ahead of him and the cluster of small concrete markers scattered around it and knew that this was where the great, echoing barks of the watchful collies had gone. And here, too, there now was only silence.

This was the main burial place of the Sunnybank dogs. There were a few others—the ancient graves down in the woods by the lake where the pets of Terhune's parents had been buried. And Lad's famous place of honor. And, for some reason, there were two other isolated graves—those of Bruce and Jean —on the hillside south of the house, high above the old rose corridor.

But here, on the hill, just behind and above the decrepit house, was the burying place of most of the Sunnybank collies. Here, where an old man and woman could look out from the house now and then and see the markers among the trees.

The big boulder—actually only a few inches of it stuck above the surface of the ground, like the tip of some ancient igneous iceberg—served as a natural centerpiece for the tiny cemetery. And on the edges of the top of the rock were carved a few of the names of the dogs sleeping alongside. The carving was not the neat, professional work found on gravestones. The letters slanted away at silly angles, almost as if a child painstakingly had etched in the letters with hammer and chisel. A workman on The Place had done it, perhaps, or the Master himself.

Wolf was one of the names on the boulder and Bob another. Scattered for a short distance around the rock were the small, rectangular stone markers denoting still other graves.

Fair Ellen sleeps here. And there is Champion Sigurdson and over there Champion Explorer. And Champion Thane. And there is the grave of Tippy, the Persian cat of the Mistress and the respected foe of so many of the collies.

The Visitor slowly read the names and then read them again. And the memories passed through his mind again as if a roster of great heroes was being called out, the names echoing across a parade ground with the flags snapping in the wind and the band playing proud martial airs. The names were to him like the names of great people in a dimly remembered history book; and they were, at the same time, like the names of the dearest friends of his boyhood, coming back to him now in a strange cloud of distant sorrow.

17

The huge success of *Lad: A Dog* brought a quick request from E. P. Dutton for another book of dog stories. Terhune, ever-anxious to increase his income and delighted over his emphatic vindication on interest in dog books, was quick to comply.

The year after the first publication of the Lad book, 1920, saw the creation of another canine hero. This time it was Bruce. The real Bruce, whose registered name was Sunnybank Goldsmith, was bred by a J. J. Griffin and was whelped on August 8, 1909. There was no doubt about his good bloodlines: his pedigree listed eleven champions. His kennel name came from a Scottish chieftain who had long been admired by Anice.

The real Bruce was claimed by Terhune to have been so excellent a specimen of collie breeding that "A score of cups and medals and an armful of blue ribbons attest his physical perfection." But, as with most of the fabled Terhune dogs, it was more Bruce's intelligence and personality that Terhune lauded than his attributes of beauty. He had, Terhune wrote, "a strange sweetness of nature that I have found in no other dog. That, and a perfect 'one-man-dog' obedience and goodness."

Though he sired a number of puppies, Bruce seemed disgusted with them and would avoid them whenever possible. Once, though, one of his sons tore off a clothesline to which he had been tied and headed for the woods, where the line got hooked on a root. All hands at Sunnybank searched for the lost puppy for a day and a half without luck, until Bruce found him in a spot where leaves had hidden him from view. It is unlikely that Bruce was being paternal, however. Male dogs are not known to recognize kinship with their own offspring.

Bruce, said Terhune, "had a melancholy dignity, behind which lurked an elusive sense of fun." In the morning, after a servant had knocked on Terhune's door to awaken him, Bruce "would get to his feet, cross the room to the bed, and lay his cold muzzle against my face, tapping at my arm or shoulder with his paw until I opened my eyes. Then, at once, he went back to his rug and lay down again. Nor, if I failed to climb out of bed for another two hours, would he disturb me a second time. He had waked me, once. After that, it was up to me to obey the summons or to disregard it. That was no concern of Bruce's. His duty was done."

When Bruce died, he, too, was buried in a place of honor at Sunnybank. And on his stone was carved "The Dog Without a Fault." It referred, Terhune wrote later, "less to his physical magnificence than to the soul and heart of him." Then he added: "Peace to his stately, lovable, whimsical soul: He was my dear chum. And his going has left an ache."

The fictional Bruce starred in a collection of six stories, which was published by Dutton under the title of *Bruce.* There is some indication that the stories had been rather hastily thrown together. Although bearing the usual Terhune hallmarks—the vivid descriptions, fast pace, and heroic collie feats of intelligence and courage—the stories have a flimsy quality, as if Terhune had hammered them out with little thought in response to a plea from his publisher for more material to sell.

The arrival of the fictional Bruce at Sunnybank results from a series of incidents so contrived as to be totally unbelievable. Outlandish as were many of the feats performed by Terhune collies, it was part of Terhune's skill that he could relate the adventures within a framework of realism and logical sequence that at least made them acceptable, if not entirely believable.

But in the Bruce stories, Terhune lost much of the credibility that was present in the Lad book and the tales sometimes seem almost ridiculous. Bruce came to Sunnybank after his mother found her way into a loose packing crate which had been vacated a short time before by another (much more highly regarded) female collie bound for Sunnybank and, as you may have realized, the dogs switched identities. It may have worked for Shakespeare, but it didn't for Terhune and Bruce.

Also much too incredible were Bruce's feats as a war dog in World War I. The Bruce stories were written during and just after the war, when the fever of the conflict still raged strongly in this country. Only two of the six stories were focused on Sunnybank. The others took place in France, where Bruce outshone General Pershing as he almost single-handedly defeated the Germans and made the world safe for democracy.

Among his accomplishments were: storming up a hill through rifle and artillery fire to get a vital message to headquarters (and thrashing a German Army dog who tries to intercept him) . . . leading an American patrol to safety through a forest of barbed wire in the midst of a thick fog and a German attack . . . seeking out and attacking a German spy who had masqueraded as a Red Cross nurse . . . and frightening a German soldier into screaming and shooting at him, thereby destroying the surprise of a major German attack.

For his heroism, Bruce suffered a shell wound in his right side, two machine-gun bullets in his shoulder, temporary deafness from shell concussion, and, finally, rifle wounds in his head, body, and leg, from which he miraculously recovered and which ended his war service and brought him back to Sunnybank as a wounded hero.

One reason for the setting of the stories was Terhune's desire to counter a wartime demand by some Americans that dogs should be exterminated to help conserve food. Earlier, in *Lad: A Dog*, he had made this the central issue of a story entitled "Speaking of Utility." One of Terhune's most unpleasant, all-purpose villains, a nouveau riche boor named Hamilcar Q. Glure, comes to call on the Master and argues: "You see, neighbor, our nation is up against it. When war was declared last month it found us unprepared. We've got to pitch in and economize. Every mouthful of food wasted here is a new lease of life to the Kaiser. We're cutting down on sugar and meat and fat, but for every cent we save that way we're throwing away a dollar in feeding our dogs. Our dogs that are a useless, senseless, costly luxury: They serve no utilitarian end. They eat food that belongs to soldiers. I'm trying to brighten the corner where I am by persuading my neighbors to get rid of their dogs. When I've proved what a blessing it is, I'm going to inaugurate a nationwide campaign from California to New York . . . "

The Master, of course, angrily refutes Glure's arguments and Lad proves the usefulness of dogs by catching a neighborhood thief after first saving him from the charge of a maddened bull.

Apparently the demands for canine extermination were still being heard, however, and so Terhune—using some anecdotes he had heard from British officers about the heroic feats of collies in the trench warfare during the early part of the war—made the Bruce stories into a "How Collies Are Helping Win the War" epic as a further argument against extermination.

The Bruce stories also displayed Terhune's readiness to inject his personal hostilities and passions into his fiction. Perhaps as a result of the war, perhaps stemming from older feelings, Terhune harbored a deep hatred for Germans and gave it full vent in the Bruce yarns. Among other things, he accuses the Germans of being dog-eaters: "The Red Cross bulletin says no less than eight thousand dogs were eaten, in Saxony alone, in 1913—the year before the war began." German soldiers fire at Bruce and other Allied war dogs merely for their own amusement. German soldiers even smell different, to Bruce. "The scent at once told him that the strangers were not of his own army. A German soldier and an American soldier—because of their differences in diet as well as for certain other and more cogent reasons—have by no means the same odor . . . " German soldiers are described as "cabbage-reeking," and there are such comments as "Like many another German, Stolz was far more adept at causing pain than at enduring it."

Even the German dogs were not exempt from Terhune's scorn: "The assailant was an enormous and hyena-like German police-dog. He was one of the many of his breed that were employed (for work or food) in the German camps, and which used to sneak away from their hard-kicking soldier-owners to ply a more congenial trade as scavengers and seekers for the dead. For, in traits as well as in looks, the police-dog often emulates the ghoulish hyena."

Another of Terhune's lifelong targets was vivisection. He constantly crusaded, both in his fiction and his articles, against the use of dogs in cruel laboratory experiments. The second of the six stories in the Bruce book combined two of his pet hatreds by employing a German vivisectionist as an arch villain. His name was Dr. Halding and he almost got away with Bruce for vivisection purposes, but was foiled when the young collie attacked him and caused him to wreck his automobile. Dr. Halding's lawyer, "whose name sounded as though it had been culled from a Rhine Wine list," filed suit against the Mistress, but the case was dropped because Halding was arrested and "interned as a dangerous Enemy Alien."

Flimsy stuff it was, of very poor quality when compared to Terhune's best dog writing, and embarrassing in its display of bitter national hatred.

Yet, there was too the recurring song of Sunnybank, and although muted in this book below the thunder of cannon and machine gun, it still was there:

Indeed, life was always wondrous pleasant there at The Place—for humans and for animals alike. A fire-blue lake bordered the grounds on two sides. Behind stretched the forest. And on every side arose the soft green mountains, hemming in and brooding over The Place as though they loved it. In the winter evenings there was the huge library hearth with its blaze and warmth; and a disreputable fur rug in front of it that might have been ordained expressly for tired dogs to drowse on. And there were the Mistress and the Master. Especially the Mistress: The Mistress somehow had a way of making all the world seem worth while.

And when Bruce returns to Sunnybank from the war:

It was late summer again at The Place—late opulent summer, with the peace of green earth and blue sky, the heavy droning of bees and the promise of harvest. The long shadows of late afternoon stretched lovingly across the lawn, from the great lakeside trees. Over everything brooded a dreamy amber light. The war seemed a million miles away.

The Mistress and the Master came down from the vine-shaded veranda for their sun-set walk through the grounds. At sound of their steps on the gravel, a huge dark-brown-and-white collie emerged from his resting-place under the wistaria-arbor.

He stretched himself lazily, fore and aft, in collie-fashion. Then he trotted up to his two deities and thrust his muzzle playfully into the Mistress' palm, as he fell into step with the promenaders.

Terhune further endeared himself to his growing public by dedicating his book of Bruce stories to his dogs:

TO MY TEN BEST FRIENDS—

Who are far wiser in their way and far better in every way, than I; and yet who have not the wisdom to know it—

Who do not merely *think* I am perfect, but who are calmly and permanently convinced of my perfection;—and this in spite of fifty disillusions a day—

Who are frantically happy at my coming and bitterly woebegone in my absence—

Who never bore me and never are bored by me—

Who never talk about themselves and who always listen with rapturous interest to anything I may say—

Who, having no conventional standards, have no respectability; and who, having no conventional consciences, have no sins—

Who teach me finer lessons in loyalty, in patience, in true courtesy, in unselfishness, in divine forgiveness, in pluck and in abiding good spirits than do all the books I have ever read and all the other models I have studied—

Who have not deigned to waste time and eyesight in reading a word of mine and who will not bother to read this verbose tribute to themselves—

In short, to the most gloriously satisfactory chums who ever appealed to human vanity and to human desire for companionship—

TO OUR TEN SUNNYBANK COLLIES
MY STORY IS GRATEFULLY AND AFFECTIONATELY DEDICATED

Despite the book's shortcomings, critical response to the collection of Bruce stories was quite good. The *Book Review Digest* for 1920 listed four favorable reviews of the book and included this comment from the Boston *Transcript:* "Few writers have portrayed collies as cleverly as has Mr. Terhune. Bruce is made to seem quite as much a personality as any of his human friends, and his actions are always interesting and never boresome."

And so continued one of the most productive and lucrative decades ever enjoyed by an American writer. A 1924 article in the

American Kennel Club *Gazette* quoted a publisher as estimating that the Lad stories and two books had netted Terhune more than $32,-000, the Bruce stories and book about $12,000, and a book and stories about Buff, another collie, more than $11,000, with all the books still selling handily in this country and in Europe, where they had found a receptive audience. The demand for Terhune's dog stories kept increasing. During one period, he sold forty consecutive stories to *The Saturday Evening Post.* The famed editor of that magazine, George Horace Lorimer, once complained to Terhune that every time he printed a Terhune dog story, the mail would bring him 2,000 more dog stories from hopeful writers which, he added, were "either written by people who know nothing about dogs, or by people who know all about dogs, but nothing about writing."

During the same period, Terhune was selling stories, with and without dogs, to such other top magazines as *The Ladies' Home Journal, Good Housekeeping,* and *The American Magazine.* In 1920, he also had a series of stories running in the *Country Gentleman* under the pen name of Stephen Dirck. It was the first time since his old ghost-writing days that he had not used his own name on his work. He was to use the name of Stephen Dirck again, years later, for an article which he felt was too personal and revealing to be written under his own name.

Money was pouring in. The Terhunes' love of travel now took them all over the United States, to Europe, even to North Africa. Bert himself planned the itinerary for each trip, down to the smallest detail. The journeys were made during non-Sunnybank winter months. He explained them this way: "I should like to stay out here at Sunnybank for twelve months a year, if it were not that even the cheapest quality of creative work must be fed sometimes on outside influences and on outside scenes and on meetings with many folk of many kinds." Dry rot, he said, is the one thing a writer must avoid, which was why they left Sunnybank several months each year for New York City and travel. Everywhere they went, Bert memorized the topography, the climate, the smells, the look of the people, as potential locales for future stories and serials.

Terhune by now was firmly established as a writer about dogs. He even took on, in late 1922 and early 1923, the editorship of a short-lived monthly publication called *The Dog Review.* But he already was beginning to have some misgivings about being so regarded.

He loved dogs, loved to write about them, and relished the financial returns that such writing brought him; but he did not want to be so completely limited. In his autobiography, he protested:

. . . in most of my serials, which later are brought out as books, a dog plays a lively part. This is through no wish of mine. Seldom does such a dog add to plot or structure. Often he gums both. Magazine editors, however, in mapping out these serials, insist that the yarn have a Sunnybank collie in it. . . .

. . . Having begun to write dog stories—having become known as the fiction exponent of The Dog—I can't stop. Again and again I have tried to branch out into something else. Eternally, editors, publishers and readers have yanked me back into the canine groove . . . I like dogs. I like to write about them. For that matter, I am kid enough to like ice-cream in big quantities. But an exclusive day-and-night diet of ice-cream, month after month, would make me crave an occasional sirloin steak or even dry bread. Besides, soon or late, people are going to grow deathly sick of my everlasting dog stories. Then where shall I be?

Once he and Anice were interviewed by a magazine writer and the first question asked was, "When did you begin writing dog stories?" Terhune, in mock anger, answered: "Here we are! Terhune the *dog* man! Every time I am introduced to someone my introducer invariably says—'You know, Terhune the *dog* man.' I'll bet if I could prove I wrote the 23rd Psalm, I should still be known as Terhune the *dog* man!" To which Anice sweetly added: "Probably the *shepherd* dog man."

Except for the two months or so a year devoted to travel and relaxation, the voluminous Terhune production continued steadily during the early 1920s. He sat at his typewriter for eight or nine hours a day, six days a week, grinding out the stories, serials, books, and occasional articles. "Some writers are inspired or temperamental or soulful," he said. "I have no time or ability to be any of those things. So far as I am concerned a writer is like any other laborer, in that he must do his eight or nine hours a day of hard work and that he can't afford to loaf around waiting for inspiration. Sometimes my day's work is worthless and I have to throw it away and start afresh. But if I let myself go idle while I waited for inspiration or until the spirit moved me to write, I should degenerate into a loafer inside of a year."

In 1921, for unexplained reasons, Terhune had severed his relationship with E. P. Dutton, the publisher that had taken a chance on Lad, and switched to the George H. Doran Company, although Dutton had two more Terhune books under contract which they published during the next two years.

Doran brought out another fabulously successful book called *Buff: A Collie and Other Dog Stories.* The writing was typical Terhune, but the book was significant in a couple of ways. For one thing, the main collie hero, Buff, was entirely a fictional creation, the first dog hero not modeled on one of the actual Sunnybank collies. Also, Buff—though possessing all the attributes of beauty, intelligence, loyalty, and courage that Terhune endlessly claimed for the collie—was not a pure-blooded representative of the breed. The dog was one-quarter pit bull terrier, while the rest was collie. The mixed breeding was on his mother's side; his father was "one of the four greatest collies in America—perhaps on earth."

Terhune's collies always were skilled fighters, their quick and slashing tactics attributed by him to their alleged wolf ancestry. But Buff, with his mixed heritage, was a super-fighter because he also had "the pit-terrier's instinct for biting hard and holding on." This was discovered, to his dismay, by one villain when he attacked Buff's adored master. The dog jumped the villain: "Just below the elbow he found his grip. Deep drove the sharp white teeth; not slashing, collie fashion, but with the grim holding power that had won a score of battles for old Upstreet Butcherboy [Buff's maternal grandsire]. On the swung canvas strip, a hundred of his bull-terrier ancestors had been made to strengthen the crushingly powerful jaw muscles they had bequeathed to Buff."

The same combination of collie and bull terrier fighting ability enabled Buff to kill a huge bulldog famed "for being one of the 'dirtiest' fighters that ever set upon a weaker foe" in one of those savage dog fights that Terhune included in most of his books and that were described in long, gory detail.

The story of Buff—a rather short one that formed only the first part of the book bearing his name—involves the dog's adoration of his master, a man named Michael Trent. Trent is set upon by two villains, drugged and kidnapped, not to return for several months.

The grieving dog conducts a hysterical search for him that makes up the bulk of the story. Finally the two are reunited and Terhune describes the scene in prose whose effect is so sentimental as to be almost ludicrous. The passage probably exaggerates the capacity of a dog's emotions beyond all credibility (though Terhune claimed it was based on an actual incident from his childhood—the reunion of his father with his pointer Shot following the return of the Terhune family from Europe).

Yet it effectively demonstrates the power of Terhune's writing and his singular ability to paint a dog so vividly that, once the passage has been read, the reader probably always will bear some memory of it. This may not be literary gold, but it is vintage Terhune and it is among the most effective pieces of writing about dogs ever created:

Fifty yards from the man Buff lifted his head as he galloped. The scent —any dog's strongest quality—told him he might now rely on sight, which is the weakest of a dog's senses. At what he saw, the collie gave tongue.

Not in the hideous wolf howl or in whimper did Buff speak now, but in a cry that was human and rending—a cry that tore at the listener's heartstrings by reason of its awful intensity.

Delirious—screaming, writhing, panting—Buff flung himself on the man he had tracked. He was at the end of the trail: And what he found there drove him quite insane.

Up into Michael Trent's dusty arms the dog sprang—a vibrant mass of mad ecstasy. Moaning, crying, sobbing like a human child, Buff sought to lick his master's haggard face and to pat him in a hundred places at once with his whirling paws.

Almost thrown off his balance by the impact, Trent spoke to the collie in wondering delight. And the sound of his tired voice sent Buff into a new frenzy of rapture. Dropping to earth, he whizzed round and round Trent in a bewildering gyroscopic flight, stomach to ground, tongue and throat clamorous with hoarse joy.

Presently, flinging himself at his master's feet, the dog lay there, moaning and sobbing, his swift tongue caressing the man's dusty shoes, his furry body quivering from nose to tail in hysterical bliss. There he lay while Trent leaned over and laid both calloused hands on his head, stroking him and talking to him in the pleasant, slow tones the collie loved.

The story of Buff was told in four long chapters; the balance of the book consisted of six short stories of varying quality. All featured dogs, all except one story were about collies. Only one of the tales took place at Sunnybank and its hero was Wolf, the son of the great Lad.

The final chapter of the book is especially interesting, for it is titled "The Sunnybank Collies," and is Terhune's account of life at his estate and a series of anecdotes about some of his now-famed collies. This was one of the earliest examples of Terhune's nonfiction pieces about his home and the real dogs that lived there. He was to write thousands of words on the same subjects over the next twenty years and it was these descriptions, as well as his fiction, that made Sunnybank so familiar and so dear to his many readers and caused them to storm his gates in ever-increasing numbers. Terhune was annoyed at the visitors clamoring to see him and his dogs, yet he had only himself to blame. No attempt was made to keep his location a secret. The final chapter of the Buff book opens this way: "Here, at 'Sunnybank,'—at Pompton Lakes, in New Jersey,—we raise thoroughbred collies."

Terhune's unabashed sentimentality about his dogs was displayed again in his poetic Foreword to the Buff book. Paralleling his dedication of the Bruce book to his ten Sunnybank collies, he opened the Buff volume with an eight-stanza poem along the same lines.

The Buff book made another hit with Terhune's growing body of admirers, and the critical reaction to it was generally favorable as well. *The New York Times* called it "a wonderful story of dog love and trust and loyalty and intelligence." The New York *Evening Post*'s Literary Review, which had taken a slightly jaundiced view of the Bruce book, said of this: "The old Terhune faults are there—little crudities of plot, phrases that reappear reminiscently, even a case or two of faulty vocabulary. But no man, even if he were to spend years on a book, could put into it more of heart and of fine understanding than are to be found in this volume."

At fifty, in 1922, Terhune was at the peak of his awesome productive powers. He had three books published during the year, in addition to the stories and articles he was selling regularly to major publications.

One of the three books of 1922 was a rather innocuous mystery, set in northern California, called *Black Gold*. Especially interesting, though, is Terhune's Foreword. In it he argued, as he was to do periodically for the rest of his life, the cause of the "popular" writer:

If you are questing for character-study or for realism or for true literature in any of its forms,—then walk around this book of mine (and, indeed, any book of mine); for it was not written for you and it will have no appeal for you.

But if you care for a yarn with lots of action,—some of it pretty exciting, —you may like *Black Gold*. I think you will. . . . There is not a subtle phrase or a disturbingly new thought, from start to finish . . . a story that is frank melodrama. . . .

If, now and again, my puppets or my plot-wires creak a bit noisily,—what then? Creaking, at worst, is a sure indication of movement,—of action,—of incessant progress of sorts. A thing that creaks is not standing still and gathering mildew. It moves. Otherwise it could not creak.

Yes, there are worse faults to a plot than an occasional tendency to creakiness. It means, for one thing, that numberless skippable pages are not consumed in photographic descriptions of the ill-assorted furnishings of the heroine's room or cosmos; nor in setting forth the myriad phrases of thought undergone by the hero in seeking to check the sway of his pet complexes.

Yet, there is something to be said in behalf of the man or woman who finds guilty joy in reading a story whose action gallops; a story whose runaway pace breaks its stride only to leap a chasm or for a breathcatching stumble on a precipice-edge. The office boy prefers Captain Kidd to Strindberg: not because he is a boy, but because he is human and has not yet learned the trick of disingenuousness. He is still normal. So is the average grown-up.

These normal and excitement-loving readers are overwhelmingly in the majority. . . . If we insist that our country be guided by majority-rule, then why sneer at a majority-report in literary tastes?

Ben Hur was branded as a "religious dime novel." Yet it has had fifty times the general vogue of Anatole France's pseudo-blasphemy which deals with the same period. Public taste is not always, necessarily, bad taste. "The common people heard Him, gladly." (The Scribes did not.)

After all, there is nothing especially debasing in a taste for yarns which drip with mystery and suspense and ceaseless action; even if the style and concept of these yarns be grossly lacking in certain approved elements. So the tale be written with strong evidence of sincerity and with a dash of enthusiasm, why grudge it a small place of its own in readers' hours of mental laziness?

With this shambling apology,—which, really, is no apology at all,—I lay my book on your knees. You may like it or you may not. You will find it alive with flaws. But, it is alive.

I don't think it will bore you. Perhaps there are worse recommendations.

Terhune's objective in writing his melodramatic mysteries apparently was well realized. The Boston *Transcript* said of *Black Gold:* "From start to finish, the story is alive:" and *The New York Times* added: "It is a book which all who like action, and plenty of it, will be sure to enjoy." A sequel mystery published the following year and titled *Black Caesar's Clan* was rated by the New York *Tribune* as "replete with thrills," while the New York *Evening Post* called it "a melodrama of excellent construction and unusual interest."

Terhune's mysteries evoked praise from reviewers and sold fairly well; yet his fans and his publishers clamored for more dog tales. He had been bombarded by hundreds of letters pleading for, demanding more stories about Sunnybank Lad. In 1922, three years after publication of the first Lad book, came *Further Adventures of Lad,* eleven more stories about the great old collie, most of which already had appeared in *The Ladies' Home Journal.* In a brief Foreword to the volume, Terhune noted that, since the appearance of the first Lad book, more than 1,700 visitors already had come to Sunnybank to visit his grave.

The new Lad collection produced massive sales. The big collie had become a national celebrity. Two reviews of the book epitomized the divergent attitudes of the reading public and the literary establishment toward the writings of Terhune.

Said the *Literary Digest*: "The book is the work of an ardent dog-lover and no one can read these delightful sketches without feeling what a privilege it is to be admitted to the friendship and to obtain the devotion of an animal like Lad."

Wrote Isabel Paterson in the New York *Tribune* : " 'Lad' is pretty hard to believe in. To have such a dog around would be worse than being afflicted with a regiment of Boy Scouts all desperately intent upon their one good deed per diem. And Mr. Terhune's rather hysterical style, his incessant piling up of the agony and adjectives, is almost equally wearing. Still, if you are a dog lover, no doubt you'll like the book."

As the public response to Terhune's collies continued to increase, the voices of the critics tended more often to be carping ones. The third Terhune book that year was called *His Dog.* Some reviewers obviously were coming to feel that enough was enough. The New York *Evening Post* commented: "Mr. Terhune's collie story has become a standard product. They are all very much alike."

Even *The New York Times*, usually enthusiastic about Terhune's work, demurred slightly: "Many people who do and who do not love dogs have admired Mr. Terhune's stories about them. But some readers feel in his books a certain lack. He writes with sympathy, but hardly with imagination; he tells us a great deal about what dogs think, but not enough about what they feel. But, on the other hand, he is never guilty of the 'pathetic fallacy' and his dogs stand firm on their own feet as animals, with no mawkishness of human sentiment."

With his books selling at a furious clip and magazines printing virtually every story and article he was able to turn out, Terhune, just six years past his hated tenure as a newspaperman, was already a major celebrity in his own right. Late in 1922, *The Bookman* magazine carried an article about a visit to Sunnybank headed "Mr. Terhune Shows His Collies." At this time Bert and Anice Terhune were spending eight months a year at Sunnybank, two months traveling or resting in the South, and two months in the New York City apartment. The apartment on Riverside Drive, Terhune told the reporter, "is no part of the city to live in during the winter. It is cold and blowy; but I can look from my windows across to New Jersey and know that back in the hills lies Sunnybank where the collies are. It is no way, perhaps, for a grown man to feel. Maybe you would call it maudlin—but it is the way I feel. For the Sunnybank collies aren't merely dogs. They are super dogs!"

The year 1923 saw the publication of one more Terhune book by E. P. Dutton, *The Pest*, a mystery about the murder of the villainous Hamilcar Q. Glure, with the ever-present collie as a character. Once again, critical reaction was mixed. *The New York Times* called it "an extremely engrossing mystery yarn." Somewhat less entranced was the Literary Review of the New York *Evening Post* which commented: "To glorify the American collie seems Mr. Terhune's transcendent mission in fiction. His devotion to this most intelligent of dogs almost reduces to the realm of the incidental the unwinding of the story that serves as a vehicle for his propaganda. Mr. Terhune's writing is agreeable, if one is in search of a particularly light intellectual content, and his style is ingeniously journalistic."

An incident in the summer of 1923, though it brought sadness to

Bert and Anice Terhune, was to give a uniquely powerful boost to his already burgeoning career as a chronicler of heroic dogs.

Terhune's skill as a storyteller and his ability to wrap the deeds of derring-do in the garb of realism and reasonable logic made his stories quite plausible to most readers. But some still remained skeptical, contending that he was glorifying the dog to the point of absurdity.

Then, on Thursday, June 28, 1923, the front page of *The New York Times* carried a story at the top of the page under a two-column headline which read:

WOLF, THE HERO OF TERHUNE DOG STORIES,
DIES SAVING THE LIFE OF A CANINE TRAMP

The nine-paragraph story began with an emotional passage reminiscent of Terhune's own style:

Wolf, son of Lad, is dead. The shaggy collie, with the eyes that understood and the friendly tail, made famous in the stories of Albert Payson Terhune, died like a thoroughbred, so when Wolf joined his father in the canine beyond last Sunday night, there was no hanging of heads.

The article went on to recount Wolf's rather irresponsible nature as a young dog and his gradual maturing to the point where he became the self-designated guardian of puppies at Sunnybank and often would herd them out of the way when a visitor's car swept down the hillside driveway into The Place.

Wolf generally went for an evening stroll, the article went on, and the previous Sunday night he had wandered over to the railroad tracks at the outskirts of Pompton Lakes. While several witnesses watched nearby, Wolf saw a mongrel dog walking along the tracks as the Stroudsburg express approached at high speed. The *Times* story ended:

The headlight of the express shot a beam glistening along the rails. Wolf saw the dog and the danger. With a bark and a snap, the son of Lad drove the stranger to safety. The express was whistling for a crossing far past the station when they picked up what was Wolf and started for the Terhune home.

The news of Wolf's heroic death was reported in newspapers across the country. In addition to the widespread publicity it gave to Terhune and his writings, the incident produced a substantial fund of credibility for the author. It demonstrated conclusively that the accomplishments of the Terhune collies were indeed possible, and that there were canine heroes. Terhune's already vast popularity and influence was increased immeasurably by the death of Wolf and the newspaper accounts of it.

18

Around the corner of the old house, The Visitor walked slowly along the circular driveway of Sunnybank. He shivered a bit as the December wind pushed at him and he drew the collar of his overcoat more tightly around him.

He wished he could have come to Sunnybank in the spring when the wistaria was in bloom. He remembered, vaguely, the words Mrs. Terhune had used to describe that: ". . . it was May; and as we came down the Sunnybank driveway . . . late that afternoon, the house was strangely luminous with wistaria. The slanting rays of the sun lighted it up from underneath, so it was all a sort of warm, radiant orchid, rather than lavender. Never had I seen a lovelier sight. . . . It was breathtaking!"

Now, as The Visitor looked up, the wistaria was savaging the old house. Vines had twisted and torn their way through the roof and the window frames, ripping them loose.

Sunnybank House had died long ago. Now the corpse was decaying. Ragged holes appeared here and there at the top of the walls, under the eaves. Windows on the ground floor had been boarded up with huge slabs of plywood to keep vandals out. Windows on the upper stories stood open to the winter floods of ice and wind, gaping horribly like empty tooth sockets in an aged mouth.

Houses are made to emanate noises; but this one stood silently, more sepulchre now than dwelling place.

The Visitor walked to the west side of the house, the front portion that faced the lake. Faint, inchoate details of many of the old stories went rushing across his mind, vagrant breezes of memory. On this ground had walked the many visitors to Sunnybank. And here, just below the front door, they had been greeted by the inquisitive, plume-wagging collies come out to inspect them.

And here was the veranda. It was not as big as he had expected. Much of Sunnybank, in fact, had been on a smaller scale than he had anticipated, though everything conformed to the descriptions in Terhune's stories and articles. But the lens of his imagination always had enlarged and widened out the scene. In fact, the veranda was only about 6 feet wide and this section at the front of the house was perhaps 20 feet long; but it had provided the locale for numberless scenes in the stories of Sunnybank.

The entire veranda ran around three sides of the house and all of its length was utilized by Terhune. The side veranda was the hunting ground for burglars who sought to enter in the dead of night only to meet the enraged jaws of the collie on guard inside. Many scenes also were played on the back veranda and in real life it was there, shielded from the hot sun, that the Master and the Mistress had found the lifeless body of Lad on that September day in 1918.

The Visitor stood on the frozen ground just below the veranda and put one foot gently on the stone steps that went up to the front door. He remembered seeing a photograph of Terhune sitting on the topmost step, his arms thrown lovingly around the necks of two of his collies, Bruce and Bobby. The Master had still been young when the picture was taken; his face was unlined and the stray strands of hair fell down across his forehead. His huge feet and legs were wrapped in old-fashioned puttee-style boots with his pants tucked into the top. Behind him was what appeared to be an old porch swing outlined against the wistaria vines that covered the wall of the house.

Now the veranda was bare of furniture. The empty expanse of stone and concrete was interrupted only by the tattered remains of what once had been screened in. The screen was in shreds, but the wooden frame still stood upright.

On this little screened porch, Bert and Anice had eaten breakfast on summer mornings, had sat with their guests until long past midnight, swapping tall tales and ghost stories in the inky night as heat lightning bristled over

the Ramapos. And here they would sit alone, at autumn twilights, an aging
couple holding hands, looking westward across the lake.

19

It was a golden time at Sunnybank, those early years of the 1920s. It
was the life Bert Terhune had dreamed of living since he had been
a small boy: he was an enormously successful writer, he had Anice and
the collies, and they lived at The Place.

Terhune's personal popularity as the result of his dog stories had
grown astoundingly large. To his great surprise at first, and for reasons
he never completely would understand, his most devoted fans and
readers were children.

Youngsters pleaded with their parents to be taken to Sunnybank
to see the collies and the Terhunes. School groups of forty or fifty
children would come slowly down the driveway in buses, the little
ones clasping autograph books and waiting to see Lad's grave and the
other, living heroes. Children from many cities wrote to Terhune that
they had, without any adult instigation, formed fan clubs—Albert
Payson Terhune Clubs or A.P.T. Clubs—in his honor. Scout troops
came to see their hero, and Campfire Girls. Terhune was always
gracious in greeting the visiting children and, though he hated to have
his work interrupted, he would leave his typewriter for a few minutes
to step outside and speak briefly with the enthralled young visitors.
"And how are you, young man?" was his thundered greeting. In 1930
Terhune estimated that he still was meeting at least 1,000 children
yearly at Sunnybank. He hated to turn away a child, once writing: "A
disappointed or a frightened child is to me the most sharply pathetic
creature in the universe. Childhood seems so pitifully early a time to

begin one's apprenticeship in the lifelong trades of fear and disappointment." Adults never could be sure of their reception—a furious Terhune might storm out and bellow at them to quit bothering him —but the children were another matter.

His popularity with children took Terhune by surprise because his dog stories had appeared originally in major adult magazines such as *The Ladies' Home Journal* and *The Saturday Evening Post*, and when collected in hard covers were considered adult books, not juveniles.

Terhune wrote of his wonderment in his autobiography.

> The chief surprise to me in all my long years as a scribbler is the fact that children read and reread my dog yarns. These tales are not written for children. They contain language I would not use in talking to a child. To me, there seems nothing about them to appeal specifically to the young. Yet, from the first, more than half of my chronic readers have ranged in years from twelve to seventeen. Never have I written down to them. Never have I softened my stories on their account.

> Yet I rejoice in their endorsement. It is not easy to win the unswerving interest and approval of a child. Children have a queer way of brushing externals aside and of striking through shimmery verbiage to the heart of a yarn. If its heart is what they want it to be, they approve. Otherwise, they will have none of it. To me their praise means more than does that of all my adult audience.

Yet, just a few pages earlier in that same autobiography, Terhune had referred to himself scornfully as "the Apostle of the Obvious and a writer for the Very Young."

The horde of visitors to Sunnybank, terribly flattering at first, soon became one of the most persistent targets of Terhune's vaunted wrath. He was hot-tempered, and the invasion of his beloved Jersey sanctuary day after day drove him to constant explosions of anger. First because of the havoc the interruptions caused with his work schedule. But also because, as he loudly complained, the visitors showed no respect for his property or for the safety of his dogs. Sunnybank was frequently defaced by tourists, according to Terhune, and on a couple of occasions his dogs were struck by their cars.

He wrote angrily: "The public at large seems afflicted with the belief that Sunnybank is a zoo; and that I am a freak of sorts. This I judge from the hordes of motor tourists who swarm into the grounds to see our collies and to waste my own time.

"I have to keep the lodge gates closed when I want to get any work done; and to mar them with a sign 'No Admittance Today.' But that is the flimsiest of barriers against the invasion."

By 1925, Terhune and Anice had counted several thousand visitors. Then they stopped counting, but the flood did not cease. Terhune related that, one summer Sunday, Anice felt guilty at the inhospitable look of the no admittance sign and urged him to open the gates. Within two hours, he said, thirty-five cars had entered. The visitors spat on the veranda, struck matches on the walls of the house, or drove their cars on the lawns. Puppies had rocks and sticks thrown at them by raucous children. One group was caught trying to build a picnic fire against the trunk of a 200-year-old oak tree. Books were taken through the open windows as souvenirs. After two hours of this, Terhune gave his wife an I-told-you-so look and ordered the gates shut again. Later, Bert and Anice compromised by agreeing to permit visitors until 10:00 A.M. on nonholiday weekdays. Otherwise the entrance gates were kept closed and locked.

Terhune's bitter distaste for the suburban sprawl rapidly encroaching on the peaceful countryside around Sunnybank and for the "motor tourists" who, to his mind, obscured the greenery like locusts was frequently expressed in his fiction, as well as in his autobiographical writings and articles about life at Sunnybank. In one of the Lad stories, fittingly called "No Trespassing!", the intruders come by canoe on the lake, intent on picnicking on Sunnybank's "emerald lawn."

In another piece—an angry essay called "Car-sick"—Terhune told of a neighbor of his who, on a pretty Sunday morning, saw two parties of motorists drive onto his property and strip branches from a dogwood tree that had just blossomed. Later he went outside and found four visitors having a picnic lunch on his lawn. "Already, swatches of eggshells and chicken bones and greasy paper and greasier wooden dishes adorned the lawn . . ." To complete their crime, Terhune wrote, the intruders were building a fire against one of the man's trees and using his No Trespassing sign for kindling.

The bitterly told anecdote reaches its climax when the neighbor's puppy is run over and killed by the retreating car of the invaders. This brought Terhune's fury to a peak because his own Sunnybank Jean had been killed by a visiting car, as had several of his cats, while another of his collies had been crippled for life.

The accidental death of Sunnybank Jean, one of Terhune's famous collies and a daughter of Bruce, sparked a widely publicized furor. The incident cast Terhune in the unfamiliar role of villain and was a great blow to his reputation and pride.

On August 30, 1930, *The New York Times* related how some visitors, a family from Detroit named Norris, had stopped at Sunnybank because the fourteen-year-old son idolized Terhune and wanted to see him. They asked permission at the gatehouse to drive into The Place and were told to go ahead. As the car rounded a turn on the downhill drive, said the news story, the ten-year-old Sunnybank Jean "suddenly appeared directly in front of the car." The driver apparently had time neither to stop nor swerve before the collie was struck and killed. The father went immediately to the house to inform Terhune and to apologize but, said the *Times*, "the author was enraged." He insisted that the visitor accompany him to a nearby Justice of the Peace, where Terhune swore out a complaint of malicious mischief against the man and his wife. Terhune later agreed to withdraw the complaint in return for a payment of $100, which the author said he would donate to a local charity.

Other papers gave additional details: one said Terhune furiously announced that his writings about Sunnybank Jean had earned him more than $9,000, whereupon Norris offered to pay him $1,000 for the loss of the collie but Terhune refused, saying $1,000 could not pay for the loss of a dead friend. Another account, obviously false, declared that Norris did not have $100 with him and was led off to jail while his family wept, until the money was received from Detroit.

Terhune was badly shaken by the negative publicity. He was concerned not only at the wounding of his reputation, but also over the possible effect the publicity might have on the sale of his books. The next day he fed a story to *The New York Times* declaring that he had received many letters of sympathy over the death of Jean, including one from the president of the National Humane Society. The story was carried under a headline TERHUNE COLLIE MOURNED.

Years later, Terhune still was defending himself over the incident.

A Book of Famous Dogs, published in 1937, gave his version of the incident, which was quite different from the story as reported by the newspapers. According to Terhune, Jean was an exceptionally friendly dog who loved visitors and being petted. When a car came down the driveway, Jean would take a position at the foot of the driveway, near the back veranda, waiting eagerly for the guests to arrive. She was thus waiting, Terhune said, on the day she died. "The car . . . had crashed the gates at the lodge and had sped down the drive at perhaps forty miles an hour," claimed Terhune, disregarding the signs warning against speeding. At the house, the car ran over Jean and she died in agony. Then, according to the still-angry Terhune, "A large woman in bright blue was among the tourists who debarked tumultously from the killer car. Breezing over to where I knelt beside my dead little collie friend she made graceful amends for everything by assuring me with a gay smile: 'I am really VERY sorry this has happened.' . . . For the only time in my life I replied to a woman's words with a torrent of indescribably foul blasphemy."

That certainly should have been the last echo of an unfortunate, if much over-publicized incident, but it was not. The whole thing was revived eight years later in every vivid detail by *The New Yorker* magazine in the summer of 1938, with a long feature by Jared L. Manley headed WHERE ARE THEY NOW? DEATH OF A DOG. The story began with the Norris family vacation trip in 1930, and proceeded to recapitulate the entire affair—from the viewpoint of the Norrises. It repeated the driver's contention that permission to drive into Sunnybank had been secured at the gate, that the car was driven slowly down the drive and that the accident was unavoidable—"The damned dog committed suicide," according to Mr. Norris. The livid Terhune, he said, shouted "some terrible things to us. He called us vandals and barbarians and trippers and tourists—things like that. He kept screaming like mad and shouting for the caretaker to get the police. He said he'd have us up. He said we'd pay for this."

A contributing factor in Terhune's long-standing hatred for "motor-tourists," or perhaps a result of it, was that he, himself, had never learned to drive a car. He did enjoy being driven around and owned many cars over the years, but was content to leave the driving to Anice or to one of his servants. He told an interviewer once that his bad hand prevented him from driving. Certainly, the inner workings of an automobile bewildered him.

Another, less troublesome burden of his fame was the vast quantity of mail that came to him. Each week brought between 200 and 300 letters. On some days, it was reported, he got more mail than all the other patrons of the Pompton Lakes postoffice put together. He was so well known that letters addressed to him at "Sunnybank, U.S.A." were promptly delivered. The letters, which he variously described as "ceaseless streams" and a "snowstorm," often irritated Terhune because many of them asked him for advice about sick dogs, or requested a photo yet failed to enclose return postage. Terhune once estimated that only about one in three such requests were accompanied by return postage and he ignored those that were not, unless they came from a child. His long-standing policy was to answer personally or to have a secretary answer for him every letter from a child. Communications from adults he got to when he could. "Some of these are deserving of swift and personal reply," he said. "More are begging letters. A few are from lunatics." He complained to a friend: "the average letter writer is a pest!"

He viewed autograph seekers with equal venom. In 1935 a club of autograph collectors asked Terhune to comment on their hobby for their publication. They probably were not too happy with his response, but they printed it: " . . . the foulest pest unhung is the person who rushes up to one in the street or at a radio studio or after a speech or banquet and thrusts a bit of paper forward with a demand it be autographed. These nuisances crowd around one in dozens."

20

On June 8, 1923, Terhune's daughter Lorraine was married at the Dutch Reformed Church in Pompton Lakes, with a reception afterwards at Sunnybank. She had been training to be a nurse in New York City and her husband was a young doctor, Franklin A. Stevens. The attitude of Bert and Anice toward Lorraine had changed little over the years as she grew. They went through the motions of being good parents, they provided her with a comfortable home and the necessities of life. Lorraine had virtually everything she needed—except love. They certainly were not cruel to her or unpleasant, but she remained a kind of afterthought. Lorraine rarely was taken on trips with her parents and was left in the keeping of relatives (although in justice it should be added that most of those trips were taken during the winter months when Lorraine was in school). Bert's attitude toward his daughter was one of benign indifference, and this was almost symbolically reflected in his writing: his daughter was only rarely mentioned in his voluminous writing about Sunnybank and his life there. Anice was a proper, correct stepmother, but she always was jealous and resentful of any feeling shown by Bert for his daughter. A typical incident occurred when a visitor heard Bert suggest to Lorraine that they go for a walk down by the lake. Anice quickly jumped up and said, "I'll go with you!" She just didn't want them to be together, without her.

In public, Bert and Anice tried to portray themselves as—and perhaps convince themselves that they were—attentive, doting parents. This effort manifested itself in Lorraine's plush wedding. A local newspaper declared that 500 guests, some traveling in special railroad cars, had come to "one of the most brilliant weddings in upper Passaic County in many years."

Two ministers performed the wedding ceremony, at which Bert Terhune gave his daughter away. After the lavish reception, Lorraine and her husband sailed for a European honeymoon, then went to live in New York City, where he was in practice. They lived together only about two years, then separated; but Lorraine never returned permanently to Sunnybank. She stayed in Manhattan for the rest of her life.

With Lorraine married and gone, Bert and Anice—both now just past fifty—were alone at Sunnybank to share their life in what he often referred to as "The House of Peace." Alone, that is, in a family sense, for they had plenty of company at Sunnybank. Taking devoted care of their household needs were two French-speaking servants from Martinique—the sisters Josephine and Pauline Andrasse, who had come to Sunnybank as shy teen-agers in 1911 and who remained for over a half century. Pauline did the cooking and Josephine, known to the Terhunes and his readers as "Fifine," handled the cleaning. They lived in a second-floor bedroom above the kitchen.

In the gatehouse lived The Place's caretaker or "superintendent," as Terhune liked to refer to him. For more than thirty years this was English-born Robert Friend, who had been brought to Sunnybank by Terhune's father in January, 1899. A slender, gray-haired, bespectacled man, he was gentle and soft-spoken and took expert care of the dogs and the grounds. He also supervised the numerous workmen over the years who helped care for the estate, which varied in size from 30 to 40 acres (Terhune periodically bought and sold small parcels of land on the fringes of Sunnybank).

Friend, who remained at Sunnybank until the mid-1930s when he retired, was mentioned frequently by Terhune in his articles and stories. He addressed Terhune as "Boss" and always referred to him as "the Boss" when speaking about him. Friend knew his place, knew what was expected of him. If he toured the grounds with Terhune and a guest, for example, Friend would walk several paces ahead of the other two, rather than more familiarly alongside them.

Terhune's attitude, and that of Anice, toward their employees at Sunnybank was quite in keeping with their generally Victorian outlook toward everything: they were restrained in their relationship with the help and rather austere, but also quite protective in a paternalistic way. They felt a very strong responsibility for those who worked for them. Employees were expected to work long and hard and those who didn't were summarily fired. Respect was demanded. When Terhune passed a workman on the Sunnybank grounds, the workman was expected to tip his hat and say, "Good morning, Sir."

If the welfare of one of his servants was threatened, however, Terhune would rush to the defense. When the local bank ran into financial difficulties during the Depression, Terhune stormed over there, demanded and got the life savings of the Andrasse sisters restored to them. The two French-speaking women, in their quiet, shy way, worshipped Terhune as long as he lived.

In 1924, the Doran Company published another of Terhune's attempts at more serious writing, or "belles lettres" as he and his wife liked to call them. It was a slim little book entitled *Now That I'm Fifty* and was a kind of musing about approaching old age, rather than autobiography. The book did not attract the following of Terhune's fiction, but the strength of his name gave it a fair sale.

Now That I'm Fifty displayed another of the trends in Terhune's writing that was to become increasingly prominent: his perception of himself as a sort of kindly, sophisticated wise man, who had many valuable bits of advice to offer his readers—not only on dog psychology and training, but on life itself. This tendency toward didacticism, always a weakness, was to become more apparent in his fiction as well as in his countless articles and essays.

His advice was not necessarily invalid. Much of it was simple, rather old-fashioned wisdom, clothed in Terhune's rambling prose. In *Now That I'm Fifty,* for example, he counseled moderation in all things, including appetite. His own prodigious ability as a trencherman had been brought somewhat under control over the years. In contrast to the quantities of food he had gorged on as an athletic young man, his diet was now made up of lighter fare. One of his magazine essays, "Stepmother Nature and I," offered advice on diet, the proper method of walking, and why one should avoid drinking ice water after exercise or taking ice-cold showers. Don't spend a half-hour lolling in a hot or cold tub, he warned, for "that makes for weakened tissues."

His daily routine during those blissful years at Sunnybank involved a lot of exercise, usually in the form he loved most—a brisk walk with his collies around his estate. He constantly referred to these walks in his writings—to the "rackety, swirling" bunch of golden collies that exuberantly joined him on the woodland hikes, shaking the hillsides with their happy barking. Sometimes after breakfast the walk would go for 5 miles. Often there would be another, shorter one after dinner and sometimes one after lunch as well. Terhune told dog writers that his collies were given 10 miles of exercise a day, but this probably was exaggeration. He also claimed that he would sometimes work until 3:00 A.M., then take a dozen collies and go for an eight-mile hike through the hills. When he returned home, he said, he felt as refreshed as if he had had a good sleep.

Anice Terhune often joined her husband on the walks around his beloved acres. In her reminiscence of him, called *The Bert Terhune I Knew* and published a year after his death, she wrote tenderly of such a stroll:

> In those days before motor madness, we used to take eight or ten dogs with us on hikes through the woods. Reaching our gate, we would look quickly up and down the road. If no carriage or car was in sight, we dashed wildly across the roadway into the opposite field, the mass of collies leaping after and around us with yelps of joyous excitement.
>
> Then up to and into the back woods we would all make our way, past showers of apple blossoms in the spring, and tents of dogwood. In the fall the glorious many-tinted maples and the bittersweet would hold us breathless.

The wonderful hikes in the woods, though, were merely breaks between periods of hard work at the typewriter. No matter what his fame, no matter how much revenue was rolling in, Terhune—as long as he was in good health—never gave up his steady, taxing work regimen. It was nine hours a day at the typewriter, day after day after day, turning out the material nonstop, with only Sundays as a time of rest.

"I planned the hours that should be spent at my desk at steady typing," he wrote, "and I allowed nothing short of a catastrophe to change them. Again and again, on a morning when I knew the fish would be biting, I have told myself I needed a day off and that I would work the better for it. Whereat my Simon Legree self has answered:

'Get to your desk and stay there. Cut out the excuses.' "

Although Terhune claimed that he threw some of his writings away as not suitable for publication, and not everything that he submitted to editors was sold, his long hours at the typewriter did produce an amazing volume of published material. His books (most of which were collections of the magazine pieces or magazine serials turned into novels) were published at the rate of two or three a year all through the 1920s. And he continued to write and sell a great mass of short fiction and articles. The *Readers Guide to Periodical Literature* for the period from 1925 to 1928 lists thirty-eight stories, twenty-six articles, and three serialized novels—all published in magazines under Terhune's name.

The stories continued to be mostly collie yarns for top magazines. The articles were sold to a somewhat wider range of publications and covered a variety of topics, although the majority of them had some connection with dogs. There were pieces in the *The Ladies' Home Journal*, for example, on "The Why of the Dog" and "The Ways of a Dog with a Man"; one for *Country Life* called "What You Don't Know About Your Dog"; and lengthy articles for *The Saturday Evening Post* on dog psychology and dog shows. And there were the typically discursive pieces in *The American Magazine* on family trees, public morals, the use of liquor, and so forth. For *World's Work* he wrote articles on Greyhound racing (he approved of it) and boxing.

He was, in short, a pro—a hardworking craftsman who could really turn it out and keep it coming, month after month, year after year.

In time, though, even the fertile Terhune brain could not keep up with the never-ceasing demand for more new stories, more serials. He was so pressed for time to fill the orders from editors that he began to run out of plot ideas. So he quietly hired some help. Alma Woodward, a feature writer on the *Evening World* during the last couple of years of Terhune's tenure there, began in 1924 to provide him with plots for serials. She would write a 5,000-word nucleus for such a project and then deliver it to Terhune, who would pay her and turn the condensed plot summary into a full-fledged serial of 50,000 words or more for *The Saturday Evening Post* or another major magazine and, later, into a book. The arrangement, which Terhune kept secret for obvious reasons, continued for five years. There is evidence that he was using similar help during the last part of his career—he was buying story ideas from a New Jersey man in the mid-1930s.

Because of his vast and dedicated readership and his own status as a semi-celebrity, Terhune and his collies were always newsworthy. In May, 1925, *The New York Times* headlined a news story TERHUNE'S PRIZE DOG LOST. The article related that the lost animal was Explorer, son of Sigurd, which at the age of eleven months had won the Fred Lake Memorial Cup as the best collie bred in the United States in 1922. Explorer had, for some unexplained reason, been loaned by Terhune to a woman in Mt. Kisco, New York, and had wandered away into the woods near her kennels. The collie had been reported seen near Tarrytown, but ran away when called. "He was trained to come only to his master," the *Times* story said, and because he was a one-man dog, Terhune feared the collie was suffering.

Two days later, another *Times* headline followed: TERHUNE GETS HIS DOG. The lost Explorer had been found by police officers near Tarrytown. The news story, echoing the fictional adventures of Lad, speculated that Explorer was trying to find his way back to Sunnybank but, "hungry and almost exhausted," had been stopped by the broad Hudson River. Terhune gave the policemen a $100 reward for their big find.

Some time around 1924, Terhune began a relationship with the McNaught Syndicate, which sold features to newspapers throughout the country, that was to last for the rest of his life. He started writing a feature called "Tales of Real Dogs," anecdotes that were culled from his huge files of dog material and his own prodigious memory. Later he wrote another feature for McNaught, "Calling All Dogs!" —a melange of anecdotes, bits of history, incidents reported to him by readers, and miscellaneous oddities such as his comments on an ad offering doggie horoscopes for the astrology-minded.

And the books kept pouring out, with twenty-seven published during the years 1920–29. By far the most successful among them were the dog stories or, at least, yarns with a dog as a featured character. In 1925, the heroic Wolf was immortalized between hard covers when a series of stories about his adventures and his eventual death under the Stroudsburg express was published under the title

Wolf. The book was dedicated by Terhune to the memory of Wolf, "A Gallant Little Collie and My Chum."

The book added Wolf to the panoply of Terhune collie immortals and this was quickly acknowledged by the critics. "Mr. Terhune," said the prestigious *Dial,* "has added another hero to his canine hall of fame; has placed another dog star in literature." And even the rather austere *Saturday Review of Literature* applauded: "Sometimes amusing, sometimes exciting, sometimes whimsical, the book is thoroughly enjoyable from beginning to end." A *New York Times* reviewer a couple of years earlier had labeled Terhune "the Boswell of the collie elect."

A Terhune mystery novel published in 1926, *Treasure* (later published as *The Faith of a Collie*), demonstrated again the divided reaction of the major literary reviewers to much of Terhune's work. According to *The New York Times,* it was "By far the best novel Mr. Terhune has yet written." The book "has many phases of interest, excelling his previous books in its variety and in the beguilement of its story."

But Harriet Henry, writing in the *Literary Digest International Book Review,* commented: "This is the sort of book that will appeal particularly to boys and to men who do not care for love stories or psychological delvings into any sort of emotions; no pros or cons of the human mind, just a straight simple story."

In 1927, Terhune made another try at a book of "belles lettres." It was a small volume of essays titled *Bumps,* based on a series he had written for *The American Magazine.* Terhune noted ruefully in his autobiography that one reviewer described it as "another Terhune dog story—this time about a fascinating collie pup named 'Bumps.'" In fact the title of the book came from an essay on the bumps provided by life for the individual and their ultimate value to him. In only one of the six essays was there any mention of a dog.

Bumps, like *Treasure* the year before, was published by Harper and Brothers. In 1924 Terhune had moved from the George H. Doran Company, which had published eleven of his books over a five-year period (including a couple already under contract and published after the 1924 move). He left Doran to go with a gifted editor named Eugene Saxton, who was moving to Harper. Saxton—he was to become one of the best-known and most distinguished editors in publishing—had made a very positive impression on Terhune while working with him at Doran and the two became good friends. (Harper would continue to be Terhune's publisher for the rest of his career, although two or three minor volumes appeared under other imprints.)

Saxton remained Terhune's editor and friend for life. So appreciative was Terhune of his editor's talents that he dedicated several of his books, including his autobiography, to him. Terhune and his wife would visit the Saxtons several times a year at their home in Manhattan, and they reciprocated with periodic visits to Sunnybank. Mrs. Saxton and Anice Terhune became part of a group of ladies who got together on matinee days in Manhattan for lunch and a visit to the theater. But Mrs. Saxton never became overly fond of Anice, regarding her as just too professionally saintly. The friendship was continued primarily because of her regard for Bert Terhune and his relationship with her husband.

Eugene Saxton's son, Mark Saxton, still remembers with awe his first visit to Sunnybank with his parents. Like most youngsters, he was a devoted admirer of Terhune and was greatly excited at the prospect of seeing the great man and his collies. It was a fine autumn day in the mid-1920s. The famous Gray Dawn, by then an elderly animal, was Terhune's only house dog at the time. After lunch, Terhune let more than twenty collies out of their pens and they accompanied him and the Saxtons on a walk around the grounds, just as the delighted boy had read about. The collies ran and barked wildly through the woods and along the lake, he remembers, but they always were under Terhune's control and clearly obeyed his command.

After the hike, they returned to the house to rest and enjoy some conversation. Mark Saxton found that Terhune, despite his great size and bulk—"he looked like a mountain moving"—was not a forbidding figure and was easy to talk to. He told Mark rather wistfully of his athletic background, regretting that he was no longer able to repeat the feats of his youth. And he related some of his favorite yarns, including one of an adventure in Siam when he went out on the town in Bangkok, did some heavy drinking, got into a disturbance, and wound up spending the night in jail.

Terhune always was very fond of Mark and his brother Alexander, who was called "Sandy," and he dedicated *The Way of a Dog* to them in 1932. Mark Saxton learned about the dedication with "absolute astonishment and utter disbelief" and became quite a celebrity to his classmates. Still fond of fencing, though he no longer took part in the sport, Terhune once gave Mark two sets of fencing foils and a pair of masks for Christmas, but warned him sternly that he must never use the foils without the mask. He also promised Mark an even better present—a collie puppy descended from Gray Dawn. But the gift would be made *only,* he said, if the Saxtons ever decided to leave their apartment and live in a rural area where the collie could thrive.

Guests such as the Saxtons were entertained at Sunnybank on the comfortable veranda facing the lake, if the weather permitted; if not, in the big living room with its bookshelf-lined walls. The main floor of the old house was dominated by one great L-shaped room. The side of the L, facing the south, was the living room, or library as they sometimes called it, with its huge fireplace and the nine-foot-long couch that Anice had had specially made for Bert.

Jutting off at a right angle to the living room was a smaller room on the lake side of the house, which had a smaller fireplace and contained Anice's grand piano and organ. It was called the music room and under that piano was Lad's old "cave."

The living room covered the entire width of the house. At either end was a Dutch door, one leading to the veranda facing the lake and the other to the rear veranda that looked up to the entrance gate. A hallway down the middle of the house led to Bert's study, a small room in which he worked at an old rolltop desk. Pictures of Bert and his friends and of the dogs hung on the walls. The hallway moved on to the dining room and kitchen area, at the northern end of the house, and to the stairway to the upper floors.

On the second floor were Bert and Anice's separate bedrooms, a guest room, and bathrooms. He sometimes said that bathrooms had become almost a hobby with him as they kept putting in more bathrooms and improving the plumbing over the years. Anice's bedroom was much the largest—26 by 32 feet, with six windows. The room was painted a bright pink color of which Anice was fond.

The third floor held a couple of additional guest bedrooms, one of which had been Lorraine's room, a small room that Bert used as a hideaway when necessary, and a storage area for surplus books.

But it was the huge living room that was most vividly remembered by visitors to Sunnybank. It was a dark, restful brown—not only the walls and ceiling, but also the old Heppelwhite and Chippendale chairs and the Sheraton desk and the grandfather clock. Shelves on one side of the room contained some of the silver trophies and colorful ribbons won by Sunnybank collies at dog shows.

As the years went by, the living room more and more took on the aspect of a museum. In addition to the ancient furniture—much of which had belonged to Terhune's parents—bear, tiger, and leopard skins were stretched on the living room and music room floors. But the real eye-catcher was on the wall behind the couch: Terhune's collection of armor and weapons. There were swords reportedly used in knighthood days, flint-rock pistols, ancient helmets and body armor. There was an Indian Khuttar, which Terhune called the bloodiest instrument he had ever seen; a double-barreled, ten-shot British pistol equipped with a concealed bayonet; a thirteenth-century coat of mail from the Tower of London; a Turkish dagger and bandolier; a sidearm sword from the Revolutionary War; a fifteenth-century executioner's sword; stilettos from India; and many more.

The presence of the weapons has added to Terhune's reputation in some quarters as a lover of violence, a worshipper of aggressiveness. Perhaps. But it may have been simply the collection of a person who liked to regard himself as "A Man's Man," the ultimate accolade of that time, and who tried to live in a style conforming to such an image. His collection was the kind of conversation-piece hobby that would have been enjoyed in that era by a wealthy man who thought of himself, and was considered by his public and his friends, as a 100 percent He-man.

A delightfully colorful counterbalance to the rather somber brown of the living room was offered at the corner where an arch joined the living room and music room. There, on a stand, Anice had placed a huge copper bowl, perhaps 30 inches in diameter, which they had purchased at a bazaar in Algiers. The bowl was kept overflowing with flowers of the season—dogwood and iris in spring, then crimson June roses, gladioli and dahlias in late summer, multi-colored October leaves and chrysanthemums from the Sunnybank greenhouse, and holly leaves and berries in the dead of winter. The changing beauty of the big flower bowl was a constant visual feast.

Terhune did most of his writing in the small study on the ground floor, the same study that figured in many of the stories. Sometimes when guests were in the house and he needed more privacy, he retreated to the room on the third floor. Another spot, when the weather was suitable, was a table and chair on the shaded veranda. Or sometimes the old gazebo.

But his most famous work area—famous because it often was mentioned by writers visiting Sunnybank to write newspaper articles about him—was a big hammock set up under the crab apple trees down on the shoulder extending into the lake. His typewriter was placed on an old, weatherbeaten desk and there, on pleasant summer days, he did his writing with his beloved collies scampering around him and occasionally nuzzling him for a pat on the head.

Anice Terhune wrote of it after her husband's death:

"It was a picture to remember! A dozen times a day I used to glance out of the windows at those broad, splendid, brown-clad shoulders, bending over the clicking typewriter, the khaki hammock, with seven or eight golden collies flowing in and out and around it."

Terhune pounded out his rough drafts in single-space form on legal-sized sheets of yellow paper and he crammed copy onto every inch of paper. Always intent on fast production, he didn't even begin new paragraphs, but simply used a paragraph symbol on his typewriter. He made corrections on the rough draft with pencil, then turned it over to a secretary for final typing. Then it was put in brown covers and mailed, either directly to the appropriate editor or to whichever literary agent Terhune was dealing with at the time. Correspondence in his papers indicates that he was represented at various points by Brandt & Kirkpatrick, George T. Bye, Inc., Nannine Joseph, and Jacques Chambrun, Inc.; but most of the time it appears that Terhune sold his work to editors and publishers on his own, without the aid of an agent.

He usually drove a hard bargain. By 1925 he was a wealthy man, but the old financial concerns never left him and he was never above haggling over the sale price of something he had written. In 1927 his old friend William Gerard Chapman of the International Press Bureau in Chicago—the man who had encouraged Terhune in 1916 to leave

newspaper work and spend all his time on free-lance writing—offered
Terhune $25 for the second serial rights to a short story originally
published in 1919. Though his income by then must have been nearing $50,000 a year, Terhune insisted on bargaining with Chapman:
" . . . $50 strikes me as a far pleasanter price for it than $25. In fact,
that's the price. You see, there are fifty people who can do ordinary
stories as well as I can. But by mere luck, I chance to be the only man,
at the moment, who writes acceptable dog stories. So let's call it $50."

Chapman wouldn't call it $50—he called the deal off. Terhune
refused to let the matter rest. Two months later he wrote Chapman
again: "By the way, you overlooked a bet in passing up my price of
$50 for the right to sell 'One Minute Longer' to your papers. It is one
of my really good dog stories; as good for grownups as for kids. You'd
have made money by offering it as a Terhune dog story. However,
that was your own business; not mine."

Chapman responded: "No one has a clearer understanding of the
popularity and value of a Terhune dog story than I, but it seemed to
me that 'One Minute Longer' was very short and was distinctly juve-
nile." A few weeks later, however, Chapman agreed to pay Terhune's
price for the rights. It took the author three months and several letters,
but he got his additional $25.

On September 2, 1926, Bert and Anice celebrated their twenty-
fifth wedding anniversary. The festivities had been announced a
month earlier with a story on the Social News page of *The New York
Times* from information supplied apparently by Terhune, who always
desired publicity. The article told of plans for a reception at Sunnybank, and pointed out that Mrs. Terhune was the granddaughter of
John Stockton, U.S. Senator and Ambassador to Italy, the great-grand-
daughter of Commodore Robert Field Stockton, former commander
of the U.S. Navy, and great-great-granddaughter of Chief Justice
Richard Stockton, a signer of the Declaration of Independence.

Among those on the guest list for the reception, the *Times* article
noted, were Mr. and Mrs. Sinclair Lewis, Vilhjalmur Stefansson (the
famed explorer), Mr. and Mrs. George Arliss (he was a major film star
of the day), former Attorney-General and Mrs. A. Mitchell Palmer,
and several of the men who had made Terhune rich—magazine edi-

tors George Horace Lorimer, Ray Long, and Barton W. Currie, and their wives.

The *Times* carried another story on the morning of the anniversary and again ran a list of some of the more illustrious guests.

The reception was lavish, attended by some 350 guests. The Terhunes housed twenty guests at Sunnybank and booked all the space in a nearby hotel for many of the others. Mrs. Terhune related years later how her husband had directed her to buy some anniversary presents for them, even though he already had given her a four-carat diamond ring as his own silver anniversary present. Bert told her he was afraid that, because their daughter's wedding had taken place so recently, many of their guests would be reluctant to send another gift. And he didn't want his wife to be embarrassed by a paltry display of anniversary presents at the reception. So he spent almost $1,000 on a silver tea service and three silver vases. Fictitious names were placed on the cards with the gifts and they were displayed at the reception.

His apprehension was unjustified; their guests flooded them with beautiful anniversary gifts. But the silver tea service from "a friend in California" was the object of the most admiration. It was, Mrs. Terhune wrote years later, "such a beautiful and rarely lovely thing for Bert to do! He did not want those silver things for himself, magnificent as they are; but he feared that possibly I might feel a bit disappointed if the gifts did not shower down upon us; and he could not have borne that for me."

As the 1920s passed their midpoint, Bert and Anice continued to live the idyllic life at Sunnybank that always had been their dream. Money had not been a legitimate concern since the explosive success of the first Lad book which, by itself, practically ended Terhune's financial worries for good, although he never stopped worrying. They would spend a winter month or two in their Riverside Drive apartment—their "flat of winter exile," as Bert called it—and were regular visitors to Europe. They also went to North Africa, Palestine, and Egypt, and spent much time in Florida and California—especially northern California, a favorite region of Bert's.

Wherever they went, Terhune was a meticulous observer of local color. They often visited Scotland, which became the scene of his 1927 book *The Luck of the Laird* (later published as *A Highland Collie*).

The Runaway Bag, published in 1925, reflected a trip made to Algeria the year before.

No matter where the writer and his wife traveled, they found that Terhune's work was known and loved. Mrs. Terhune described one visit to a London haberdashery where she was buying gloves for her husband. When she gave her name, the clerk "threw a sort of side-wise, English spasm, and gasped: 'Can it be? No—it cannot!' " When Mrs. Terhune assured the thunderstruck clerk that her husband was indeed the writer of dog stories and books, he gasped again that he "never expected to be able to sell a pair of gloves for the hand that wrote those stories!"

Another time, in Pitlochry, Scotland, the Terhunes attended services in a small church. As they entered the church, a Scotsman unexpectedly greeted them by name. He told them he had once seen Terhune speak on a visit to the United States. "And I rread yourr tales! I could neverr forrget you! We're glod to weelcome you to Pitlochry!"

Charles B. Driscoll, the syndicated newspaper columnist, declared that he had been in many interior towns in Spain, Russia, and South America and usually found that the only American writers to be represented in the language of the country were Jack London and Terhune. There is no question, Driscoll wrote, that "Mr. Terhune has long been one of the most widely-read of all writers in the English language."

Driscoll once related in his column the story of a young girl who lay near death in a hospital in the Eastern United States. Someone gave her a copy of *Lad: A Dog* and a relative read the stories to her. According to Driscoll, the girl became so absorbed in the Sunnybank tales and so attached to the book that she kept it under her pillow. She recovered from her critical illness and insisted that it was her interest in the Lad stories that kept her alive through the crisis and the beauty of the book that gave her the will to live. In gratitude, she spent months preparing a carefully hand-lettered, three-color rendition of The Gospel According to St. John which she sent to Terhune. It became one of his prized possessions. As Driscoll related it, the story fittingly ended with the girl and her husband becoming close personal friends of Bert and Anice.

Terhune's name was by now a household word. *The New Yorker* carried a full-page cartoon by Gluyas Williams entitled "Literary Renegades," with the subtitle "The Albert Payson Terhune Collie Who Failed to Stop a Runaway." The cartoon showed a man—obviously Terhune, with his long jacket, knickers, and puttee-type boots —shouting in rage at a collie which sits, blithely, tail wagging, while heading rapidly into the distance goes a runaway horse bearing a screeching female rider. Terhune and the collies also turned up on thousands of postcards bearing Sunnybank scenes. Whether he made money from the sale of these postcards is not certain, but considering his unceasing concern for the monetary end of things, it is hard to believe that he did not share in the proceeds.

Weekdays at Sunnybank were for work—Terhune on his writing, his wife on her music and more frequently as the years went by on writing of her own. Anice had dabbled in writing ever since her marriage. After his career blossomed and their life at Sunnybank settled down into a comfortable pattern, she took up writing more seriously and sold articles and verse to *The Ladies' Home Journal* and stories to *McClure's, Good Housekeeping,* and *The Atlantic Monthly.*

Anice had three novels published during the 1920s; books about New England village life shortly after the turn of the century. Her first one, *The Eyes of the Village,* introduced a character called Em, who also was featured in the other two, *Boarder Up at Em's* and *The White Mouse.* The books did not sell very well but were treated kindly by reviewers. *Boarder Up at Em's* was described by the Literary Review of the New York *Evening Post* as "altogether delightful reading."

Most days Bert and Anice breakfasted together, perhaps on the veranda, then Bert and the dogs would go off on their morning hike. Afterwards, each of them went to their desks for several hours of sustained work. Lunch and some moments of relaxed conversation were followed by more work in the afternoon. Then more hiking or some chores around the kennels, or perhaps a row on the lake at twilight. Bert had a specially made paddle almost 6 feet long that could, when he felt like it, propel his canoe around the lake at virtually motorboat speed. After dinner they would sit on the veranda, usually holding hands, and talk, or perhaps Anice would play the piano while Bert sat near the fireplace and read, the collies dozing at his feet.

Sometimes, when Anice played a popular song and the spirit moved him, Bert would sing along. His voice, rich and resonant when he spoke, had the appeal of a piledriver when he sang. And he knew it. Once, while driving to a picnic with some relatives in an open car, a bee flew in and buzzed angrily around, looking for an inviting target. While everyone flinched and leaned away, Bert said confidently, "No problem, folks. I'll just sing to it and watch what happens." He began singing in his usual ear-splitting tones; the bee quickly flew out of the car.

On weekends, Sunnybank often was filled with houseguests. Sinclair "Red" Lewis sometimes was there, and explorer Vilhjalmur Stefansson, old newspaper pal Robert Wells Ritchie, biographer William Inglis, editor Ray Long, and many other writers, actors, musicians. Bert's nephew, Frederic F. Van de Water, himself an author and one of Terhune's closest friends despite their seventeen-year age difference, was often a guest at Sunnybank (his birthplace) along with his wife and son. Fritz Van de Water always worshipped Terhune. Their family was a large one, with many nieces, nephews, cousins, but neither Terhune nor Van de Water had much concern with family ties, and their relationship with their relatives—except for each other—was never very close. The growth of Terhune's fame and fortune led to considerable ill-feeling on the part of some relatives, who felt that he had become much too self-important. Some of them blamed Anice, accusing her of being a snob who regarded her own family as much superior to the Terhunes. But the truth apparently was that Bert never had much taste for family gatherings and always preferred to steer an independent course. Fritz Van de Water felt much the same way.

Fritz's son recently described a Sunday morning ritual that he remembered from those years at Sunnybank. Pauline Andrasse would cook a mammoth supply of waffles and after the Terhunes and their guests had eaten as much as they could, the leftovers would be gathered up in bags. Then all the collies would be let out of their kennels and taken for a romp around the grounds, treated with bits of waffle as they went. "You can imagine the ruckus twenty or so dogs can stir up," Van de Water said. "As visitors we didn't mind, of course, but some of the neighbors found all that noise a bit much to take, especially on Sunday mornings."

Charles Driscoll, the newspaper columnist, loved Sunnybank and the Terhune hospitality so much that he and his friend, V. V. McNitt of the McNaught Newspaper Syndicate, visited The Place every spring and fall for seventeen years.

Houseguests were treated royally and fed sumptuously. The cook was expert at preparing such exotic dishes as terrapin, and she was well known for a rich, heart-shaped dessert biscuit. Meals were served on one set of china encrusted with silver or another encrusted with gold. Two beautiful silver peacocks served as table centerpieces and there were delightful old luster candlesticks. The warm wood tone of the big dining room table was not obscured by tablecloths; dinner was served on individual placemats by the two quiet servants, who always shyly addressed Anice in French if they had to ask a question.

Terhune loved the companionship of successful people; he relished good conversation and good liquor, cigars and story-swapping. He had been a joiner for years and met many of his friends through New York clubs. His favorite came to be the Century Club, which he loved for its quiet rooms and what he deemed to be its intellectual atmosphere. The intellectual tone was muted each year at the Century Club's "Roman Revel" where Bert, ever the ham, became something of a tradition for his skit appearances as an Arab sheik. He had, wrote one club member in describing the annual show, "a laugh like a howitzer blast—in joy or rage, he bellowed!"

Another of Bert's favorite clubs, the Adventurers, a few years later in 1935 gave him a testimonial dinner and made him a lifetime member.

One of Anice's great joys at Sunnybank, in addition to her houseguests, was her periodic musicales. She and four men friends formed what they came laughingly to call the "Sunnybank Quintet." The men and their wives drove to Sunnybank on a Sunday afternoon, and the day and evening were spent in playing chamber music, with Bert and the wives as the more or less voluntary audience. After playing for several hours, they would have dinner, then return to their music. In the evening the tone was lighter—Anice would sit at the organ and the musicians would improvise their favorite melodies from opera or songs by Stephen Foster. During the winter the mini-concerts would take place in the living room; when the weather improved, they would play on the veranda. Writing years later of her musicales, Anice admitted that Bert sometimes walked into his study to do some writing while the concert was on, but she quickly added that he always left his door open so he could continue to hear the music.

21

The early and mid-1920s were, in every way, years of joyous melody for the Terhunes and for Sunnybank, interrupted only occasionally by a discordant note. Perhaps it was a review of a new Terhune book which dismissed it too readily as just another of those Terhune dog yarns; perhaps a critical letter in a canine magazine; or an incident like the one which occurred in 1933 after Terhune had been presented by Columbia University with an Alumni Medal of Excellence for his literary achievements. He always had hoped to receive an honorary degree from Columbia, but the honor never came, so he settled with a great deal of satisfaction for the alumni medal. The award was given to him by one of the professors he once had found so boring, President Nicholas Murray Butler, and Terhune treasured it, taking it home to Sunnybank where the framed scroll and medal occupied a special place on his wall. Later he was told that someone had referred to the award as "Terhune's dog license." The writer, always deeply sensitive about his work though he constantly deprecated it himself, was so hurt by the remark that he removed the award from the wall, put it away in a drawer, and never again made mention of it.

He was quick to resent anything he interpreted as a slight. Once, at the Dutch Treat Club in New York City, he and Fritz Van de Water were riding up in the elevator when Van de Water introduced him to Henryk Van Loon, the historian and artist. Van Loon also was a huge man, about Terhune's size, and after they were introduced said jokingly, "You look like a man who could wear my cast-off clothes." Terhune's face reddened and he shot back: "If they're any better than those you have on, I'll be glad to look them over."

As the Terhune dog stories and books continued to fascinate his ever-eager readers during the 1920s, a new set of canine heroes followed as the literary descendants of Lad, Bruce, and Wolf.

There was Bruce's son Bobby (Sunnybank Robert) who, with Jean, was part of the first collie litter bred at Sunnybank, born on December 23, 1917. There was Treve (Champion Sunnybank Sigurd), bred by John Quigley and born in August, 1920, and Treve's fine offspring Explorer and Cavalier and Jamie and Sigurdson. And there was Explorer's son, Thane, whelped on March 26, 1927. Terhune described how he came to award that name to the puppy:

I had been saving up that half-royal Scottish title for years, waiting for a dog that should merit it. In this pale-gold youngster's deepest eyes, almost from birth, I read the true "look of eagles": the look I had been watching for, so long. In his ungainly and pudgily overgrown baby body, I read a future of mighty bone and lionlike symmetry and of tremendous coat. Here was a born champion. Here was a pup preordained to wear my stored-up name of "Thane."

Terhune's prophecy of Thane's value as a show dog was vindicated. The collie won his fifteenth championship points in five straight shows and became a champion at the age of seventeen months in September, 1928.

The unexpected death of Thane was important enough to be reported in *The New York Times* in April, 1929. The story said that the champion two-year-old collie had died of congestion of the lungs after being sick for only a few hours. Noting that the young dog already had been the hero of several magazine stories and that a book about him was "in the making," the paper described Thane as the pick of the Sunnybank kennels, told of his triumphant dog show career, and said that Terhune reportedly had refused an offer of $3,000 for him. Several experts, according to the *Times,* had rated Thane as the best collie in the country.

Though "congestion of the lungs" was the announced cause of

Thane's death, Terhune privately contended for the rest of his life that the prize collie had been cruelly murdered. He told friends that Thane had been fine when a group of visitors walked around The Place, stopping at Thane's run along with the others. The next morning, he was dead. Terhune declared that bits of glass were found in Thane's food dish and that an autopsy disclosed glass fragments in the dog's stomach. He did not say who he thought had killed the dog.

But of all the collies Terhune wrote about during the late 1920s and early 1930s, undoubtedly the most popular and engaging were Fair Ellen and Gray Dawn. And they were in fact the last of the great, celebrated collies of Sunnybank.

Fair Ellen was described to Terhune's readers in the final chapter of a collection of Terhune stories published in 1932 under the title *The Way of a Dog.* She was the only female in a five-puppy litter born in February, 1922. The sire was Champion Sunnybank Sigurd (Treve) and the dam was Sunnybank Alton Andeen, a Canadian-bred bitch.

Fair Ellen was, wrote Terhune, "the downiest and goldenest and prettiest and strongest of all that baby collie family; the greatest litter of pups, taken by and large, we have been able, thus far, to raise at Sunnybank." Two of her brothers, Sigurdson and Explorer, became dog show champions; another, Cavalier, also performed well in the show ring.

Between ten and twelve days after their birth, the four male puppies opened their eyes. But not Fair Ellen. Finally, when she was about a month old, her eyelids opened to disclose that her eyes were covered by thick membranes. When older and stronger, surgery might be able to remove the membranes and give her normal sight. Until then, the blind puppy was raised with her four rowdy brothers and she quickly demonstrated her intelligence and pluck, learning to use her nose and hearing to guide her around the puppy yard. Terhune began watching Fair Ellen closely, marveling at her apparent ability to reason and also noting that her brothers treated her with a strange gentleness.

At three months old, Ellen was operated on. The surgery was not successful; the membranes were removed, but the eyes still were sightless. Terhune made plans to put the collie to death, but was talked out of it by his wife, who argued that the blind dog seemed happy and content with her life and unaware of her affliction. Why condemn her to death?

And so Fair Ellen was allowed to live on at Sunnybank. Terhune began taking her on short hikes around The Place to familiarize her with the land. "Just at first," he wrote, "she bumped into countless obstacles before I could come between her and them. But I noticed —as earlier in the puppy-yard—that never did she collide with the same obstacle a second time. She had an uncanny memory for locations and for the spot where she had suffered collision. Also, she learned the topography of the grounds with startling swiftness."

One day, as Terhune and his blind collie walked along the lake edge, Ellen stopped and then turned and slowly, carefully walked into the gradually deepening water of the lake. Then she began to swim out. After a few minutes, she raised her head in apparent confusion and Terhune realized she was trying to get her bearings. He called her name and she quickly turned and swam directly back to him. From then on, she enjoyed frequent swims in the cold lake water, needing only Terhune's quiet call to find her way back to shore.

He also began to take her on his long hikes through the Sunnybank woods and sometimes up into the nearby Ramapo Mountains. "I slowed my pace to enable her to keep up with me in the funny exploratory gait she had taught herself—a choppy wolf trot, the head a little to one side and with the forelegs thrown far forward so as to give warning of any obstacle. (At even the light touch of some weed, in her line of advance, she halts at once, to avoid collision.) Soon she mastered and vastly enjoyed the art of making her way through woodland and up and down hill, at my heels, guided by scent and sound of my step."

Terhune said that Fair Ellen was the only Sunnybank dog who had not been taught to obey, implicitly and immediately. She was not trained because such training involves discipline and he could not bring himself to discipline a blind dog. Yet, he said, she did obey, by instinct rather than by training.

Because Fair Ellen carefully remembered every collision with an obstacle and took pains thereafter to detour around that obstacle, Terhune said that everyone at Sunnybank became more orderly as a result, trying to be sure that nothing was left lying around, out of place, to become a hazard for the courageous little collie.

When Ellen was almost a year old, Terhune consulted a veterinarian about the wisdom of breeding her and was advised that her blindness probably would not be transmitted to her offspring. A few months later, she gave birth to a litter of ten puppies. At first, the blind mother seemed unsure how to care for the newborn babies and was nervous and excitable. Terhune spent a cold night with her, calming her and making sure she did not harm the pups. After a few hours, her maternal instinct began to assert itself and she started to care properly for the tiny collies. Later the always-gentle Ellen became a ferocious defender of her young, storming out to attack any other hapless dog who ventured within 50 feet of the puppies.

Fair Ellen showed other strange powers. Here is how Terhune described them:

> . . . several of our pigeons will fly homeward to their cote, and their course will bring them into earshot of Fair Ellen. Immediately, barking in excitement at the game, she gives chase. Sometimes for a hundred yards or more she can follow directly beneath them, changing her own course instantly when they wheel or when their flight shifts. Always she remains precisely below them. The soft winnowing of their wings, often too faint for human ears to catch it, is her guide.
>
> Here on the hill-and-lake region of northern New Jersey, thunderstorms are frequent. Some of the collies do not like these storms. Some pay no heed at all to them. Ellen loves them. They fill her with a gay exaltation. She barks in clangorous delight at every peal of thunder.
>
> Among the hills it is impossible for the human ear to locate at once the direction of a scarce-heard distant mutter of thunder; nor for us to guess, by the sound, from what point of the compass the far-off storm is approaching. But Ellen is never at a loss about this. At the first growling whisper of the miles-away thunder she gallops toward it, in a straight line, barking and wildly wagging her tail. Not once has she been mistaken in this.
>
> Invariably—if the storm comes up at all—it comes from the exact direction toward which she galloped to greet its first distant onset. Not once, but perhaps a hundred times, we have noted and verified this.

Terhune claimed that several collie breeders had made him good offers to buy Ellen, for her puppies were good quality and had no eye trouble. But he always refused, wanting her to stay at Sunnybank, where she was "beautifully happy."

Fair Ellen lived for almost twelve years. Terhune wrote her eulogy as the final chapter of *The Book of Sunnybank,* published in 1934, a year after her death. He reported that thousands of persons had come to Sunnybank expressly to see Ellen and that many journalists had written accounts of her life.

"As the years crawled on," Terhune wrote,

Ellen's jollity and utter joy in life did not abate. Gradually her muzzle began to whiten. Gradually the sharp teeth dulled from long contact with gnawed bones. Her daily gallops grew shorter. But ever the spirit of puppy fun flared forth as when she was young.

She would romp with me, wildly, as always she had done. The seemingly noiseless slipping of my fingers into the side pocket of my leather coat, where always lie a handful of animal crackers, would bring her rushing up to me from many feet away; in gay expectation of the treat.

Fair Ellen outlived her three mighty brothers. Then her own time came. Terhune wrote about the deaths of his beloved dogs in a way that was simple, unashamedly sentimental, and decidedly affecting. The few lines that follow, as they relate the end of Fair Ellen's unusual life, are other wise significant as well. They were the closing lines of the last original book to be written by Terhune (though by no means the last Terhune book to be published):

On the afternoon of July First, 1933, Ellen and I went for one of our daily rambles—walks whose length was cut down nowadays by reason of her increasing age.

She was in dashing high spirits, and she danced all around me. We had a jolly hour, loafing about the lawns together. Then, comfortably tired, she trotted into her yard and lay down for her usual late afternoon nap.

When I passed by, an hour later, she was still lying stretched out there in the shade. But, for the first time in twelve years, the sound of my step failed to bring her eagerly to her feet to greet me. This was so unusual that I went into the yard and bent down to see what was amiss.

Quietly, without pain, still happy, she had died in her sleep.

I can think of a thousand worse ways of saying good-bye to this thing we call Life.

Gray Dawn was, in many ways, a dog of another color.

He was a son of Bruce and he was a blue merle collie. The most famous collies of fiction, such as Terhune's, and of film (such as Lassie), have been sable and white in color; that is, a coat of some shade of gold or brown mixed with white areas. Lesser known to the public, but also popular among collie fanciers, are those animals all-white in color and those with tricolor coats, a combination of black, white, and tan. Probably the least-known type of collie (and the oddest looking to the unfamiliar eye) is the blue merle, which has a coat of silver gray with some blue highlights.

According to Terhune's account, Gray Dawn was born in the midst of a raging rain and sleet storm in December, 1918, just a few months after the death of the great Lad. He was the only puppy in a litter of nine to survive, because his dam—terrified by the thunder and the wind of the near-hurricane—had broken out of the building in which she was preparing to birth her litter and dashed out into the storm. The other eight puppies died of exposure to the storm after their birth, but Gray Dawn survived by chance; he had become lodged down against his mother's side and was sheltered from the sleet and wind.

In the morning, with the storm over and the sky still choked with angry gray clouds, the surviving puppy was given the name of Gray Dawn.

He was different in more ways than just his color. Most of Terhune's collie heroes, though displaying the expected puppy mischief, were also quick to show typical qualities of intelligence, loyalty, and pluck. But Gray Dawn, growing into an unusually large puppy, was, wrote Terhune, "unbelievably awkward . . . in eternal mischief . . . in everlasting trouble." After one episode in which the puppy tore the Mistress's dress and then fell against and shattered a porch jar that had come from Syria, Terhune shouted, "I'm beginning to hate the sight of him!"

But the Mistress, who was always characterized by Terhune as patient, calm, kind, and immensely wise, answered: "Pick him up some time, and look straight down into his eyes. You'll see something there that will show you he isn't all clown. I never saw a steadier, stancher look in any dog's eye, except Laddie's. Dawn is going to turn out all right. Don't worry."

Some time later, after Gray Dawn had fled in fear from an angry mother hen, Terhune put down another black mark after the puppy's name: "He's a coward. Yellow all through!"

The puppy's propensity for accidents and his apparent lack of courage made Terhune determined to sell him and he received an offer from a fancier who saw a future show champion in the collie pup. However, Terhune then described a rather contrived-sounding incident in which he was attacked by the same hen that so terrified the puppy and Gray Dawn, despite his fear of the chicken, came storming to the Master's defense, driving the angry hen away from him. Terhune outlined the significance of the incident in his usual dramatic fashion:

After the first moment there was no laughter in his heart. He knew what that gallant attack on a dreaded enemy had cost the craven puppy in nerve and will power.

Dawn had been cringingly afraid of the pugnacious Plymouth Rock; but love for his Master had overcome terror. . . . To his infantile idea, the Master was undergoing the same agonizing and terrifying treatment from the hen that he himself had had a few days earlier. To save his god from such torment the puppy had risked another dose of hideous pecking and wing beating.

Great was Terror. But infinitely greater was Love. Paladins of old, bravely giving battle to fire-breathing dragons, had been spurred on by no purer courage.

The incident changed Terhune's mind about selling the jaunty gray pup. He was to spend the rest of his days at Sunnybank, the newest member of The Place's collie hall of fame. Gray Dawn continued for the rest of his life to be what Terhune called a "huge, ungainly brute," but he became a much-loved pet, first of Bert and Anice and later of the millions of loyal Terhune readers who came to know him.

During the mid-1920s, stories about Gray Dawn began to appear in *The Ladies' Home Journal.* The big gray collie had the usual quota of Terhune-type adventures—catching a burglar at Sunnybank, saving a little girl from death by snatching her from in front of a speeding car, finding his way back to The Place from New York State by boarding the Nyack-Tarrytown ferry across the Hudson River, rescuing the Mistress from a forest fire, etc., etc.

The Gray Dawn stories were collected in a volume under that name and, in slightly expanded versions, were published in 1927 by

Harper and Brothers. The book was among the most popular of Terhune's writings and Gray Dawn quickly became one of his foremost collie heroes. So popular, in fact, was the big merle collie and so strong the demand from readers for more of his adventures that the later Terhune book *The Way of a Dog,* published in 1932, contained five additional Gray Dawn stories. A blue merle collie named Gray Dawn also figures in a Terhune novel called *Grudge Mountain* (later published as *Dog of the High Sierras*) but the story is wholly fictional; Sunnybank and the Terhunes are not part of it.

As usual, the critical reaction to Gray Dawn was mixed. *The New York Times,* a consistent supporter of Terhune throughout his active career, said: "Another of those always interesting and entertaining Sunnybank collies is the central figure in Mr. Terhune's new book. It is by far the best dog story that Mr. Terhune has yet written."

But one could almost hear a sigh of boredom in the comment of the *Saturday Review of Literature:* "The stories are undeniably creditable productions, but many persons who have liberally sampled Mr. Terhune's past offerings in the same vein may reasonably think that it is time he gave his collies a permanent rest."

It was Gray Dawn's rather paradoxical personality that so endeared him to Terhune's readers. Capable—according to Terhune— of an act of near-heroic courage at one moment and the most outrageously clumsy accidents at the next, he was one of the most surprising, and hence interesting, of the Sunnybank collies.

In a brief epilogue to the original book of Gray Dawn stories, Terhune related two incidents to illustrate the collie's diverse behavior. Once he merrily hurled himself against Terhune with all the force of his 80 pounds and knocked the author headlong into Pompton Lake. Another incident took place while Terhune was sitting up all night with his blind collie Fair Ellen as she gave birth to her first litter of puppies. "Gray Dawn," Terhune wrote, "followed me to the brood-nest shed. He stood outside it, on guard (stood, not lay or sat), for nine hours, waiting for me to come out. When I joined him there at sunrise his shaggy coat was thick with frost and he was stiff with cold and inaction. He had remained thus, on sentry duty, through the chill of the winter night, instead of seeking his warm kennel—just for the doubtful privilege of being near the human who was his god."

Those two incidents, Terhune declared, "typify the two extremes of Dawn's erratic nature. Between the two boundaries is an infinite mixed area of white loyalty and bumptiousness; stanchness and puppy-like flightiness; calm wisdom and tumultuously noisy idiocy; aggressive high spirits and the most painfully acute sensitiveness."

Gray Dawn died in his sleep on Memorial Day, 1929, at the age of ten and a half. He was, Terhune said, "the last of the great Sunnybank collies."

The death of Gray Dawn was kept secret for two months. Terhune and his wife were aware of the dog's popularity; hundreds of visitors had come to Sunnybank expressly to see him and people all over the country had sent him, Terhune wrote, parcels "containing everything from sliced chicken to candy." They feared that announcement of the death of their latest famous collie would bring a new onsurge of visitors to see his grave, along with reporters and photographers.

Finally, almost as if they were announcing the passing of a noted movie star or political leader, the Terhunes disclosed during the summer of 1929 that Gray Dawn had died.

Of his death, Terhune wrote: "I missed him and I still miss him, more bitterly than a mere collie should be missed. His going took something unsparable out of my life."

They were, indeed, golden years, those years of the 1920s at Sunnybank. Bert Terhune lived the kind of life that had been his dream since childhood, the same dream possessed by many other aspiring writers: he lived with a wife he loved in a place of sylvan beauty, raising fine dogs and writing stories about them for an audience that eagerly seized his words and paid him dearly for the privilege of reading them. There were no valid financial worries any longer—only good, hard work and brisk walks through the autumn woods, the roaring fire and gentle piano music on a snowy night, and the faithful collies.

Now and again there was, for a moment or two, the old pain—the old feeling of shame that the writing had not been on more serious themes, that the language had not been more slowly, more carefully crafted, that the critics had not been more appreciative, more respectful of his talents. But the pain, the regret, lasted for only a moment, then was gone again.

It was a perfect time. Here is the way Terhune described it, in these closing words of his autobiography:

Every year we come back to Sunnybank from our short winter exile in time to witness each separate detail of the spring Miracle. Here we stay until January.

It is good, on winter evenings, to lounge in front of the big hearth fire with the house dogs asleep around us; and to listen to the roar of the big storm or to the scratch of snow against the windows; to hear, on bitter nights, the rifle-crack of mile-wide splitting ice on the lake, or the groan of battingly imprisoned air under the twenty-inch thick ice sheet.

It is good to sit like that, reading or chatting together, and to know we are gloriously at home after our many-years' journey.

It is good to tramp over the frosty hills at sunrise in the tingling cold, a swirl of collies dancing about us, the sun in our faces, the dawn-wind in our eyes.

It is good to feel the tug of the rod and to hear the hum of the reel, in shadowy pools on hot summer days. It is good to row lazily homeward across a sunset-scarlet lake.

It is good to loaf on the deep veranda, the drowsing collies at our feet, on moon-drenched spring nights; the soft air heavy with the scent of wistaria and honey-suckle.

It is good to talk and laugh here with the many friends whom the years have left us and who seem to like us and to like this dear home of ours.

It is good to have the congenial dual work which makes short our days and which makes tenfold pleasanter our after-hours of loafing.

It is ALL good; incredibly good; a happiness that never has palled. It is our golden Indian Summer.

If this impossibly perfect life of ours might endure—!

PART THREE

The Downward Slope

22

But of course it could not endure. The long final chapter began on a cold, clear December night in 1928.

Terhune loved to walk—around his estate, up into the Ramapo hills, or along the nearby roads, still mostly country lanes in spite of the ever-increasing encroachment of the automobile, the invader that Terhune so detested. And when the moments came that he found himself stalled at a crucial point in a story, he often would leave his desk, pull on his heavy jacket and visored cap, and go out into the cold for a brisk hike to clear his mind. It almost always worked, he said. The impaling twig on which his story was hooked would dissolve in the clear country air and he usually would return with the rest of the manuscript etched in his mind, almost written by the wind.

He had reached such a momentary block while working on the night of December 13 and left the house in search of his customary remedial exercise. He elected to walk along the edge of the "high road" so often mentioned in his works, the two-lane Oakland Road that cut through the middle of Sunnybank as it ran past, dividing the house and the lakeside acres from the forested hillside and pastures above.

It was shortly after nine o'clock as he walked about a mile from Sunnybank. He suddenly saw a car coming toward him, driving on the wrong side of the road at, he estimated later, about 50 miles an hour. The speeding car struck Terhune on his right side as he tried vainly to dodge it and hurled him into a roadside ditch. The car did not stop.

The impact had thrown Terhune almost 30 feet. The glasses he had been wearing and the cane he had been carrying on his hike were flipped so far by the force of the collision that they never could be found.

Unconscious for a time, Terhune came to and found that he could not move his right arm or leg. He dragged himself to the edge of the road and with his left hand began waving his handkerchief at passing cars in an attempt to get help. Car after car passed him. Finally a young couple from the nearby town of Oakland stopped and helped him. They recognized him and took him back to Sunnybank. They wanted to help him into the house, but he declined with thanks, saying he didn't want to frighten his wife.

Anice was playing the piano. She turned to see Bert holding painfully to the fireplace mantle. He told her that he had had a little accident, had been knocked down by a car. Seeing immediately that he was in shock and seriously hurt, she got him into bed and called for a doctor.

Terhune's accident was big news for a few days, but the newspaper reports indicated that the famed author had not been seriously hurt. Doctors were quoted as saying that, pending further study of X-rays, they believed no bones had been broken. A day later another medical report was issued saying that Terhune had been badly bruised and also had suffered "internal bruises and blood congestion caused by tissue being crushed against bone." In general, though, the news reports indicated that Terhune had had a miraculous escape from serious harm.

His own later accounts of the incident told a much different story. It was rather typical of Terhune, as a professional writer always on the lookout for material, that he made full use of his accident as grist for his typewriter. By September of 1929, nine months after his accident, he had published in *The American Magazine* an account of the mishap titled "I Am Ashamed of Myself." He sold another article about it to *Reader's Digest* and still another to *Physical Culture Magazine.* He was still making use of the near-tragedy in 1941, thirteen years after the incident, when the *Reader's Digest* carried still another piece about it: "I Said I Would Fight—And I Did."

In these articles about his injuries, Terhune declared that his right arm and leg had been left almost paralyzed. Sedated by morphine for the pain, Terhune was told by one doctor that his right leg should be amputated along with three fingers of his right hand and perhaps the entire hand. He also was told, he wrote later, that he never would walk again, that his heart had suffered some damage in the accident, and that the shock of the mishap probably would prevent him from ever doing any more creative work.

It's a bit hard to determine whether those were actual statements by the attending physicians or simply Terhune's dramatized scenario. In his articles about his comeback from the injuries, Terhune was prone to such overblown declamations as:

"I told the gloomy prophets that they were wrong. There would be no amputation. Nor would there be a helpless and workless lifetime in bed. I said I was going to fight. I was going to win. And I did."

It does appear, though, that Terhune's much more serious estimate of his injuries, when contrasted to the newspaper stories, was accurate. It took months for him to achieve even partial recovery from the injuries and his health would never again be the same. He was confined to bed for several weeks and on crutches for months after that.

The doctors' pessimistic forecasts, Terhune wrote, were like a pail of ice water hurled in his face. They shocked him out of his morphine fog of helplessness and made him determined to get better. He began a daily round of painful exercise, after first telling the doctors he would accept no more drugs for relief of pain. "For many hours a day, at short intervals, I flexed and twisted the numbed leg and arm. It was grueling work; the more so because for about three weeks it seemed hopeless. Then gloriously pringling pains began to blossom forth, and with them the ability to make some feeble rudimentary use of the crushed sinews. Day by day there was more and more life and more wholesome hurt in arm and leg." The dramatic account of his refusal to accept more drugs for his pain was confirmed by a letter written by Anice to a personal friend on Christmas Eve, almost two weeks after the accident. She described her husband as still extremely ill and "suffering bitterly," but said he had done without "morphia" for the last two days at his own request.

Terhune estimated that it took him two months to learn to walk properly on crutches, a process that included a number of falls. He graduated then to a single crutch and later to a cane. Ten months after the accident, he was walking normally again, although with a slight limp. But the old, robust physique was gone for good. He was almost sixty, and his giant body would never quite recover from the shock of the accident and the near-nervous breakdown that followed, the "shell shock" as Terhune used to call it. He soon resumed his work, but the long, hard hikes through the woods and up into the Ramapos were gone forever, and the bracing, exhausting swims in the cold waters of Pompton Lake were past. The golden time had ended. Now the road turned slightly, almost imperceptibly, downhill.

There was one ironic touch to the accident and its aftermath. Just as had happened with the real-life death of Wolf under the wheels of a train, Terhune's newsmaking injuries provided new evidence that the Sunnybank collies acted in real life very much as Terhune described them in his popular stories. On December 27, 1928, *The New York Times* ran a story headed TERHUNE IS RECOVERING; FAITHFUL DOG REFUSES TO LEAVE BEDSIDE OF INJURED AUTHOR. The *Times* story related that Gray Dawn had refused to eat for the first twenty-four hours after the accident and since then would eat only at the bedside of his master. Once, when a doctor's probing caused Terhune to cry out in pain, the collie went for the doctor's throat. After that, the loyal dog had to be taken from the room and locked outside whenever the doctor arrived to examine his patient. The entire front page of the tabloid New York *Graphic* for December 28 was devoted to a photo of Gray Dawn lying at the bedside of the recuperating Terhune. The headline across the top of the photo read: FAITHFUL DOG GUARDS STRICKEN NOVELIST!

News of the accident brought flowers and telegrams to Sunnybank from all over the country. One letter came from a man who claimed that he had served two prison terms for felonious assault and offered to find the driver of the hit-and-run car and serve a term for manslaughter.

In fact, the driver of the auto, a young man, came to Sunnybank the day after it happened, having read about it in the paper, and admitted to Mrs. Terhune that he had been at the wheel. He claimed that he did not stop because he thought the impact had resulted from his car striking a low-hanging branch of a roadside tree. He said he had been late for an appointment and had been speeding. He asked to see Terhune to apologize personally, but the author refused to see him.

"Bert did not sue him," Mrs. Terhune wrote years later, "and we refused to give his name to the police or to the reporters, though they tried very hard to discover it.

"I don't quite know why we were so considerate; but I think our feeling was that he had done so much harm to Bert that even if he were caught by the police and made to suffer, it could not give Bert back his health. . . . He was criminally careless, of course, but did not mean to do any harm, and he tried to atone."

In an effort to soothe his shattered nerves, Terhune and Anice decided to travel to Europe. He always had loved boat trips and thrived on the sea air, beginning finally to overcome the insomnia that had been tormenting him. In London, the Carlton Hotel had their favorite suite ready for them. They soon discovered that they were the only occupants of that floor, all the other rooms had been closed for redecorating, but the hotel was so sensitive to Terhune's feelings that they made his old quarters ready for him. He needed his crutches to get around London, but was resting much better and was greeted warmly by the English, who loved his books. The trip was a great tonic for him.

When the crutches were permanently discarded, they were mounted for a time on the wall of Terhune's study as a trophy of his fight against pain and his victory over the dire forecasts of the medical men. His writing resumed, with almost the same vigor as before, and Terhune proudly declared later, "the next year I . . . had the second most lucrative season of my entire career."

The year of 1929, as Terhune's strength returned and his writing began to approach again its old flood-level proportions, also saw the return of the unconquerable Lad. The now-celebrated Sunnybank collie, who had been dead for eleven years, was the star of a new collection of stories titled *Lad of Sunnybank*.

Once again down the familiar driveway "trotted the huge mahogany-and-snow collie. He was mighty of chest and shoulder, heavy of coat, and with deepset dark eyes in whose depths lurked a Soul."

In a brief epilogue to the volume of ten new Lad tales, Terhune explained why he had again returned the great collie to fictional life:

About eleven years ago my earliest stories of Sunnybank Lad appeared in book form. It is more than fifteen years since the first of these was published in the *Red Book Magazine.*

The stories themselves had no claim to greatness, nor even to literary merit. I know that as well as you do. But Laddie was great enough to counterbalance any defects of his chronicler, and to bring unlooked-for success to my tales of his adventures and of his strange personality.

Better than that, the stories won for the grand old collie a host of friends, both here and in Europe, friends to whom he was as real as though they had known him in the flesh.

Many of these friends have written to me, again and again, asking to hear more about Lad.

So I have ventured to write this latest book, hoping to please Lad's old-time admirers and perhaps to gain other friends for him, by making our long-dead collie chum live anew in its pages.

The new book pleased Lad's admirers and quickly became one of Terhune's best selling works. It is among the dozen or so Terhune titles which remained in print until the 1970s and continued to delight new readers who met Lad for the first time.

At the end of the twenties, Terhune still hewed to his long-time schedule of daily writing, pounding out the prose without cease, toiling with all the hour after hour faithfulness of any artisan. During this decade he had published twenty-seven books and hundreds of short stories, articles, and essays. He was solidly wealthy, with more coming in every day as his dog stories went on selling and selling and selling, and his reputation as one of the world's most popular writers was firmly secured.

Now, perhaps, he could find the time to ease off the highly commercial, manufactured fiction that had been so financially rewarding for him and turn more often to a more contemplative kind of writing.

In 1930, Harper and Brothers issued two of Terhune's books. Both of them reflected his desire to assume the role of a literary elder, a statesman with words of well-aged wisdom to give to the world. One was entitled *Proving Nothing*—a collection of nine essays on various subjects. The critics received the volume gently, but with the built-in condescension that always was reserved for Terhune's more serious writings. The New York *Herald-Tribune* said of it:

"Terhune has a knack in telling things which makes you remember what he says. He writes without constraint and with a simplicity which comes from knowing his own mind and what he wants to say. His chapter on his mother has sincerity without sentimentality; it is good writing because it makes no attempt at being fine writing."

Also in 1930 came the book which Terhune had been planning for years—his autobiography. He called it *To the Best of My Memory*. In publicizing it, Terhune told reporters that he had written his autobiography primarily to prove to editors and his public that he could write about something besides dogs. "I know that when a man writes his biography that means he is through," he told a writer for the New York *Sun*. "But I simply had to write it; it demanded to be done. Now maybe they will believe me when I say I know something else but the collies."

It was, considering what is known of Terhune's life, a rather strange autobiography: an old man telling rollicking stories of the adventures of his youth, a collection of "Oh, yes, and that reminds me—" anecdotes. In talking to reporters about the book, Terhune readily conceded this. "It isn't a story of my life at all," he declared. "If it were, it wouldn't be very good reading." Rather, he explained, it was a series of yarns that he felt would hold the reader's interest. The book was Terhune's reminiscence of his childhood at Sunnybank and later his early struggles to establish himself as a writer. It dwelled with almost loving prolixity on the newspaper years that Terhune always professed to hate so much, telling stories about the characters with and for whom he had worked at the *Evening World*. Of the 272-page work, 150 pages are devoted to the years at the newspaper. There also is a bit about the dogs and the glorious life at Sunnybank, about The Place itself and the depth of Terhune's feelings for it.

But strangely absent from this autobiography is much about the man himself, his thoughts and dreams and frustrations. Perhaps it is a throwback to a Victorian era of public reticence. But in this late twentieth-century day of published confessionals and unrestrained self-revelation, one reads Terhune's account of his life with a sense that much more is held back than revealed. Terhune's short, tragic first marriage is not referred to at all, and his daughter is mentioned only once or twice, in passing.

In the autobiography, Anice is set on the same pedestal that she occupies in the guise of the Mistress in Terhune's Sunnybank fiction and articles, remaining wise, calm, patient, ever gracious, and beloved by all.

Bert believed every word that he wrote about Anice. In talking about her to interviewers, or even to friends, he would make such comments as: "She is fit to 'look on the face of God, and live.' If there is a better Christian or whiter soul on earth, I never met such," or "She is the gentlest person I have ever known, the most charming, and the bravest." A writer for a women's magazine, after visiting Sunnybank and observing the very real devotion the Terhunes displayed for each other, gushed: "33 years they have been married and never was a couple more in love. Genuinely, quietly, entirely."

Anice, in reality, was somewhat more human. She *was* delicate and talented, with a cameo-like beauty. But she also was vain and so determined when she wanted something that her relatives had long before nicknamed her "The Duchess." She was described by a close friend as the kind of person who, when she went to the bank to cash a check, always demanded new money.

Like her husband, Anice displayed a great deal of pride and sensitive feelings. She once presented her minister with a pair of ornate brass candlesticks for the church. They were duly and gratefully placed on the altar. But the choirmaster soon complained that, when the large candles were lit for the service, the fumes from the burning candles were bothering the choir. The minister quietly removed the candlesticks and took them to the parsonage where they occupied a place of honor. The following week, Anice came to services and immediately noticed the absence of the candlesticks. When she went to the minister about it and he explained what had happened, she angrily demanded them back and returned them to Sunnybank.

As the years went on, Anice more and more occupied the role of a sort of grande dame, a dowager of Victorian times. She invariably dressed in white or pink, with the matching broad-brimmed hats that her husband liked. Her dresses were longer than current fashion called for and, when guests had dinner at Sunnybank, Anice usually changed to a floor-length gown.

She was rather ethereal, living in a perpetual make-believe world of books and music, sheltered from hard reality or worry. She was, as one friend recalled her, a bit "pixilated." And yet there was an underlying firmness, a resolve about her that never should be discounted. One long-time observer of the Terhunes said that Anice "molded Bert into the public figure that he was, she toned him down, guided him, and moderated his behavior. In many ways, she created him." Ethel Vreeland, her closest friend, said that Anice was far removed from the Dresden doll image created for her by her husband. "She made most of the decisions," Mrs. Vreeland commented, "leaving Bert happily writing his books and raising his beloved collies."

To the Best of My Memory represented one of Terhune's periodic forays into a more serious kind of writing and he reacted with great sensitivity to the reviews of each such effort. In the case of the autobiography, of course, there was more concern than ever about the reaction of the literary world, for this book was one of the culminations of his writing career. He had finally begun to cut down his writing pace. The story plots were becoming ever harder to dream up, and the words came more slowly. For the first time, he was beginning to give some thought to retirement. And so the autobiography had massive importance to him. Once again he waited impatiently to see what the critics would have to say.

They treated the book with kindness and, in some cases, surprising appreciation.

Said *The Bookman:* "His story is informal and witty; just journalistic enough to make excellent reading."

And the New York *Herald-Tribune* commented: "That Terhune possesses a large measure of writing skill, this autobiography proves. The chapters describing his boyhood are rich in incident and racily objective. He understands people as he understands dogs."

Among the richest plaudits were the comments of Charles McD. Puckette in the always respected *New York Times:* "This is a first-rate autobiography. It is a human document which bears the stamp of truth . . . literary autobiography is the richer for the story of a life well and frankly told. A reviewer who opened the volume gingerly with fear lest the narrative be, let us say, 'As told by a Sunnybank collie,' remained to be grateful, among other things, for chapters on newspaper work on Park Row which were to the life. The 'best' of Mr.

Terhune's memory is good indeed."

But there also were, inevitably for Terhune, the carpers. They never would concede that the man had any literary talent: he remained the commercial hack, to be treated with benign paternalism when he tried to write seriously.

The reaction of the *Saturday Review of Literature* typified the attitude of the artier echelons of the literary establishment toward Terhune:

Albert Payson Terhune's new autobiography is a lovable and unimportant book. People like Mr. Terhune's stories because he is a good writer without being a great writer and because—and he is himself quite aware of both facts —there is no pretense or pose about his work, even when he is telling the story of his own life. Hence the agreeable human tone of his autobiography and hence also its relative unimportance . . . it is not likely ever to lack readers entirely. Literary historians of the future are not likely to compete with one another to secure copies of *To the Best of My Memory,* but anyone who is at all interested in the intimate life of America in the early twentieth century, in the development of the American newspaper, or in the growth of the American popular magazine will find here a wealth of unique source material.

The same review also complained that "one regrets to find so much cheap, ill-informed writing in the book."

Although the writing began gradually to taper off, life continued at Sunnybank much as before, broken occasionally by the vacation trips Terhune loved so much. When they came back from those trips, especially when they were aboard ship, they were eagerly greeted as major celebrities by the newsmen assigned to meet the boat. And Bert, who relished publicity as much as ever, usually had a colorful yarn for them. He always wanted the reporters to consider him "good copy." In April, 1930, for example, back in New York from Europe, Terhune told the newsmen that he had discovered a strange and ferocious breed of dogs living high in the French Alps. He had heard stories of such a breed, he said, and wanted one, so drove into the Alps in search of it. He wandered through the Alpine woods for a full day and finally found a dog the size of a Great Dane, with a head somewhat like a Saint Bernard. Its hair was reddish and curly and it had forelegs and shoulders like that of a bulldog. The animal charged him, Terhune declared, but then stopped and began sniffing him in friendly fashion. "By using all his knowledge of canine traits," the newspaper story declared, "Mr. Terhune succeeded in making the dog friendly." The curly dog story ended with Terhune stating that he accompanied the dog to a nearby mountain settlement but found that the natives were very jealous of their unusual dogs and refused to sell him one.

As Bert and Anice grew older, they began to reduce the size of their famous collie kennel. Breeding was diminished and more puppies were sold than in the past. The collies in residence, once as many as forty, were now much fewer. By 1934, the popular journalist Mary Margaret McBride wrote in a feature story of her visit to Sunnybank that there were no longer any puppies there, just "old dogs living out a peaceful end to their days."

And as the years slowly passed and the ubiquitous automobile continued its conquest of the Jersey hills and woodlands, Terhune kept up his stubborn, hopeless battle against oncoming civilization.

The New York Times reported in November, 1930, that the board of freeholders of Passaic County had decided to go ahead with its planned modernization of Oakland Road in spite of the vigorous objections of Terhune. He had fought against the road improvement for two years in order to preserve what the newspaper story termed "the rustic beauty the author loves so well." Terhune had angrily told reporters, "It is as if they wanted to turn the face of Venus de Milo into a platter. Her features are very good to look at but they don't serve any purpose. My beautiful trees and land will be despoiled to make room for a great concrete sheet."

It was a lonely as well as unsuccessful fight. The *Times* reported that Terhune was the only one of the thirty-eight property owners involved to object to the widening and paving of the road.

But he occasionally won a small victory and suburbia was checked for a moment or two in its headlong rush across the countryside. The *Times* reported a couple of months later, in January, 1931, that Terhune had after all won part of his battle: some of the old trees along Oakland Road would be preserved. The board of freeholders had agreed that, in widening the road to 40 feet, a realignment would be made to avoid destroying the roadside trees.

And at Sunnybank, Terhune continued to plant trees and flowers for the future, fighting a patient rearguard struggle. As the nearby hillsides began to fill with houses and stores and the exhaust of the automobile, Sunnybank remained a place of quiet beauty, still one man's paradise.

23

The Visitor walked slowly along Wanaque Avenue in the borough of Pompton Lakes, New Jersey. He had left Sunnybank for a while because all the dammed-up memories of The Place had flooded in on him too quickly, and he wanted a time to be away from it, to think about it and savor it. So he had climbed into the rented car and pulled back out through the old metal gate of Sunnybank. There was no need to pause for last looks back, for he would come again after his early afternoon break for one final look around before leaving for good.

He had turned to the left and driven north along United States Highway 202, the old Oakland Road that had been modernized over Terhune's violent objections and now was a busy, curving two-lane concrete highway moving up through the Ramapo Valley toward the New York State line and the distant summits of the Catskills.

A short distance along the road and then another left turn onto the Schuyler Bridge across Pompton Lake. The bridge, a low concrete structure barely above the waterline, had been named for Captain Arent Schuyler, one of the original settlers of the area in the 1690s. Near the bridge, The Visitor slowed his car for a moment and studied an old building that stood with a sturdiness that belied its age and historical significance. Here George Washington had come with his staff to attend the wedding of a member of the Schuyler family who had served as his aide.

This same old house has still another claim to fame, one of much more recent vintage. For a town of just a few thousand people, Pompton Lakes has been unusually well publicized. First, of course, came its international fame as the home of Bert Terhune and of Sunnybank. The Place actually was not located in Pompton Lakes at all, but in the neighboring Wayne Township. The dividing line, then and now, runs down the middle of the lake. But Terhune always regarded Pompton Lakes as his home town because it was the nearest town. He got his mail there and stubbornly refused to acknowledge his legal residence in Wayne Township by listing his address in his books and articles, and in reference sources, as "Sunnybank, Pompton Lakes, New Jersey."

Pompton Lakes' other claim to fame came in the 1920s and 1930s, when the old house near Schuyler Bridge became a training camp for fighters and was used by many of the leading boxers of the period as they prepared for upcoming bouts. Newspaper stories beating the drums for a coming title fight would carry the dateline "Pompton Lakes, N.J."

Joe Louis trained at the camp for many of his fights, as did Primo Carnera, Max Baer, Sugar Ray Robinson, Jack Sharkey, and many others. Bert Terhune, lifelong lover of boxing and a fighter of considerable ability in his own youth, paid frequent visits to the camp just a few minutes from his home, trading ring stories with the old-timers on hand and doubtless taking a turn now and then at the heavy bag.

After he drove across the bridge, The Visitor was at the fringe of the town, Bert Terhune's town of the books and stories. Sometimes, wanting to fictionalize the place names in the yarns, he would refer to Pompton Lakes as "the nearby village of Hampton," but Terhune's regular fans always knew what he meant. One of the Gray Dawn stories, for instance, begins: "A half mile of fire-blue water and another half mile of fields and woods lie between The Place and the friendly little hill village of Hampton." Sometimes the city of Paterson, a few miles to the east, would be called "Paignton."

The Visitor pulled to the side of the road and parked for a moment. He was on the village side of the lake, looking back across the familiar fire-blue water at Sunnybank. The lake somehow seemed much smaller from this side, more an enlarged pond, really.

From here, Sunnybank looked incredibly sad. Though it was a sun-filled winter day, the old estate on the opposite shore sagged in a shroud of gloom, as if the sun's rays could not penetrate it. The tottering house looked even more of a wreck than it had from close at hand—the grounds showed more clearly from a distance their unkempt despair. But the most sorrowful thing about the view was the sense of emptiness that permeated the other shore. As The Visitor sat on a busy water-side street, the cars muttering by in either direction and children's laughter filling the air from a nearby schoolyard, he looked across and saw no motion at The Place, no living thing. Only the oak trees standing firmly against the pushing December wind, the gray, diseased old house, the fragile little gazebo down the front slope.

Sunnybank hung on, waiting for someone to come back. The Visitor sat there for a few moments more, looking across the icy expanse of water at the aching, frigid silences of The Place. Then he started the car and drove on into the town.

He walked up Wanaque Avenue, wondering with irritation why it was difficult in a town this size to find a decent place to get a hamburger. Then the irritation and hunger subsided as he remembered that he was walking the street that Bert and Anice had walked and so often employed as a locale in the stories. He had seen the town post office in its present location, where it was at the time of Terhune's death, and also the savings and loan building that had housed the post office during the twenties and thirties, when much of the staff's time was spent in sorting the hundreds of fan letters that poured in from Terhune devotees all over the world. Bert and Anice, often accompanied by one or two collies, made a daily ritual of driving into town for the mail, and this routine little journey played a part in some of the stories.

The Visitor walked along the sidewalk to the Emanuel Einstein Free Public Library of Pompton Lakes and up the stairs to the second-floor reading room, looking for historical information about the Terhunes and Sunnybank. He decided to check the library card catalogue for books by Terhune, and discovered that the little library possessed almost every one of the sixty-odd books published by Terhune. He asked the librarian for a few of the rarer ones and spent an hour or so looking over such works as Caleb Conover, Railroader *(1907) and* Water! *(1928). Because these volumes are not among the vastly popular Terhune dog books or even his less popular autobiographical works, they are fairly hard to find; most libraries have ignored them.*

The Visitor skimmed through these books and decided that it was reassuringly fitting Terhune's home town library should have so nearly complete a collection of his work. For Terhune was hardly universally loved, even among

*the neighbors whose town had been made so well known to the reading public.
It was rather heartwarming to know that, whatever they thought of him as
a person, they had made sure that Pompton Lakes would maintain for posterity
a full record of his work. It seemed a neighborly gesture of tribute, or at least
of appreciation, that Terhune would have respected and been grateful for.*

24

He was a man of mercury. Proud, stiff-necked, opinionated. Prone to
violent flareups and later shame and regret.

Terhune was a giant and he roared with a temper worthy of his
physique. Since boyhood he had cultivated a vocabulary of choice
swear words and he quickly called them into play when he was
aroused. Yet many people who knew him would, when talking about
him, stress his gentleness and kindness. He was a complex man, a
crosshatching of contrasting traits.

Hal LeRoy, the dancer and musical comedy star, who became a
good friend of Terhune during the last years of the writer's life,
described him as "the most gentle man God ever put on earth." The
wife of Terhune's minister said that Bert was "very humble . . . a
gentle, wonderful person." He was the kind of man who would
telephone his minister—Rev. Gerrit Heemstra—each Christmas and
ask if it would be all right if he and Anice came over so they could
watch the Heemstra children open their presents.

As his wrath indicated when the automobile from Detroit acciden-
tally killed his collie Jean, Terhune could have an ugly temper, and
be unwilling to accept apology or excuse. Yet this was the same man
who for many years made an anonymous donation to his church
before Christmas to purchase toys for the children of needy families

in the congregation. The children would be asked what toys they hoped for and Terhune made sure that their wishes were fulfilled. His secret philanthrophy went on for years and was continued, after his death, by his widow as long as her financial circumstances permitted.

He was a fighter, a man of passion. He hated people who desecrated nature, vivisectionists, unbidden visitors, people who were unkind to animals, and a good many others. He trumpeted his dislikes again and again in his writings and was not at all reluctant vigorously to defend his stands in personal discussions as well. And those heated arguments usually were waged with skill.

Terhune's personality was clearly abrasive to many people. Anice acknowledged his mercurial temperament when she wrote: "Some people who did not know Bert as well as I did have said that he was quick-tempered. He may have been, with other people. I don't know. He was not so with me. Anyway, I like people with quick tempers! They clear the air like a summer shower and then the sun comes out brighter than ever. I know that I would not have had Bert changed in any way, even one single bit. Impulsive, I admit that he was. Excitable as a blooded race horse! He could use sizzlingly lurid language on occasion; but it was only skin deep." But she insisted he always was quiet, calm, and patient in a real crisis.

Various townspeople of Pompton Lakes tangled with Terhune on one thing or another over the years and he built his share of enemies. But there were also many devoted friends among his neighbors. His public attitude toward Pompton Lakes and its people always was a very warm one: "I love every inch of the mile-distant village of Pompton Lakes; with its bright shops and its brighter homes and its friendly folk. When my wife and I come back from an absence we are welcomed as dear returning comrades. . . . Much we like the people there. They are our loved friends, one and all."

But the love that Terhune claimed for Pompton Lakes and its people was not always reciprocated. "You have to remember," a long-time resident of the town said recently, "that Pompton Lakes was and is a mill town, a town of blue-collar working people. Many of them enjoyed the fame that Bert Terhune brought the town and respected him for it, but others resented him and felt he was putting on airs, especially when he would stride down the main street all dressed up in his khaki jacket and puttee boots, looking for all the world like a Great White Hunter."

Another elderly resident of the town, who disliked Terhune with a passion, described him as "a big, fat slob . . . a good man until he got delusions of grandeur. As the years went on, he became a figment of his own imagination."

He was *the* local celebrity and sometimes people long remembered a very brief encounter with him. An eighty-seven-year-old lady recently described her only meeting with Terhune in these words: "I was walking up Wanaque Avenue in Pompton Lakes and approaching me was this big man. As he came near me, I knew who he was although I had never met him. He gave me the warmest smile and in a very kind, deep voice said 'Good Morning!' and I returned the greeting and that experience made my day. I have never forgotten it."

Mrs. Clarence L. Vreeland, close friend of Anice for more than fifty years and whose husband was Bert's physician, said: "I don't think he was popular, except with his friends—he was busy and could be brusque—but with his friends he was delightful. He had a *temper* and it exploded, but it meant nothing. In a way he and my husband were alike and I used to say they swore companionably at each other and were the best of friends. He was anything but vain. In some ways he was rather humble. He was busy and didn't waste time on outsiders. I noted that the people who criticized him the most were the most subservient when they met."

Although he—and his dogs—often were inhospitable to visitors, some testified to his kindness. Among them were young writers who came to him for advice and help. Fred Temby, a veteran newspaperman of the area, wrote a few years ago in a reminiscence of Terhune that he "was especially cordial and helpful to writers and to those who took this field seriously." Temby added that Terhune "was a man for the individual, a champion of the masses, a liberal, a philosopher, and perhaps the greatest of all, just plain 'Bert,' friend of all."

Temby described his first meeting with Terhune in the mid-1920s. He went to Sunnybank uninvited to ask Terhune's advice about writing. Although he had not been expected, Terhune was very pleasant to him. Asked how one learns to write, Terhune replied: "There is only one answer: to write! Some are successful quickly, some take longer. You must write, write, write unceasingly until you begin to sell." The two men also got into a brief discussion of religion and Temby asked him if he thought there was one true religion. Terhune replied, *"Which* religion doesn't matter. If your goal is out in the distance, it doesn't make any difference which path you take as long as you don't deviate in your progress toward the goal."

Loring Holmes Dodd in his book *Celebrities at Our Hearthside* wrote of Terhune: "I have said he was kindly. He was extraordinarily so. It came to you in the look from his eyes, in the warm, quiet tones of his voice. He was indeed a gentle giant."

Terhune's deep and often-displayed love for children becomes one of his most ironic qualities when the strained and distant relationship with his daughter is recalled. Perhaps, in some measure, he was extra kind to the youngsters he encountered in order to assuage his guilt at his own failings as a father.

One fine day many years ago, two small boys decided to sneak into Sunnybank and see the famous collies. They had hardly climbed over the stone wall at The Place and started down the hillside when they were met by an enraged Terhune, who demanded to know what they were doing there. He shouted that they must learn the meaning of trespassing and the sanctity of private property. Then he ordered the two terrified boys to accompany him to the house, where he would telephone their parents to inform them of the boys' guilt. When they arrived at the house, Terhune handed the phone to one of the boys and told him to call home. After the boy had given the number to the operator and was waiting for his mother to answer, Terhune softly added, "Ask if you can stay for supper." The boys did stay for supper, spent a marvelous hour playing with the collies, and then were driven to their homes by one of Terhune's employees. One of the boys was Edward Sisco, who grew up to become a state senator and also mayor of Wayne, New Jersey, in which position he helped save Sunnybank from subdividing many years after Terhune's death.

A small Pompton Lakes girl once was standing on the sidewalk with a friend, admiring the toys in a store window. Terhune came down the street and observed them, then took the girls inside the store and told them to pick out any toys they wanted. The bill was on him. When the girl went home and told her father about the incident, he was very concerned—not knowing who the stranger had been—and rushed down to the store to try to determine the name of the man and what his motives had been. The storekeeper laughed and said, "Oh, that was Bert Terhune. He does that sort of thing all the time."

Terhune's view of women, as deduced primarily from his writings, was the rather stereotyped one of males of his time—respectful, chivalrous, more than slightly paternalistic and noticeably superior. A passage from one of his Bruce stories is revealing:

"Toward men—except those he had learned to look on as friends —the collie always comported himself with a courteous aloofness. But he had seemed to regard every woman as something to be humored and guarded and to be treated with the same cordial friendliness that he bestowed on their children—which is the way of the best type of collie."

In his public statements, too, Terhune made clear his feelings that a woman's place is in the home. He told a New York reporter in 1934, for example, that what this country needs is "more wives who concentrate on the ideal of maintaining a charming home."

Although not all his neighbors in Pompton Lakes and Wayne Township regarded Terhune with strong affection, they did respect and honor him for his achievements as a writer. On September 14, 1935, the Passaic County Board of Freeholders, with which Terhune had fought for years over the widening of Oakland Road, voted to change the name of that road to "Terhune Drive" in honor of the famed author and his clergyman father. There was substantial irony in this honor, given Terhune's incessant battle against improvement of the road to prevent it becoming what he had called "a scab across the countryside," given his hatred for the ever-increasing flow of automobile traffic carried through Sunnybank by the highway, and the tragedies associated by Terhune with the "high road"—his own brush with death and the maiming of several of his collies by automobiles. Yet Terhune—whose substantial ego always welcomed recognition— gracefully accepted the renaming.

Nonetheless, he never lost his contempt for the board of freeholders. He always liked to associate with newspapermen and was a faithful member of the Pica Club, a newsmen's hangout in Passaic County, where earnest drinking was one of the major club activities. At one club meeting, according to local legend, a member of the board of freeholders passed out cold after some heavy imbibing. Terhune looked down at the supine man and gravely proclaimed to the gathering, "There is nothing lower than a drunken Freeholder."

Other local honors came after his death. In 1948 the New Jersey Bell Telephone Company named a new telephone exchange, Terhune 5, in his memory. In 1965 a new elementary school in Wayne Township was named the Albert Payson Terhune School. At present several New Jersey legislators are trying to have the collie named as the official state mascot as another perpetual memorial to Terhune.

25

One group that always had strangely mixed reactions to Terhune as a person and as a writer was the dog people—the breeders, dog show judges, and others intimately associated with the breeding, training, and showing of purebred dogs, and, even more specifically, the collie people. Their diverse reaction seems strange because of Terhune's fame as the great fictional advocate of the dog, its ardent champion and popularizer, especially of the purebred collie. One would expect virtually all dog people to look upon Terhune as a hero. But, in the dog world, as in his personal relationships with people, Terhune's vociferous opinions on highly debatable subjects, his trigger temper and earthy vocabulary made him many enemies.

Terhune of course had been a dog lover since his childhood, had long wanted to write about dogs, and early in his career began accumulating voluminous files about the adventures of dogs in history, in fiction, and in modern America as described in newspaper stories.

When Lad and Bruce grew older, he began to consider breeding purebred collies at Sunnybank. After the first Terhune-bred litter was whelped in December, 1917, additional litters followed at the rate of three or four a year. It soon became necessary to sell off most of the puppies resulting from the breedings in order to avoid being overrun by collies. The result of this was the eventual establishment of "The Sunnybank Collie Kennels." Terhune listed himself as owner, but the operation of the kennel was supervised by Robert Friend, the superintendent. Friend's name was given equal billing with Terhune's on the kennel letterhead and Friend also was the one who generally took Sunnybank dogs into the ring after Terhune began entering dog shows. The letterhead also bore the kennel motto ("To Win Without Boasting, To Lose Without Excuses") and, in later years, small photographs of Sunnybank Lad and Champion Sunnybank Sigurd.

The kennels themselves, behind the house, were not pretentious. They consisted of roomy wire runs, each with a wooden dog house raised to keep it dry and to give the dogs a shaded spot underneath for hot days. Each run also was shaded by the big trees on the lawn. In winter, the floors of the dog houses were piled deep with cedar shavings, though many of the collies preferred to sleep out in the snow, even in freezing weather. The small barn near the house was equipped with stalls for sick dogs and for the birth of puppies in warm weather. Cold weather whelpings took place in the heated greenhouse. Three separate runs, 100 hundred yards away, were kept for use by bitches sent to Sunnybank for breeding purposes.

Due more to Terhune's fame as an author than the show quality of his dogs—especially at first—possession of a Sunnybank collie quickly became a status symbol among dog owners and Terhune-bred dogs were in great demand for many years. Terhune had firm policies: a puppy never would be sold unless Terhune had a chance to meet and talk with the prospective buyer, a puppy would not be sold to anyone living in an apartment, a puppy could not be shipped to its new owner—he must come to Sunnybank in person to pick it up. He also was very cautious about permitting the use of the Sunnybank prefix in a collie's registered name, and once estimated that he allowed only about one of every ten puppies he sold to bear the Sunnybank designation. In spite of the restrictions, Terhune wrote: "I could sell five times as many pups if I bothered to breed five times as many. Buyers have come to Sunnybank for them from a score of states. Two have come from as far away as California."

Over the 23 years that the Sunnybank Kennel was actively engaged in collie breeding, Terhune bred 49 litters and a total of 147 puppies. The last litter at Sunnybank was born on January 15, 1940, about two years before Terhune's death.

Ownership of a Sunnybank puppy became such a conversation piece that it was claimed by many more people than there were puppies born at The Place. Terhune was amused, and at times irritated, by countless letters he received from people telling him that they owned a son or grandson of Lad. In fact, Lad had only one offspring who survived puppyhood and that was Wolf, who left no descendants. It seems rather strange, considering the fame of Sunnybank Lad and Sunnybank Lady, that Terhune elected to bestow the names again on two puppies born in August, 1927. Both were sold. The Sunnybank name also was perpetuated by at least one Terhune fan. As recently as the late 1960s, an Illinois collie bearing the registered name of "Sunnybank Lad" was entered in dog shows.

Just how much of an expert Terhune really was on dogs in general and collies in particular always was a matter of strenuous debate among dog people . . . and sometimes between Terhune and his detractors. Throughout his career, he was challenged—both on specific statements he made about dogs and canine psychology and on his general expertise on the subject.

One example of this was a dispute that developed late in 1936. Terhune had written in the *Reader's Digest* that a dog can smell fear in a human being. A New York doctor, skeptical, asked the American Medical Association for its opinion and the AMA responded that Terhune's scientific facts were false. But newspapermen then rounded up several animal experts who testified that animals somehow can recognize human fear. A similar question was asked in 1975 of Dr. Frank Miller, a veterinarian who writes a syndicated column "Wonderful World of Animals." Dr. Miller's answer was: "Yes, dogs do pick up bad vibes (and certainly fear is one) fast, and partly by scent."

Terhune once told an interviewer that by the early 1920s he was judging dog shows coast to coast and there is evidence that he judged collies in Oakland, California, in 1923. This would seem to imply that he had been licensed as a judge by the American Kennel Club. In fact he must have been judging in an honorary capacity then, for a recent check of the records shows that Terhune was not licensed by the AKC until the late 1920s. The fact that he *was* licensed by the AKC as a judge of collies, no matter when, indicates that he had satisfied that very demanding organization concerning his knowledge of purebred collies. Terhune also proudly served for several years in the 1920s as a member of the board of directors of the AKC. It is doubtful that the AKC would have elected him to its board, despite his vast popularity among readers, if it had felt—as did some of his most vociferous critics in the dog world—that he was a fraud, an imposter who really knew next to nothing about dogs. Rather than subduing his critics, however, his election to the AKC board exacerbated his relations with some important dog breeders, who were furious that a coveted seat had gone to Terhune. The writer faithfully attended board meetings during his tenure at the AKC and played an important role in improving the *Gazette,* the major AKC publication. As an active member of the club's publication committee, he argued that the AKC should be represented by a high-quality magazine. He backed up his stand by contributing without payment articles and stories to the *Gazette* that would have brought him large sums from general magazines. In an effort to encourage the use of the *Gazette* as an advertising medium, he ran a large ad for the Sunnybank Collie Kennels each month, even though more advertising was the last thing his kennel needed.

Most of the public criticism of Terhune appeared in magazines for dog breeders and owners, or "the fancy," as they like to term it. Sometime after Terhune's initial burst of fame as author of the Lad stories, an article appeared in which it was alleged that Terhune's knowledge of collies was superficial and sentimental and that, although his kennel was successful, the author really didn't know much about collies from a dog show perspective and that the Sunnybank-bred collies were poor show specimens. It was that article, which Terhune said he found mildly annoying, that caused him to begin entering his collies in area dog shows.

Terhune's attitude toward dog shows and showing remained inconsistent throughout his career. He would protest bitterly against some of the practices involved in the grooming of certain breeds—

grooming so extensive that it almost amounted to alteration. And he would argue that few of the pampered show dogs were also family pets. "The bulk of them," he once wrote, were

"kennel dogs," dogs bred and raised after the formula for raising and breeding prize hogs or chickens, and with little more of the individual element in it. The dogs were bred in a way to bring out certain arbitrary "points" which count in show-judging, and which change from year to year.

Brain, fidelity, devotion, the *human* side of a dog—these were totally ignored in the effort to breed the perfect physical animal. The dogs were kept in kennel buildings and in wire "runs" like so many pedigreed cattle—looked after by paid attendants, and trained to do nothing but to be the best-looking of their kind, and to win ribbons. Some of them did not know their owners by sight—having been reared wholly by hirelings.

The body was everything; the heart, the mind, the namelessly delightful quality of the master-raised dog—these were nothing. Such traits do not win prizes at a bench-show. Therefore fanciers, whose sole aim is to win ribbons and cups, do not bother to cultivate them.

To many of the dogs in a show, Terhune added, the activity is "a form of unremitting torture."

It was such opinions, expressed in Terhune's usual positive style, that quickly made him a controversial and sometimes ardently hated figure in dog circles. The quotes above are taken from one of the original Lad stories, so his controversial status developed almost concurrently with his early reputation as a dog writer.

But the dog show bug, as Terhune himself admitted, is a virulent one and the author and his wife soon succumbed to it. Provoked by the magazine accusation that Terhune's collies were not of top grade show quality, he soon began entering his collies in shows and in his writings began to appear statements that the dog show game was "the straightest show on earth. Not an atom of graft in it and seldom any profit."

The Sunnybank collies started to get their share of blue ribbons at shows in the New York-New Jersey area. An article about Terhune, written some years later, claimed that at the Bergen County (New Jersey) Kennel Club Show in the spring of 1919, Terhune collies won "fifteen blue ribbons, two silver trophies, and two special prizes."

The occasional dog show victories, however, still could not silence

Terhune's critics in the sport. He relates in his autobiography that a magazine called *Field and Fancy* carried an attack by an anonymous writer who charged that Terhune's dogs were able to win only at small shows. The author couldn't claim to be an expert, the article said, until one of his dogs had won a blue ribbon at the Westminster Kennel Club Show in Madison Square Garden, the Super Bowl of dog shows.

As Terhune related it: "So I took two of my eleven-month home-bred pups—Sigurdson and Explorer—to that year's Westminister [sic —Terhune repeatedly mis-spelled the name by adding a second "i"] show at Madison Square Garden. Being puppies, they were allowed to come home at the end of the first day . . . With them we brought four blue ribbons and a reserve winner's rosette, won there, as well as several medals and more than $150 in cash prizes. It was the first and last time I have shown dogs of mine at Westminister. But I think I proved I could do so without disgracing them or my kennels."

The wins at Westminster didn't silence the skeptics, then or over the many years since. Some argue that other collie pups entered at that same Westminster show did far better in the ring than Terhune's entries, while others maintain that the Sunnybank puppies were entered in so many different classes at the big show that their showing was far from outstanding. But the crowning glory of a rough collie and a very important factor in the judging of this breed at a dog show is certainly the coat, and an article about the Sunnybank collies in a 1924 issue of the AKC *Gazette* declared: " . . . their coats bloom with what is truly an unusual luxuriance. Anyone who saw Ch. Sunnybank Sigurdson and Sunnybank Explorer at the 1923 Westminster show, can testify to that. They carried, by far, the heaviest coats in the show."

Another attack surfaced a while after the Westminster event, again in the pages of *Field and Fancy.* A writer minimized the Terhune showing at Westminster and challenged the author to prove that his dogs could earn championships in the show ring.

A dog earns the coveted right to carry the title of "Champion" (awarded by the AKC) before his name only through his ability to win fifteen or more championship points at AKC-approved dog shows. Points are awarded to the male and female designated as "Winners Dog" and "Winners Bitch" in each breed classification. The "Winners Dog," for example, is chosen from the winners of several male classes such as puppies 9 to 12 months, Bred-by-Exhibitor Dogs, and American-bred Dogs. Selection of the winner is made by a judge, who has been licensed by the AKC after demonstrating his intensive knowledge of the breed to be judged. The judge carefully studies each animal entered, checking its body structure, its teeth, its gait, its coat, and every other physical attribute. The winner theoretically is the dog that most closely conforms to the "standard" for that breed—the description of the ideal dog. Hence the reference to such competitions as "Conformation Shows." The number of championship points given to the "Winners Dog" or "Winners Bitch" is determined by a complicated formula, which is based partly on the number of dogs entered at that particular show (the more entered, the greater the number of points given, up to a maximum of five) and partly on the number of specimens of that breed registered in that area of the country.

The AKC requires that a certain number of points must be earned at "major" shows (i.e., shows with sizable entries), that the two required major show wins are judged by different judges, and so on. It is a concerted effort to be sure that a championship is not easily earned and that it represents a very high assessment of an individual dog by qualified judges at several different shows. In some cases, ambitious owners enter their hopefuls in dozens of shows over a period of years before finally securing enough points for a championship—if, indeed, they ever do.

Nettled by the charge that he had to win a championship to prove the quality of the Sunnybank collies, Terhune wrote: "So I set to work at it; winning the coveted championship title for four of my dogs in fairly fast succession: Sigurd ('Treve'), Sigurdson, Explorer, and Explorer's son, Thane. I made champions of these Sunnybank collies in three successive generations—son, sire, grandsire." Thane won his fifteen championship points in five straight shows, finishing at the age of just seventeen months. At three successive shows in September, 1928, Thane was named Best of Winners and Best of Breed. In one show he bested an international champion.

Terhune also set up rigid limitations on the showing of his collies. No Sunnybank dog was exhibited at a show more than 100 miles from home. Indoor shows and benched shows generally were avoided because of Terhune's concern for his dogs' comfort and because he felt that the danger of their contracting distemper was greater at such shows. His dogs always were handled in the ring by Robert Friend or himself; unlike many owners, he never would permit a professional handler to "campaign" his dogs (take them on a dog show circuit).

Terhune was very much an outsider at dog shows. Many of the other collie breeders were aristocrats who traveled to the big shows (often by train) with a retinue of handlers, trainers, and grooms. Terhune came by car, accompanied only by Robert Friend, sometimes Anice, and with one or two collies. He generally was looked upon as an upstart, a nobody. Another thing that drove the other breeders and handlers frantic with rage was the huge crowds of people that descended on the dog show with only one objective—to see the great writer and his famed collies. At one show, held in a huge armory, the show superintendent set up his office on a balcony high above the armory floor. It could be reached only by climbing several flights of stairs. One professional handler, sick and tired of all the people asking him where they could find Terhune, directed each such questioner to the distant balcony. "That's Terhune right up there," he would say. "Go right on up."

It was not only the skepticism over the quality of his Sunnybank dogs that enmeshed Terhune in continuing controversy with other dog people. He was forever making sweeping, uncompromising public statements about collies and dogs in general, and they frequently got him into hot disputes.

Many collie breeders considered him an arch enemy because of his incessant criticism of certain changes over the years in the breed's physical makeup. The author kept up a steady drumfire of complaint about the changes imposed on collies by the breeders, both in his fiction and in his magazine articles about dogs. For instance, in one of the early Lad stories, the Master walks around a dog show and views some of the other collies:

"Look!" he said boastfully to his companion, pausing before a bench whereon were chained a half-dozen dogs from a single illustrious kennel. "These fellows aren't in it with old Lad. See—their noses are tapered like tooth-picks, and the span of their heads, between the ears, isn't as wide as my palm; and their eyes are little and they slant . . . and their bodies are as curved as a grayhound's. Compared with Lad, some of them are freaks. That's all they are, just freaks—not all of them, of course, but a lot of them."

"That's the idea nowadays," laughed the collie man patronizingly. "The up-to-date collie—this year's style at least—is bred with a borzoi (wolfhound) head and with graceful, small bones. What's the use of his having brain and scenting-power? He's used for exhibition or kept as a pet nowadays—not to herd sheep. Long nose, narrow head—."

Later in the same story, Lad wins the blue ribbon at the dog show because the judge is an old Scotsman who "had scant patience with the ultra-modern, inbred and grayhoundlike collies which had so utterly departed from their ancestral standards."

Rumors had long been circulating that the modern collie was descended in part from the Russian Wolfhound (Borzoi). Terhune's implication that such was the case, along with his angry denunciation of the changes wrought in the breed and other charges that the narrowing of the collie head had led to a smaller brain and lesser intelligence, made him the object of violent criticism in many collie circles.

Another of Terhune's oft-repeated claims was that the collie was a direct descendant of the wolf and owed many of his attributes— particularly the fighting prowess which Terhune was so fond of demonstrating—to his wolf ancestry. One pure-bred Terhune collie utilized "an instinctive throwback to his wolf forebears of five hundred years earlier." Lad is attacked by a vicious mongrel who "to his dismay . . . found himself fighting not a helpless dog, but a maniac wolf." Terhune also noted that "Atavism is mysteriously powerful in dogs, and it takes strange forms. A collie, too, has a queer strain of wolf in him—not only in body but in brain . . ."

In fact, the ancestry of the collie is very much a mystery; there seems to be no substantial evidence that it is a direct descendant of the wolf. Many scholars of dog genetics do feel that the domesticated dog was descended from a particular race of wolves, but that would have been eons ago, certainly long before the several hundred years assumed by Terhune. Collie ancestry is largely unknown because the breed was developed by Scottish farm people who did not concern themselves with such things as pedigrees.

One of the little things in Terhune's writings that irritated many dog people was his constant use of the word "thoroughbred" to describe a dog of full-blooded ancestry. It probably was pointed out frequently to him that "thoroughbred" is a term applied to certain horses, while the proper term for a dog is "purebred." But, perhaps out of sheer stubbornness, Terhune kept describing a full-blooded dog of whatever breed as a "thoroughbred."

Terhune's refusal to concede error about dogs applied just as much to his personal life. A local veterinarian took care of sick dogs at Sunnybank and he and Terhune became good friends. One day the vet came to Sunnybank to look at a dog that had been under the weather and informed Terhune that the dog had worms. Terhune always wormed his own dogs and he indignantly told the vet that he was wrong; the collie could not possibly have worms. The vet insisted he was right and the argument got hotter and hotter. The two men were screaming at each other when Terhune, characteristically, stopped in the middle of a sentence and said, "Care for a libation?" The vet allowed that he could stand a drink. The liquor was served, then the furious argument resumed. After a few more drinks the two men were feeling no pain, but still raving at each other about the dog's medical problem. Finally, Terhune shouted, "All right, you stubborn son of a bitch, take the collie in to your hospital and check him out. If he has got worms, I'll pay you a hundred dollars!" The vet took the dog with him, examined him carefully, and confirmed that the dog did have worms. He sent Terhune a bill for $100 for professional services rendered and Terhune paid the bill without protest. It was, the doctor later told friends, the only time he ever won an argument from Bert Terhune.

Many of Terhune's nonfiction magazine pieces, after his short stories had established him as a dog writer, were on the psychology and habits of the dog. In this he gave a rather inconsistent performance, at times praising and adulating the dog to the point of near-fantasy, at others seeming to take sheer delight in debunking what he considered to be silly legends about canine attributes or mythical prowesses.

In 1926, for example, in an article published in *Harper's Magazine,* Terhune wrote: "From the beginning of time, dogs have taken it upon themselves to guard the humans they have accepted as their deities and to gamble life, right blithely, for those humans' sakes. That is the chief reason why I am silly enough to wonder if dogs are not better worthwhile, fundamentally, than are humans. If it is supremely senseless to toss life away that a loved one may live, then most of the rank and file of us humans are anything but senseless. We leave that to the dogs."

Later in the same article he wrote: "There are a score of reasons why I am inclined to put the dog ahead of man, in all but brains and speech. One of them is the dog's genius for forgiveness. If he is your pal, if he has elected you his god, there is nothing he will not forgive you."

In the same *Harper's* piece, though, Terhune scorned the old myth that anyone whom dogs and little children like can be trusted, while those so disliked should be watched carefully. "That," declared Terhune, "is as ridiculous as is the aged maxim about trusting a man who looks you squarely in the eye. Dogs and children—or the other way around—like or hate people for the same reason we grownups like or hate people. Namely, for no logical reason at all, but for some occult attraction or its opposite."

After admitting that a dog was not his superior in judging character, Terhune resumed his fulsome praise of the animal:

From childhood, I have had dogs around me. For the past thirty-odd years, I have made an intensive study of them. The more I learn, the more I find I have yet to learn. But it has not taken me that time, nor a tithe of that time, to discover that they are our superiors in nineteen things out of twenty. Intellect (not intelligence) and the dubious blessing of speech—in these two matters we are their betters. In a hundred others—in swerveless loyalty, in forgiveness, in foursquare honesty, in humor, in stamina, in adaptability, in conscience, in pluck, in sacrifice, in all five of the so-called 'senses' (exception vision), in normality, and in many another fine detail—they are immeasurably beyond us.

Terhune's critics over the years would contend that he was such a fraud that even his own collies neither liked nor respected him. But all the available evidence supplied by people who visited Sunnybank and saw Terhune with his dogs indicates quite the opposite—that Terhune had firm control over his dogs, that they gave every indication of worshipping him just as was indicated in his writings, and that he had a thorough knowledge of their behavior. Just a couple of examples follow.

The musical comedy star Hal LeRoy was at Sunnybank one day and was talking to Terhune when a fight began in one of the dog runs. There was a great deal of loud barking and snarling. LeRoy worriedly asked Terhune if he didn't intend to stop the fight. "See that collie coming over to the run?" Terhune said calmly, pointing to an approaching dog. "He'll take care of it." The collie ran over to the run where the fight was in progress and barked once. To LeRoy's amazement, the fight stopped.

On another occasion a reporter for the *Evening World,* Terhune's old newspaper, was visiting Sunnybank to interview the author. Terhune was showing him the kennels when all the collies—a breed known for readily voicing its emotions—began an ear-splitting, excited barking. The reporter's story of the incident read, "In a deep and almost thunderous, yet kindly voice, he called out 'Quiet!' and every dog stopped barking as quickly as if every one of them had completely lost their voices."

Another custom that Terhune often wrote about and that was quite true was his insistence on personally putting to death his dogs that were incurably ill. He would feed the dog a last meal of favorite food, perhaps a delicacy normally forbidden in quantity, such as a bowlful of sugar lumps, and then put a bullet in its head with his Colt .38. Many other dog people, who preferred leaving such distasteful tasks to their hired men or perhaps to their veterinarian, were horrified at Terhune for doing it himself and in such primitive, if no less merciful, fashion. Terhune would answer only, "I am a sure shot," and let it go at that. He apparently was motivated by a belief that his dog's last seconds alive should be spent with its beloved master, rather than a stranger, and that the animal should die happily, savoring an unexpected treat.

One of the pieces of information that Terhune so freely dispensed got him into a public wrangle in the mid-1930s with the American Medical Association. Terhune had written a brief article for the August, 1936, issue of *Reader's Digest* in which he discussed how to avoid being bitten when confronted by a belligerent dog. Terhune declared with great assurance that a dog that approaches with head held high and loud barks does not plan to bite. But if the animal comes on with head down and emitting low growls, it probably has serious intentions. The best resort for the human target, Terhune advised, is to stand with feet together and hands on chest. That pose may so puzzle the dog that it will forget about biting in its curiosity.

Whether Terhune's advice saved anyone from being bitten is not known, but what aroused the wrath of the AMA was his further advice on what steps to take if a bite actually occurred.

If you are bitten by a dog, Terhune wrote,

remember this—not once in many thousand times is the dog rabid. Rabies exists, but it is very rare. Of the almost uncountable bites inflicted during a term of years on attendants in the New York City dog pounds, not one caused a case of rabies.

If the bite is where your lips can reach it, suck it out thoroughly. Then bathe it in lukewarm (not hot) water and paint it with iodine. And don't worry. You are in no danger. If you are afraid the biter had rabies—which he almost never has—use the same treatment but paint the wound with carbolic acid instead of iodine.

After Terhune's article appeared, he was furiously taken to task by Dr. Morris Fishbein, feisty long-time editor of the *A.M.A. Journal.* Fishbein called Terhune's advice "subversive" and emphatically warned that dog bites should never be self-treated but referred immediately to physicians or public health officers. He cited statistics from both Ohio and England to show that a substantial number of biting dogs were proved to have rabies and that, in one study, more than a third of the persons bitten by rabid dogs eventually died.

The very least that should be done, Dr. Fishbein went on, is to cauterize the wound and place the animal under close observation for signs of rabies, with the Pasteur treatment to be started as soon as the dog shows signs of the disease. He reiterated that rabies is a disease that is always fatal in human beings once it develops.

Although the Pasteur treatment had been in use almost fifty years at that time, many people still did not utilize it and this, Dr. Fishbein concluded with an angry flourish, "can be attributed largely to ignorance, carelessness, indifference and the widespread dissemination of such advice as that found in Mr. Terhune's article."

Terhune's rather cavalier attitude toward the danger of rabies was nothing new and stemmed in part, probably, from his long-held horror at the suffering perpetrated on innocent, healthy dogs due to the once-common "mad dog scare." He began one short story, "The Fetish," with a typical description of a big mongrel who was "sick of mind and of body. He craved only to get out of that abode of men and to find solitude in the forests and hills beyond the village." The mongrel trots down the main street of a town, flecks of foam dripping from his mouth. Someone yells "mad dog!" and a crowd begins to chase the desperate dog, who eventually is shot to death. "When some such suffering beast is seen, on his way to solitude," Terhune declared in describing the incident, "we humans prove our humanity by raising the idiotic bellow of 'Mad Dog!' and by chasing and torturing the victim. All this, despite proof that not one sick dog in a thousand, thus assailed, has any disease which is even remotely akin to rabies. Next to vivisection, no crime against helpless animals is so needlessly and foolishly cruel as the average mad-dog chase."

Such incidents—a howling mob chasing an innocent dog down a village street and shouting "Mad dog!"—recurred often in Terhune stories. His abhorrence for cruelty led him to an obstinate blindness to the real dangers of rabies, as his "advice" in *Reader's Digest* shows.

Some two years earlier, Terhune had been involved in a dispute in Hackensack, New Jersey, over a plan to make rabies inoculation compulsory in the wake of a rabies scare. There was much argument over the plan, some dog owners expressing fear of the possible ill-effects from inoculation. *The New York Times* quoted Terhune as saying that he never had inoculated his own dogs and would not do so. The American Kennel Club, he said, had successfully opposed similar statewide legislation in New Jersey. At that time it was not regarded as a move that would be of much value. "Personally," Terhune concluded, "I do not approve of inoculation. I do not believe it is necessary or efficacious."

Terhune was not alone among dog people in his short-sightedness on this issue. The same news story quoted an executive of the AKC as saying, "Whether it (inoculation) is good or bad, I don't know, and the veterinarians are divided on the question. Personally, I am a little afraid of it."

For all his opinionated preachments on dogs and dog behavior, Terhune was capable of public humility with regard to his knowledge of the subject. He wrote in his autobiography:

All my life I have made an intensive study of dogs. Thirty years ago I knew everything about them that could be known, and much more. After three decades of much closer study of them and their ways, I find to my dismay that I know almost nothing at all about them. I have scarcely scratched the surface. That is not false modesty. It is sickeningly true.

The sum total of my canine knowledge and experience and observation is this: Anything can happen; and usually it does . . . I have learned much from my dogs—far more than ever they have learned from me. But to this day there are a hundred things about their mentality—or its lack—that are sealed mysteries to me and to every other human.

Though his credentials as dog expert were (and still are) challenged from time to time, there is no doubt that Terhune had a profound influence on public opinion with regard to dogs and that he was particularly instrumental in establishing the venerable collie as a breed of unusual durability in terms of popularity. The American Kennel Club keeps careful records of the numbers of purebred dogs registered in each breed category and has done so for many years. The AKC registration lists provide a reasonably accurate reading of the popularity—at least in a numerical sense—of the more than 120 breeds recognized by it.

The taste of the American people in dogs, as in most other things, tends to be fickle and short-lived. Many breeds vault up to canine stardom, then almost as suddenly descend back into comparative obscurity. The notable thing about the collie is its consistency. Collies became popular in this country in the 1880s, due in great measure to the publicity given to their finding favor with Queen Victoria of England. They were often exhibited at the early dog shows in this country. So Terhune cannot be credited with originally creating the American popularity of the breed. But what has set the collie apart from most other breeds is the way in which it has consistently remained among the most popular, year after year, decade after decade. The collie has seldom ranked among the top two or three breeds, based on the registration figures; but it has rarely dropped out of the top ten and most years has been ranked somewhere between fifth and tenth in popularity among the some 120 recognized breeds. (The latest AKC figures show that the collie has dropped from the top ten. But if the past is any criterion, it soon will return to favor.)

This consistency of appeal over many years was due in great part to Terhune's unceasing idealizing of the breed. His worship of the collie was devoutly replicated by thousands of his faithful readers, and later by their children, and still later by *their* children. Even today, with a few Terhune books still being sold in book stores and many others enjoying a steady readership through library circulation, the long-dead author continues to have some influence on the steady popularity of the collie. Admittedly, though, the collie has had another and—thanks to electronics—much more powerful champion in recent years: a handsome sable-and-white male collie (or collies) who has gained fame as a female impersonator under the name of "Lassie." The canine television star has taken over from Terhune the continuing task of collie advocacy and obviously done the job well.

But there is no question of Terhune's influence on the popularity of the breed. *Sports Illustrated,* in a 1968 article on Terhune, noted: "Most of the collie breeders going today got into the sport of dogs because of Terhune." Many of those collie people still worship Terhune as a near-god and Sunnybank as the Garden of Eden. Discussion of The Place, the Master and the Mistress, Lad and Wolf often will bring tears to their eyes. The magazine quoted one leading collie breeder: "Everything I am and ever have been in collies is because of the Terhune books."

Yet Bert Terhune is still, years after his death, a controversial figure who is sometimes the object of scorn and hatred. The old feelings do not easily die. A man long active in the world of collies asked to reminisce about Terhune wrote only this: "George B. Shaw said don't hate them, just ignore them. My Mother always said Let the Dead Rest. Mr. Terhune's own dogs did not even like him." Another noted collie breeder, who knew Terhune rather well, answered a similar request by saying: "I knew Mr. Terhune for many years but since I cannot say anything good about him, I will make this as short as possible. Considering what a large man he was physically, he was the smallest person I ever knew."

One collie club in this country, when asked in the late 1960s for a donation for the restoration of Sunnybank, engaged in long and heated debate on the issue. Some of the older members got up to condemn Terhune as an irritable egomaniac, who was rude and hostile to worshipping fans who came to visit him and who had spread maliciously false rumors about the collie and the alleged lessening of brain size and intelligence. But the Master also had his loyal defenders. Finally, after bitter argument, the club decided to make a relatively small token pledge to the campaign. The modest gift would fulfill its responsibility without cutting too deeply into its treasury on behalf of a long-gone writer who was so passionately disliked by some of its members.

Perhaps the most important thing about Terhune and the dog people is that hundreds of families came to own collies because of him. And these big, grave, sweet-tempered animals brought much joy to those who loved them. In a very real sense, Bert Terhune was responsible for this. It is possibly one of the nicest epitaphs a writer could wish for.

26

After the publication of his autobiography in 1930, Bert Terhune began gradually to slow down his writing career. But he still had a few dog yarns in his stockpile and the following year Harper published *A Dog Named Chips.* The book, which included six stories previously published in *The Ladies' Home Journal,* was not among Terhune's best sellers, but it did have some significance as one of his few book-length works about a dog that was entirely fictitious. The hero was a mongrel whose ancestors, Terhune wrote, probably represented at least fifty different breeds.

Actually, Chips should properly be referred to as a heroine, for the book concludes with a rather silly revelation that the little mongrel scamp previously thought to be a male and referred to throughout the book as "he" has just given birth to a litter of puppies—one of the most contrived, unbelievable episodes of which Terhune ever was guilty.

The weak ending of the book, perhaps a reflection of Terhune's declining energy and imagination, contributed to a negative review in *The New York Times,* which had given him an almost unbroken string of approving reviews over the past dozen years. The *Times* commented:

"This is his first attempt to create a real fictional dog character and evolve stories for it to disport itself in. The dedication of the book admits that Chips is wholly a product of the imagination. It must be said that reality serves Mr. Terhune better than fancy in the making of dog stories. For neither his canine hero nor the four [sic] stories about him in the book bring to the reader conviction of reality, or even of possibility."

The next year, 1932, saw the publication of two more Terhune books which represented almost the last of his original writing, although a number of additional books bearing his name were still to appear.

The first of the two new books was another of Terhune's extremely popular collections of short pieces—some of them stories with fictional characters, others featuring the Master and the Mistress and the dogs of Sunnybank. *The Way of a Dog* started off with five more stories about Gray Dawn, the last of which detailed the death of the big gray dog.

Terhune still was able to add another captivating personality to the long cast of Sunnybank stars. One of the pieces in the book, "The Biography of a Puppy," was a fascinating account of the birth, puppyhood, and early training of Sandy—"Sunnybank Sandstorm"—a son of Gray Dawn. He had been chosen by Terhune as his latest house dog—the position of honor involving freedom to roam and sleep inside the house which had been accorded to Lad, Wolf, Bruce, Gray Dawn, and a few of the other collies, those judged by Terhune to be the noblest of the many litters birthed on The Place. The piece on Sandy was written with all the old Terhune magic.

Terhune's dedication of *The Way of a Dog* noted, with considerable accuracy, that the book was "This latest (and probably last) book of my dog stories." It also was one of his best-selling books.

The other Terhune book published in 1932 was, according to his wife, "the book that meant more to him than all else he ever wrote." Terhune's upbringing in the house of a clergyman and his own deep, lifelong religious commitment had produced in him a longing to write a work of religious significance. Several years prior to 1932, he had begun submitting to *The Ladies' Home Journal* a series of sketches in which the character and personality of Jesus were compared with qualities attributed to the great figures of the Old Testament. It was the type of didactic, proselytizing religious writing that would irritate the ecumenically minded today, for the comparisons made by Terhune were inevitably at the expense of the Old Testament personages, whose essential inferiority to Jesus always was emphasized. It was a rather fundamentalist approach to Christianity, a working out in literary form of Terhune's aggressive, passionate religious faith. The style of the writing, though, was typical Terhune—simple, colloquial, fast-paced, readable. In other words, altogether unscholarly.

Terhune was delighted at the response to the magazine sketches. "The host of letters that came to me," he wrote, "told me I had brought a new meaning and a new hope and comfort to my readers, in these sketches of Christ. That gave me the courage to put my words into a more lasting form."

He then set to work refining and expanding the magazine articles into a full-length book, which was titled *The Son of God* and published by Harper in 1932.

Terhune admitted in the book that he had never read any of the classic scholarly books about Jesus, but based his work on his own long, careful study of the four gospels. Included in *The Son of God* was Terhune's explanation of Jesus's cry on the cross, "My God, My God, why hast Thou forsaken me?" Rather than expressing a sense of abandonment by God, Terhune argued, Jesus uttered the words to remind his hearers of the Twenty-second Psalm, which begins with the same words. That psalm, wrote Terhune, was a messianic prophecy; after Jesus alluded to it by reciting its opening lines, he went on to say, "It is fulfilled," which, according to Terhune, was later mistranslated as "It is finished" or "It is over." Thus the cry of Jesus, Terhune declared, was not an expression of agony but one of consummate triumph and completion.

The work never approached the astronomical sales figures of Terhune's dog books, but he and his wife were nevertheless deeply proud of it. And it was reasonably well received by the reviewers. The *Book Review Digest* for 1932 listed four reviews, two of which were rated as favorable and two as leaning to the favorable side.

Perhaps most meaningful to Terhune was the reaction of competent critics for major religious publications. H. D. Gallaudet wrote in *The Christian Century:*

The plan of the book is as effective as it is simple. I am not sure but that it is unique. Yet the method is so obvious and the result so striking, that one wonders why nobody has done exactly this before . . . You may not be moved by the author's theology. And some of his rhetorical asides will probably leave you cold. But I wonder if many of us could improve on his simple portrayal of the loftiest heights of character manhood has ever reached, in this human picture of *The Son of God.*

The year of 1933 marked a watershed in the literary career of Albert Payson Terhune: it was the first year since 1917, since the still-struggling early stages of his rise to success, that not a single Terhune book was published. The great mechanical man of writing was slowing down, the legendary production beginning to fail. There was an almost imperceptible hush falling across The Place.

He made a comeback of sorts in 1934 with his last book of original writing. Another nine books were published during the remaining years of his life, but all were either collections of his old short stories or reissues of old magazine serials under new titles as short novels of mystery or melodrama.

The new book in 1934 was one of his best ever. *The Book of Sunnybank* was a collection of tender, almost elegiac short pieces about The Place and its inhabitants (later published under the revised title *Sunnybank, Home of Lad*).

The book had its share of dog yarns to satisfy the demands of Terhune's loyal readers. But it had much more as well: some historical background about The Place, a colorful, evocative description of the changing seasons at the lakeside estate; a verbal trip through some of the main rooms in the old house; the adventures of the real-life Chips at Sunnybank—an Irish terrier who came after and was named for the fictional Terhune mongrel hero-heroine; an affectionate description of the birds, cats, and other animals who lived at Sunnybank and were regarded by the Terhunes with love equal to that given their dogs; a few more protests against the continued encroachments of the motor tourists; some philosophical comments by Terhune on old age and its tribulations; a discussion of genealogy in dogs and men; and finally another touching portrait of his blind collie Fair Ellen, whose life had ended while Terhune was writing the book.

The Book of Sunnybank was written with deep feeling; there was a haunting sense of farewell about it, of completion, as if it was to be Terhune's final testament to his readers, his wife, and his beloved home. The book's sales were not huge, although it had been fondly greeted by reviewers, many of whom reacted as if they were being reunited with a loved old friend who had been away for a while.

Here is one passage from *The Book of Sunnybank.* It typifies Terhune's ability, at his best, to write descriptive passages of beauty, perception, and imagination, while yet confining himself to simple, understandable language that avoids the self-consciously "poetic" nature writing of so many writers loved by the literary establishment.

This is how Terhune described the coming of spring to his home:

Thawing days and freezing nights. Slowly, slimily, the frost begins to crawl out of the ground, making Sunnybank a foul quagmire.

It is Spring's sorry advance notice. Its one redeeming feature is a song sparrow that wakes me in the morning amid the dribble of wet eaves or the hammer of March rain on the roof.

Through the vileness of the weather he sings a gloriously triumphant announcement that spring is here. Which it is not. But I bless him, none the less, for his optimism. Groundless optimism is so much more bearable in a bird than in a human.

The grass remains dust-gray and the wet air breeds a golden argosy of snuffles and the earth is rotted. Mud takes on all the worst features of mucilage. Cross-country walks are a sticky burden.

But the song sparrow can see farther into the murk than I can. He keeps on insisting that winter is gone and that the dead world is nearing resurrection.

This "charming, rambling, human book," as *The New York Times* called it, was augmented in its original edition by pictures taken by the great photographer Margaret Bourke-White.

Terhune had been a writer for almost forty years, had been earning his total living from it for almost two decades. He was a rich man and a much beloved one. Thousands of readers throughout the world fairly worshipped him. Every library worthy of the name owned at least a dozen of his books. He was the embodiment of popular literary success.

Yet at sixty-two, his writing career almost finished, he still ached with the knowledge that the pundits of the printed word did not take him seriously (although his stories were selected occasionally for such anthologies as *O. Henry Prize Stories* and *The World's Greatest Short Stories.* One Terhune buff was able to locate thirteen separate volumes of "best" stories in which works by Terhune were represented). He was still just a dog writer, with all the demeaning implications of the phrase. There were moments, now and then, when Terhune brooded about this and thought that he would have been willing to trade it all —the money, the string of much-read books, the legions of loving fans —for just one important work, one major book that would have the Menckens and the Wilsons and the Woolcotts on their feet, roaring with applause.

And then again, he would think of more arguments for his old brief that the popular writer was often as talented, if not more so, than his more prestigious counterpart.

Insisting in his autobiography that the approval of the "lowbrow" means as much as that of the literary critic, Terhune declared:

We demand majority rule in our government. Why sneer at it in our literature?

I have not read a line written by Harold Bell Wright or by Zane Grey. I do not expect to read any of their work. But I do not believe either of those two men would have been able to pile up an avid reading public of millions of men and women, for each of his books, unless those books had had as much merit in their own way as had anything of Walter Pater's or of D. H. Lawrence's or of Hergesheimer's; or of any other writer's, past or present, whom the cognoscenti extol and at whom the multitude yawn.

Marlowe and Ben Jonson, whose plays could not draw large enough audiences to pay for heating the theater, sneered at Shakespeare as the cheap favorite of the groundlings . . . Marlowe is half-forgotten today . . . Shakespeare endures . . .

God forbid that I should place Zane Grey or Harold Bell Wright on any such pinnacle of promised immortality! I say only that the public at large loves them and their kind; and that the public at large has shown no lasting devotion for any one of twenty writers whom the intelligentsia from time to time have acclaimed. Also that the enduring approval of the general public has more than once been proved correct by posterity.

Terhune had waged a similar argument in *The Saturday Evening Post* in 1925: ". . . to save my soul I could not write . . . about psychic concepts or soul complexes or about characters who think luridly and who do nothing. It is an art to write these things. I do not possess that art. I am too low-browed even to want to attain to it.

"All I can achieve is the writing of stories wherein folk do things instead of being content to think them: stories wherein something happens and happens hard. Not idyls of self-analysis or autobiographic psychology."

Yet, after all the challenges to the literary establishment and its standards of greatness, after all the spirited defenses of the vastly popular, yet critically unappreciated writers such as himself, the small, quiet cry of pain occasionally would be heard:

"None of my fiction for well over a decade has been an attempt at literature. But it seems to interest a goodly number of non-critical people. With that I am content. Or if I am not, I am nearer content than I have any right to be. True, I dreamed long ago of adding something to my country's and my century's literary store. I am not able to do that. So I must do what I can.

"It would be rank hypocrisy for me to say I would not give one of my legs to be able to write as any of a dozen better men and a half-dozen women can write. But I can't. So I must write as I can."

27

After *The Book of Sunnybank* in 1934, the writing was almost done.

Additional Terhune books continued to stream into the stores—one more in 1934, one in 1935, two in 1936, three in 1937—but they were all old works recreated for a new market. Never having completely recovered from his accident and with new illness coming into the picture, Terhune found himself physically unable any longer to attack book-length works. In his early sixties he was still a powerful-appearing mountain of a man. But the strength of the giant was fading now and he was less able to ignore the almost constant pain from his old injuries.

He continued, during these years, to turn out short dog anecdotes and historical vignettes for the McNaught Syndicate and an occasional piece for the *Reader's Digest.* And he had more time now to do some articles for children's periodicals such as *St. Nicholas* and *Scholastic*—gently philosophical essays on life and mundane how-to pieces on puppy care and training. But the glib flood of dog stories, the hard-action serials for the mass circulation magazines, the books of essays . . . these were no more.

He did, however, find the strength to do some writing for a new medium—one that brought him wide exposure, good money, and many additional fans: the burgeoning new medium of network radio.

Terhune had a deep, rich speaking voice and could handle himself well in front of a microphone. During the late 1920s he was a frequent guest on local radio interview shows and later made periodic appearances on some of the important network shows of the day. One evening in 1933, for example, he was the special guest star on "The Salada Program, sponsored by Salada Tea, featuring Emily Post and songs by Sydney Nesbitt, the singing aviator, with Muriel Pollock and her Salada Strings."

In 1933, he also discussed the possibility of doing a regular radio series for the makers of Milk Bone dog biscuits. The show never materialized, but shortly afterward another one did that would make Terhune—for a few years at least—a radio celebrity.

The series was the creation of an independent radio producer named Bruce Chapman. Chapman had suggested to a friend whose advertising agency represented Spratt's Patent, Ltd., an English manufacturer of dog foods, that the company consider sponsoring a radio program. The client was receptive and Chapman proposed a series of dramatized dog stories written by Albert Payson Terhune.

When Chapman first called on Terhune to broach the idea, his objective was only to secure the use of Terhune's name and his writing ability.

He found that Terhune not only had a deep voice that was perfect for radio, but also a natural bent for telling stories in a compelling way. Another thing that appealed to Chapman was that Terhune talked and told his stories in a simple, unaffected way, with no trace of pompousness. The producer quickly revised his idea and asked Terhune if he would consider appearing on the Spratt's series as the featured narrator of the stories, in addition to doing most of the writing. Terhune's response was that he didn't know a thing about doing a radio series, but that if Chapman would guide him and help him put the stories into proper radio form, he would give it a try.

Chapman had considerable experience in adapting the work of well-known authors for radio dramas, so he entered into a partnership agreement with Terhune. A basic narrative was written by Terhune and turned over to Chapman, who rewrote it into a fifteen-minute radio drama narrated by Terhune and utilizing a small dramatic cast of actors. One of the unsung heroes of the cast was a busy radio animal imitator named Bradley Barker, who provided most of the dog sounds. The program was given a late Sunday afternoon time slot on the NBC Blue Network and went on the air. (The starting date of the program is not certain; Chapman states that it first went on the air in the fall of 1932, but NBC records show a starting date of January 21, 1934.)

Each program began with the announcer saying: "Again Spratt's takes pleasure in presenting that famous author of dog stories, Albert Payson Terhune, who brings you each week a true story of the affection, intelligence and heroism of man's greatest friend—his dog."

Terhune himself opened each story with the words, "Good afternoon—I hope you'll like it!" and the phrase quickly became closely associated with him by the radio audience.

Spratt's supported the program with considerable promotion, including full-page ads in the *Gazette* of the American Kennel Club and that, coupled with Terhune's tremendous popularity among dog lovers, was enough to ensure a large audience for the program. At that time the NBC broadcasting empire was divided into two radio networks—the Red and the Blue. The Blue Network included more of the so-called superpower radio stations, the stations around the country that broadcast with exceptionally high power and thus commanded particularly large audiences. According to Chapman, the Terhune program had the highest Crosley rating (the major audience survey of that time) for its time period and also the highest Crosley rating of any fifteen-minute radio drama then on the air.

Most of the scripts were based, not on Terhune's stories about Sunnybank collies but rather on tales about dogs, many of them true, that appeared in newspapers or elsewhere and had caught Terhune's eye.

Those were also the days of various regional network groupings and scripts for the program indicate that, in addition to the NBC Blue Network, it was heard on the Mountain Group, the Orange Network, the Mutual Broadcasting System, and the NBC Pacific Coast Network. The program remained on the air until the spring of 1936, usually as a late Sunday afternoon feature, although it was carried for a while on Saturday and briefly on other days of the week as well.

It maintained its high ratings as long as it was on the air. The series run ended only because of a sharp rise in the price of wheat, which caused a severe dip in Spratt's earnings in the United States and an eventual decision, spurred by the Depression, to eliminate all advertising in this country.

Bruce Chapman said recently that he found Bert Terhune a delight to work with during the run of the radio programs. "He was the easiest man in the world to get along with," Chapman said. Terhune always called Chapman "Chief." Whenever a difference of opinion arose over a script or a production problem, Terhune would give in and say, "You're the expert on radio, Chief, let's do it your way." Their invariable post-program routine was to head for 21, the popular New York restaurant and bar, where Terhune would relax and enjoy a double Swiss S, his favorite cocktail. The two men became good friends and Chapman continued to assist Terhune for the rest of his life, first as an adviser on Terhune's other radio appearances as a guest star and later as a sort of unofficial business manager and counselor, and sometimes as an agent.

After his own series ended, Terhune occasionally was asked to appear as a guest on such major shows as the "General Electric Circle Program" and the "For Men Only" show. On the latter program, Terhune's comments about dog behavior included an explanation of the different meanings of dog barks, illustrated by the invaluable Bradley Barker. Another show that periodically invited Terhune to be a guest was the CBS "Heinz Magazine of the Air," on which the author would write and deliver a true dog story from history.

The additional income from his radio appearances, although not huge, was welcomed by Terhune. The Depression had had its inevitable effect on book sales and Terhune's income, though still comfortable, was sharply reduced from its level of the late 1920s. The style of living of the Terhunes, however, was not changed a bit. The comfortable, almost baronial life at Sunnybank, the entertaining, the trips—all remained as before. Terhune never could bring himself to deprive Anice of the life she so loved and he himself would find it very difficult to change. So they went on as before, but the reduction in his income forced him to go into his capital to maintain their way of life.

Fame and celebrity had been very sweet to Terhune despite his cries of protest at the invasion of his privacy; he had been one of the world's most popular writers for some fifteen years and had loved every minute of it. Now, in the mid-1930s, there were signs that the fame was beginning to slacken off, although Terhune still was beloved by thousands upon thousands of faithful readers. But the drop in book sales, the loss of income, the slowdown in his writing caused by advancing age and failing health—all these things combined to make

Terhune occasionally depressed, to feel that the world somehow had passed him by, that he was now out of vogue, on his way to being utterly forgotten.

Terhune decided that perhaps more personal publicity would remedy the situation. So he hired a publicity agent—Amy Vanderbilt, a young journalist who was moonlighting with some free-lance public relations jobs and who later was to gain her own fame as columnist and author. She wasted no time in getting Terhune's name into print.

In July, 1934, *Time* Magazine had favorably reviewed a Columbia picture called *Whom the Gods Destroy,* written by Terhune and starring Walter Connolly and a very youthful Robert Young. There was not a dog in the film and *Time* called it "ideal cinema material: sad, intelligent, dramatic . . . " In the course of the review, in a passing reference to Terhune's fame as a writer, *Time* described him as mild-mannered. The innocuous comment gave the aggressive Miss Vanderbilt the opening she had been seeking.

Operating apparently on the old-time publicist's principle that getting a client's name into print is the important thing, whether the report is favorable or not, Miss Vanderbilt fired off a letter-to-the-editor that appeared in an early issue of *Time:*

What is this calumny I find in the usually accurate *Time* . . . about Albert Payson Terhune? Mild-mannered, is he? Let me be the first to rush to this anything but phlegmatic gentleman's defense. In the matter of temper, not temperament, among writers possibly only Theodore Dreiser betters him. That prognathous jaw is forever setting itself in grim determination that someone "shall be cut from ear to ear." He gets actively annoyed on the slightest provocation and his huge fists contract in his more or less consistent effort to control himself. He trembles on the brink of explosion most of the time. His indignation is righteous and his anger is of the inspiring kind that would end in a knockdown drag-out fight—if he hadn't spent 62 years learning to keep in leash. He collects, as a matter of fact, all manner of weapons and murderous devices. His manners are anything but mild. Only dogs, old ladies and children escape his tongue lashings.

She wrote that Terhune had just turned down a suggestion that his old Raegan stories from *Smart Set* magazine be republished in book form because the return of those "sophisticated" stories might hurt the sale of his dog books. "He prefers to remain an Apostle of the Obvious," Miss Vanderbilt concluded, "and to know the joy of a wide and appreciative audience. And then too, Mr. Terhune enjoys his great prosperity."

The letter was blatantly obvious press agentry, but it was signed Amy Vanderbilt, Business Manager, *The American Spectator,* New York City.

News stories about Terhune began to appear that were obviously inspired by a publicist looking for a gimmick. CATS ARE WORLD'S GREATEST SPONGERS, TERHUNE AVERS read a headline in the New York *World-Telegram.* The story provided a series of typical Terhune assertions about cats—the kind guaranteed to incense cat lovers but also certain to make good copy and thereby insure getting Terhune's name before the public. "Men hate cats and women love them. . . . the cat is the only animal man has never conquered . . . the cat is the only animal that won't do a lick of work . . . . . . cats have reduced comfort to a fine art. They are the world's greatest spongers. . . . . A cat simply does not know what loyalty is. . . . To find a cat with loyalty would be like finding one with five ears."

The news story closed with a typical Terhune technique—the unexpected kicker. " 'Are dogs more intelligent?' he was asked. Mr. Terhune looked a little uncomfortable. 'I am an honest man,' he said, 'and I must admit that the answer is no. Cats do some marvellously intelligent things. They will learn by themselves to unlatch a door or to hit a faucet handle until they turn the water on. A dog would never learn that.' " The ending of the story resulted in banner headlines all over the country: TERHUNE ADMITS CATS SMARTER THAN DOGS.

The *World-Telegram* later headlined another story: TERHUNE, BREEDER OF FAMOUS COLLIES, WOULD NEVER THINK OF FUNERAL FOR DOG," and said the author felt a funeral for a dog would be just as ridiculous as a marriage ceremony. The comments were made when Terhune was interviewed aboard ship as he and Anice returned from a trip to Bermuda. He also gave the reporter his oft-repeated quote that "I'd no more kiss a dog than I would a goat."

The silliness of most of the publicity gimmicks apparently didn't bother Terhune, who was delighted with the increased attention being given to him by the newspapers along with his new career as a radio personality. But he was disappointed that the fresh publicity had little effect on the depressed sale of his books. They continued to sell steadily, but the nation's economic crisis had brought the sales figures considerably below previous levels and Terhune's income, while remaining comfortable, no longer was spectacular. His old friend William Gerard Chapman wrote to offer him $25 for newspaper syndication rights to an old Terhune story and the offer was accepted, Terhune commenting: "Naturally, the price is a joke. But then ALL literary prices nowadays are a joke—a joke on the poor cuss who does the writing. Because an unsophisticated slice of the public is interested in my scribblings about dogs, I have kept both nostrils above water (even if not so very far above it) during the past six famine years. God grant I may continue to do so!"

Some time in 1935, Terhune was suddenly confronted by death. He began having persistent trouble with his throat—pain and occasional hoarseness—but he attributed the problem to his heavy smoking of cigarettes and cigars and for a long time refused to heed Anice's pleas that he see a doctor about it. Finally he gave in and went to see Clarence Vreeland, the Pompton Lakes physician who was his good friend. Dr. Vreeland warned Terhune that he must consult a throat specialist without any further delay. The writer reluctantly agreed, concerned now but still insisting that nothing serious was wrong.

The specialists confirmed Dr. Vreeland's suspicions: Terhune had cancer of the throat. They told Terhune their diagnosis and added that his hope for survival was slim, but that major surgery offered the only chance.

It was typical of Terhune that he made full use of the medical crisis as the subject for a lengthy magazine article.

The article was published in the January, 1936, issue of *The Atlantic Monthly* and appeared under the pseudonym of Stephen Dirck, which Terhune had used for a few stories many years before. "I Set My House in Order" was essentially an account of how he had prepared to die.

"I am a writer," he began the piece. "Not of the first rank; yet I make my living that way. I am not signing my real name to this. I can write more frankly under an alias in telling what I am going to tell. I do not care to be connected with it by name, for reasons you will understand."

After getting the verdict from his doctors, Terhune related, he asked whether the surgery could be at all delayed. Three months, they told him, no more. He resolved to make the best possible use of the time.

His reaction to the news was neither fright nor sadness: "I found myself viewing my prospects with an almost indifferent calm . . . I have never thought more clearly or with less emotion." He did not want immediately to break the news to Anice and instead told her and their friends that his illness was a heart problem, which had been an aftermath of a flu attack.

His first concern, as it seemed always to have been, was his financial situation: " . . . I had been fortunate enough to arrange, long ago, that my family should have our home and a comfortable income in the event of my death; but the depression had cut deep into my funds, as into everyone else's. It had pared down the volume and the prices of my work. It had tangled my fiscal affairs."

Desperately intent on building up the value of his estate in the time remaining to him, Terhune resumed a semblance of his old superhuman literary production schedule. "I grabbed every form of writing job I could find, were the pay good or poor. I took work that once I would have deemed miles beneath my notice, from sources that would not appeal to the average writer of any standing, sometimes at incredibly low rates.

"When a man goes on a hunt for such work there is more of it to be found than one would suppose. I did it all, to the best of my mediocre ability. For there was a strong chance that some of it might carry my name when I should be a memory. I did not want even the pettiest monument to me to be fashioned from slipshod scribbling. Wherefore I put into the labor all the skill I had in me."

One of his greatest pleasures from this hectic ninety-day period of incessant work came from the writing of a four-part serial for one of the top magazines that had bought so much of his material over the years. He looked on the serial as his valedictory to the readers of that magazine. He wrote with even greater speed than usual, but it flowed smoothly, he enjoyed writing it, and was satisfied with it. After he sent it in, the editor of the magazine responded that the serial was the best, most spontaneous work he had done in a long time.

His doctors, still worried over the delay in the surgery, tried to persuade him to have the operation immediately, but Terhune refused. He kept writing. "There was no heroism or even pluck in my sticking to my desk for nine or ten hours a day during those months of waiting," he wrote in describing the ordeal. "There was nothing much else to do. I did not feel like going out. I did not feel like doing any of the myriad gay things which strew my average winter. I was too tired. I was in too much pain."

The three months of writing at forced draft paid off. He earned more from the output of that period than he had during the previous eighteen months.

In addition to working frantically to earn as much additional money as he could during the three-month waiting period, Terhune also tried to straighten out his financial records and put everything down on paper to make it easier for Anice.

And, much to the regret of those who have attempted to study his life, he apparently used the period to destroy many of his personal papers and old correspondence. He commented in the article, " . . . there were letters and papers which would have caused needless pain and which would have revived needlessly cruel memories. These I got rid of, in the course of setting my house in order."

It was this rather desperate expunging of all bitter memories recorded on paper, apparently, that partly accounts for the scant information on Terhune's first marriage. In the personal papers that were left behind for posterity, there were only one or two bits of correspondence with his only child.

The rest of Terhune's *Atlantic Monthly* article about his wait for probable death was devoted mainly to telling how he conducted himself during that difficult time. Some of his reactions were described in typically blunt, outspoken fashion.

Often in stories, he noted, the doomed hero goes to those he has wronged or who have wronged him and asks or grants forgiveness, as the case may be. "To me," he commented, "this seems the sloppiest and most ignoble conduct imaginable. There are a few—a very, *very* few—people with whom I am still on passively bad terms. Perhaps the fault is mine. Perhaps it is theirs. What does it matter whose fault it is? In each instance it is a perfectly good grudge. As such it stands; and thus it shall stand (as far as I am concerned) until doomsday.

"I would sooner have cut my tongue out than to have gone to any of these people and told them I was in imminent danger of death, and to have made my peace with them on that basis. . . . If the grudge was worth carrying through life, it seemed to me worth carrying through death."

Terhune did make it a point to seek out five old friends who had drifted away with the years, and to spend some time with them.

Awaiting death, would he make his peace with God? Terhune said he would have none of this. It seemed to him "cowardly and unsportsmanlike to live a regrettable life and then, at the Gates of Death, to howl for divine mercy." Anyway, he added, he believed that God had guided him throughout his life and he felt no need for a sudden reunion.

His attitude toward those around him? Again, Terhune was coldly honest about himself: "I should like to be able to add that I went around, during this period of waiting, with a glorified smile on my face and with an inspiredly helpful word to everyone who came near me. But I did nothing of the kind. Looking back, I seem to remember that I displayed for the most part all the lovable friendliness of a sick wildcat.

"I was played out. I was suffering acutely. Moreover, I was not seeking to leave sugar-coated memories behind me among those I loved. It would take off some of the grief and loneliness if they could remember me as cranky—a man not greatly to be missed. Besides, I was too busy setting my house in order to have time to pretend to be a patient and softly smiling saint.

"My supposed remnants of flu, and the genuine heart trouble which I pretended was a part of it, served as ample excuse for any surliness and for the declining of all declinable invitations. I am sorry for those who had to be around me. Luckily there were few of them. (I am sorriest, a millionfold, that at the end my wife had to know what was the matter. I tried harder to spare her the knowledge than you would be interested in hearing.)"

After the tense ninety days were over, Terhune had the operation. He tried to give the impression in his article that the threat of a major disease had been a false one: "And they found . . . that they had been almost wholly wrong in their diagnosis! My ailment was not what they had foretold." Then he added, quite contradictorily: "It yielded readily—if temporarily—to the operation."

"In due time," he went on, "I was shipped home, cured. I had somewhat the feeling of a non-swimmer who has nerved himself for a plunge into a bottomless lake and who finds the water is only six inches deep."

Despite Terhune's published allegation that the doctors had been wrong, the available evidence indicates that the diagnosis of cancer was confirmed and that although the surgery halted its progress for a time, the course of the disease was incurable. He was ill for most of the remaining six years of his life and was forced to undergo a series of additional operations in further efforts to arrest the spread of the malignancy. "He was in and out of hospitals for operations," his wife wrote later, "forever having to undergo some new torturing treatment in the hope of a permanent cure and always coming out of the ordeal a little weaker than before."

He fought to keep the operations from interfering with his radio commitments while his series for Spratt's remained on the air. He insisted that the operations be done in stages so that he would miss as few programs as possible, telling his doctors to take out only enough so that he could be on the air again the following week. His producer, Bruce Chapman, noticed in their after-broadcast visits to 21 that Terhune was drinking more in an effort to dull the pain. But the liquor never had any noticeable effect on him and Chapman says he never saw Terhune drunk.

He could not stop writing entirely, not so long as his brain worked and he still had the strength to put forth the words. But his output was only a fraction of what it had been in his prime. On December 18, 1936, he invited the newsmen out to Sunnybank and declared that after his sixty-fourth birthday, three days later, he would go into partial retirement.

After thirty years of writing for nine to eleven hours a day, six days a week, he told the reporters, henceforth he would do only two or three days of easy work a week. "I'm going to cut out all the serials, articles, stories and lecturing," quoted *The New York Times,* "but I'll continue my weekly syndicated article on dogs, write a book once a year, and give occasional radio broadcasts. If I'm to get any fun out of life, I'd better start now."

Despite his confident announcement (or perhaps his pretense of confidence), there were to be no new books. But he did continue to turn out the syndicated pieces and an occasional article. Frequently he was asked by editors for a new story, but always refused on the ground that he was retired. "The real reason for this retirement," wrote Anice after his death, was that "he no longer had the physical strength to write or even to think up any more stories. He was tired clear through. He wished no one to know how ill he was; and we kept it secret as far as possible. No one knew, except those who had to know."

In response to a letter from William Gerard Chapman about the possibility of a story, Terhune answered: "If you'd like to talk terms on an original dog story, I'm listening. Though it's an even chance I'll not get to writing it. As I told you, I'm tired of working and am loafing more (and more happily) than ever before. My new syndicated series . . . calls for less than a day's work a week. My other syndicated feature calls for less than a day's work a fortnight. (I love to brag about my new self-chosen leisure, as a kid over his 1st sweetheart) . . . remember, I've done a good bit of hustling, this past 40 years, and have a few pennies laid by."

But a short time later, in another letter to Chapman, Terhune's mood was more sober and he made a passing reference to the end of the road: "I have dropped out of the writing game . . . I grow very old and very tired. I am not hungry; nor (God willing) shall my wife and daughter be, after my death. So I have slowed down greatly on my old wild speed and I am trying to get all possible fun out of life, while still the getting is good."

The market for Terhune books continued strong and his publishers had to scramble to come up with new—or what passed for new—material. In 1940 Harper and Brothers published a Terhune novel called *Loot!* (later published as *Collie to the Rescue*). In answering a friend who sent congratulations on the new book, Terhune pointed out that *Loot!* originally had been written as a magazine serial in 1928, and "Even then it was such dime novel drivel that I refused to send it out as a book." But in the summer of 1939, three publishers had begged him for a manuscript to meet the demands of his still-clamoring fans and he told them he would never write another book. Then Harper asked whether he had any old serials lying around that had never been published as a book. He sent them *Loot!* and commented to his friend, "It was a case of 'my poverty, and not my will, consents.'"

Ill as he was, tired as he was, he still had the knack at times. And he still could draw an endearing portrait of a dog that, told in simple, uncluttered language, was powerful in its effect upon the reader. Such a portrait—of Sunnybank Bobby—appeared in the *Reader's Digest* for November, 1941, just a few months before Terhune's death, as part of the magazine's famous series on "The Most Unforgettable Character I've Met."

In between the operations and the periods of extreme pain, there were times of comparative peace and well-being for Terhune. He continued to enjoy his daily round of life at Sunnybank and to go with Anice on occasional trips.

The joyous old days of conviviality, of a house filled with guests were over. Terhune's poor health had forced him to give up his clubs, except for rare visits, and he began to lose contact with most of his old friends, the newspapermen, the explorers. Bruce Chapman, by then acting as a sort of agent for Terhune, remembers that he was invited out to Sunnybank for dinner every three or four months. It seems that Anice kept a list of Bert's old friends and invited each of them out periodically so he would not completely lose touch. "I think he was feeling rather lonely at that stage," Chapman says. "He enjoyed talking to me about what remained of his business affairs because it meant a lot to him to know that he was still involved, that people still wanted his work, that he could still be a bit active."

Hal and Ruth LeRoy became good friends of Bert and Anice Terhune during the last few years of Terhune's life after purchasing a Sunnybank collie puppy. The show business performer and his wife lived nearby in New Jersey and called Terhune to inquire about the availability of a puppy. After the author subjected them to his usual searching interrogation to make sure they were qualified to own a collie, he agreed to sell them a puppy for $90, with half the money going to Anice's favorite charity for blind children and the rest going to cover kennel expenses. The transaction led to a friendship that resulted in the LeRoys visiting Sunnybank five or six times a year.

Even friends were required to make an advance appointment to visit; the old rules against unexpected visitors still held firm. Arrivals were met at the entrance gate by superintendent Robert Friend or his successor (Friend retired in the late 1930s and died in 1940), who had a paper indicating the names of those with permission to visit that day.

After a polite warning from the superintendent about driving slowly down the winding driveway, the visitors would proceed on their way, passing signs reminding them to "Drive 5 M.P.H." and "Drive in Low Gear." Often the slow-moving car would be met by Break and Chief, two of the remaining old collies, who would serve as a tail-wagging advance guard down to the house where Bert and Anice usually awaited them on the veranda.

In good weather, most of the visiting was done on the veranda, except when Bert felt well enough to go for a walk around The Place. He still wore the costume he had made famous—the long khaki jacket, its pockets stuffed with dog cookies, the puttees and heavy work shoes. On one hand was a battered gold ring ("All my dogs have teethed on this"). When he could, he would take the remaining puppies for a short walk around Sunnybank and then come back for the older dogs and take them as well. On occasion he and Anice would drive around the neighborhood, looking for unwanted dogs that had been abandoned by their owners. Such animals were brought back to Sunnybank and given a home. They were fed and exercised in the same fashion as his prize collies. "These are my lost stray pals!" he would boom out, when showing them to LeRoy. LeRoy remembers particularly one such stray—an Airedale named Gypsy. On one of their walks, a collie pup kept wandering away from the group. Each time, Gypsy patiently went after the puppy, picked it up in her mouth, and brought it back to the others.

Terhune never lost his love for spinning yarns. As he and LeRoy walked past one of the kennel runs, he would growl, "That collie over there is one of the most fabulous I ever owned." Then he would proceed to tell a long story about the dog's adventures or misadventures.

On the veranda, Bert and Anice would sit together, always holding hands. "They were like young lovers," Mrs. LeRoy recalls. "They were inseparable."

After settling down with a drink—"Are you ready for a libation now?" Bert would quickly ask—they usually wound up talking about LeRoy's show business experiences. Bert could never get enough gossip and reminiscences; he never had lost his love of the theater and his worship of show people. "Tell me some more about your experiences in the Ziegfeld Follies," he would beg LeRoy. Once he asked his guest if he would mind dancing for him. LeRoy did an impromptu tap dance on the old veranda for his audience of three and after his big finish was given a wild ovation by the delighted Bert and Anice.

Terhune always was a fine host, greeting his guests warmly and making them feel very much at home. But, LeRoy remembers, when he became weary or perhaps when the pain became too much to bear, he had no hesitation about dismissing them. He would suddenly stand, stick out his big hand, and quietly say, "Well, thank you for coming."

And there were the annual visits of newspapermen to Sunnybank in December to mark Terhune's birthday and to hear his opinions of world events and also the predictions, which he claimed had been of uncanny accuracy. He had first invited the newsmen out to The Place in 1936 when he announced his partial retirement from writing. He found their visit so enjoyable (and so welcomed the stories about him that followed) that he resolved to make the Sunnybank press conference an annual pre-birthday occasion.

In 1937, after a year of semi-retirement, he commented, "I have found the art of loafing a very difficult one to learn." With war raging in Asia, he warned that the press can make or break a war, and declared that the American people "are idiots enough to be dragged into war by newspaper propaganda." He called on the press to "keep its head so that the populace will keep its head." Unless editors and the reading public "get sane," he insisted, the United States would be dragged into the burgeoning war between China and Japan. He told the reporters he had predicted the Asian war two years earlier and would now predict that Japan would eventually lose "unless she can get the support of banks," a prospect deemed doubtful by Terhune.

A year later, in December, 1938, Terhune celebrated his sixty-sixth birthday with the observation that he was finally developing a liking for the "art of loafing."

When spring came and the weather turned gentle again, they

would still manage to pack a picnic basket and walk slowly up the hill and into the woods across the highroad that now bore his name. A few of the last, old collies who still lived at Sunnybank would join them and tag happily along, barking merrily and spooking squirrels. And for a moment or two, they would recapture those glorious woodland hikes of the golden time when they would lead a band of noisy, joyous collies into the trees.

Anice Terhune wrote fondly of one of those last picnics in her reminiscence of her husband and then added:

"It is good to remember such things now. It is good to reach out and hold onto them, when all the little picnics are over, when the young, dappled green leaves of the forest dance only in my memory; when the pure sweet voice of the 'Spring Song' mingles forever in my heart with an old wood-brown corduroy coat, and a battered tweed cap with a shy, smiling little spring flower tucked gaily in its visor!

"Such memories are golden—priceless!"

Whenever Bert felt stronger, and the doctors approved, they left Sunnybank for a short trip. They often would drive up to New England, Anice always at the wheel, perhaps to the old Red Lion Inn at Stockbridge, Massachusetts, a long-time favorite, or to the Old Tavern at Grafton, Vermont, or some other ancient, peaceful inn in the New England hills. Sometimes the trip would be to West Dummerston, in the southeast corner of Vermont, to visit the hilltop home of Fritz Van de Water, who by now had a long string of published books to his own credit. The two men loved to sit for hours, swapping yarns about the writing business and the many characters they had come to know during their careers.

The Terhunes took many short, leisurely drives over the back roads of Vermont and Massachusetts, enjoying the scenery or occasionally stopping to visit a friend. Bert came to love New England more and more, becoming, as his wife said, almost a son of the area by adoption.

One of those visits to the Berkshires brought Terhune together again for the first time in some years with Mark Saxton—son of Eugene, his long-time editor—who had been thrilled as a child with the privilege of visiting the fabled Sunnybank and of having a Terhune dog book dedicated to him. The elder Saxtons had a summer house at Mill River, Massachusetts, and Bert and Anice came to lunch one day. Mark was now a fledgling writer himself and his first book had just been published. He was looking forward to his reunion with the famed author he had idolized as a child and to talking with him, as one writer to another, about the craft.

When the Terhunes arrived, in a car driven by a chauffeur, Mark was shocked at the change in Bert. He had lost a great deal of weight and looked sick and very tired. He spoke with some difficulty—there was a hoarseness and a sense that he spoke with effort and pain—and he did not talk any more than necessary.

Before lunch was served, Anice sat with Eugene Saxton and his wife in chairs on the lawn while young Mark showed Bert around the grounds. There was an old barn on the place, with a few cows and pigs, and they went there first. Mark remembers still that he was smoking a cigarette as they entered the barn and Terhune rather sharply asked him to put it out. He seemed almost mortally afraid of fire.

The Saxtons' property included a wooded hill covered with beautiful white pines. Terhune asked Mark if they could ride up to the top of the hill. Only in a farm truck on a rough road, was the response. Despite his condition, Terhune asked if they could take the ride—he said the hill was too pretty to miss. They drove to the summit and Terhune stood silently for moments, drinking in the view. As they stood there, Mark Saxton became aware for the first time that Terhune was dying. "There was an overwhelming sense of finality about that moment," he said.

During the visit, Terhune promised to read and evaluate Mark's next book. And when it was sent to him, he responded with a note of fulsome praise: "You've done it. Just as I knew you could and would. *The Broken Circle* is gorgeous . . . tremendous . . . a masterwork." Then followed the inevitable bit of self-denigration: "And all the time I'm writing this clumsy praise, your knowledge of me and my own so-called work tells you that my admiration is worthless from a literary viewpoint."

But soon the traveling would pall and they would both feel the call of Sunnybank. And always, when they turned their car toward home, there came that same gladness that Terhune had felt as a child of five or six. It never had left him—the joy of knowing that he was on his way back to Sunnybank.

He had expressed his longing in one short paragraph of a piece of inconsequential fiction he had written many years earlier:

Spring was in the brain. Soon it would be in the air. I found myself picturing my loved Pompton mountains all radiant in a shimmering misty green-and-pink veil;—hearing in imagination the beat of the male swans' wings against the water as they battled all over the lake;—smelling the million blended scents of the young wet forest;—dreaming of shad and of bock.

One of those pleasant short motor trips almost killed Terhune. He had made what was to be his last radio appearance in April, 1941, on the very popular network program "The Cavalcade of America," for which he wrote and narrated a script about the life of Henry Bergh, founder of the Humane Society. The long hours of rehearsal required to synchronize his narration with the cast of radio actors used in the dramatization and the tension of preparing the major program took its toll on the ailing writer. The end of the broadcast left him in a state of near-exhaustion. But he was buoyed by his anticipation of a long-planned trip with Anice to Williamsburg. After a couple of days to rest from the exertion of the radio show, they left on the trip. Terhune, according to his wife, was feeling better than he had in weeks.

The first night, however, they stopped over at a hotel in Washington and Terhune became violently ill with food poisoning. Mrs. Terhune blamed it on mushrooms he had enjoyed that day with a steak at a small roadside restaurant, despite her warnings on taking a chance on the food. Doctors were summoned to the hotel and managed to bring the food poisoning under control, but Terhune had a heart attack and went into a coma. A heart specialist told Mrs. Terhune that her husband was dying. She insisted that an oxygen tent be set up in the hotel room, even though the doctors felt it was hopeless.

"I just couldn't let him die like that, away from home and among strangers!" she wrote later. Though it was the middle of the night, an oxygen tent was obtained and set up in the room. For two days they waited, and she remembered praying constantly, "Dear God, if he must go, please, *please* let me get him home to Sunnybank first!"

After two days, with Terhune still in a coma, the doctors decided they could chance moving him to a Washington hospital. The place was so crowded that the only spot for Anice to sleep was on a cot crammed into the bathroom of her husband's hospital room.

Two more days passed and Terhune began to regain consciousness. He showed improvement and some of his old spirit, asking when he would be well enough to be taken home. The heart specialist, according to Anice, said to her: "We can only call this a miracle, Mrs. Terhune. For when they get that far, they don't come back!"

It now was May, 1941. Though this time the trip was made by ambulance, Bert Terhune returned again to Sunnybank.

28

The final few months of Albert Payson Terhune's life were spent at Sunnybank in the haze of approaching, inevitable death. As the autumn of 1941 arrived, Terhune regained some of his strength after his collapse in Washington, but he obviously was nearing the end. There was no question of it in Anice's mind and probably not in his, although they did not speak of it. She stated later that Bert expressed optimism about getting well until just a few days before he died.

The bear of a man, with appetite to match, no longer cared to eat. He had lost more than 100 pounds. Drinking and smoking no longer interested him, either. He had been fond of long, thick cigars; now he would only puff occasionally on a cigarette for a few moments. He was, said Anice later, "gentle, polite, uncomplaining, but not interested."

Right up to the end, though, Terhune continued to be a working writer. Longer works were out of the question, of course, and even short magazine articles were beyond him. But he still managed to type out, or on bad days to dictate, the brief little "Tales of Real Dogs" for the McNaught Syndicate, which had bought his work for so many years.

In these waning days, these tenderly ebbing days, he seemed to hold ever tighter to his beloved Sunnybank. They rarely left The Place now. For hours, Bert and Anice—whenever the autumn weather was warm enough—would sit quietly on the old veranda, holding hands, and looking out across the familiar "fire-blue lake" to the Ramapo Mountains beyond. Often they would sit for long intervals without speaking, just touching each moment as it passed them by.

When winter approached, a winter that was to plunge the country into a new global war, they would go into the loved old house and sit there, and wait. Bert, when he felt comfortable enough, would read or listen to Anice play the piano for him, as she had for forty years. Or she would busy herself with her collection of ancient parchment music sheets, sometimes pausing to show her husband an interesting discovery.

Bert still took an interest in the upkeep of his home. One decision which for a while kept his mind off his condition was the purchase of a modern refrigerator to replace the huge, ancient icebox that covered one entire wall of the Sunnybank kitchen. When the new refrigerator was delivered, Anice—whose knowledge of things mechanical was as limited as Bert's—peered inside it and protested, "You can't tell me those little ice cubes are going to keep that big refrigerator cold!"

Around Thanksgiving, 1941, Terhune underwent still another operation. It was to be his last surgery although he would undergo many more blood transfusions. He remained in the hospital for several weeks, then was brought back to Sunnybank just before Christmas for his sixty-ninth birthday.

Christmas always had been the most special time of the year at Sunnybank. Each year Anice composed a carol which was imprinted on a Christmas card that also featured a new photograph of Sunnybank and was sent to their many friends. In her honor, the choir at church would sing the original carol at Christmas services. Strolling carolers were welcomed at Sunnybank on Christmas Eve and fresh cookies and hot chocolate always were ready for them. And for his December 21st birthday, Bert would welcome the small band of newspapermen for his holiday press conference and his predictions of world events. On Christmas Day, Bert would telephone his minister and ask permission to call so that he and Anice could enjoy watching the minister's children open their presents.

But at Christmas, 1941, Anice could not gather her thoughts to compose the carol. And Bert was too sick to invite the newspapermen. Nobody cared about his predictions any more because in a world two weeks past Pearl Harbor the more dire predictions had come to pass. There was a war to be fought and a military disaster to be overcome. No one would heed the self-indulgent prophecies of a sick, tired old writer in a faded house among the New Jersey hills.

On Christmas Eve, Bert watched from the couch as Anice trimmed their traditional tree in the living room and then, as had been their custom for forty-one years, Bert completed the trimming by putting the last bit of decoration into place. There was a quiet peace about Bert now; the old irritability and occasional abruptness were gone for good. He told Anice that this birthday and Christmas were the nicest he had ever had. And he said to her several times, "I did not know anyone could be as happy as we are!"

Anice and the two faithful maids, the Andrasse sisters who had been with them for thirty years, looked after his every need, but he asked for little. He was content just to take every additional minute that was given to him to be with those he loved, at Sunnybank. By now, he could walk only with the aid of a cane and he became continually weaker, but he remained cheerful. Reading took more strength and patience than he could summon, so he and his wife spent much of their time listening to the radio. Their special favorite was an amateur talent program for children that originated in New York City; they listened to it with great enjoyment each week.

A few weeks before he died, Bert had a last reunion with his beloved nephew, Fritz Van de Water. The two men sat together in the living room at Sunnybank, drinking Scotch and talking over old times. It was a great tonic for Bert and they stayed up most of the night. After Bert's death, Van de Water wrote of his uncle: "At heart, he never seemed more than 25. . . . He loved good food, good drink, good revelry and laughter." Then, writing of that last visit together:

"He was in almost constant pain, but he had the strength of an elephant and a mighty will to live. He knew his number was up, yet on that night of our reunion he showed not only no trace of self-pity but no hint of surrender or of resignation. Writing was his avocation; living—zestfully, gaily, strongly—was his occupation."

Bert Terhune's death at Sunnybank was described in the following words by his wife in her reminiscences, published the year after his death:

When the knowledge came to him, three days before he died, that he must leave me, he had no fear for himself—only wonder. The strong, unshakeable faith that was so great a part of him never wavered.

"This is very strange," he said. Then—"I've played the game the best I know how."

His only concern was that he must leave me. His only wish was to have me close beside him, as I was, through all those last precious hours. His mind was perfectly clear throughout. . . .

Over and over he murmured:

"I shall come back. I shall be here at Sunnybank with you always. I promise you that! When you walk in the rose garden I shall be there with you! When you wander about the place, when you sit by the pool, when you sit on the veranda and watch our 'Light at Eventide' I shall be with you—I shall surely be here! You must believe me!"

Albert Payson Terhune died at Sunnybank at 8:00 A.M. on Wednesday, February 18, 1942. The official certificate of death listed the causes as pulmonary edema, myocarditis, and carcinoma. Funeral services were scheduled for the following Saturday. The ceremonies would be at Sunnybank and burial would be in the graveyard behind the Pompton Reformed Church in the little tree-shaded plot that he and Anice had prepared for themselves, 50 yards or so from the other family graves.

Terhune lay in state in a casket that was placed in front of the fireplace in the living room he had made so famous in his writings. He was dressed in a beautiful red robe that had been a favorite of his.

The funeral was attended by 250 persons and there were 20 honorary pallbearers. Bert Terhune left Sunnybank for the last time in a hearse that slowly climbed the twisting drive through the hillside oaks, passed through the entrance gates and onto the highway now bearing his name, the road that Terhune had both loved and hated and on which he almost had been killed by a speeding car. Then slowly down the long hillside above the lake, past the old dam, and onto the quiet streets of the small town he had called home. Those who rode in the procession to the cemetery still remember the infinitesimally slow pace at which they moved toward the church cemetery. The funeral procession was led by a platoon of marching policemen that held the speed to near-zero.

Throughout the solemn proceedings, Anice Terhune remained composed and gracious. She had been brought up to believe that one did not give vent to deep emotions in public. Neither she nor Bert's daughter wept during the services.

At the cemetery the mourners gathered around the gravesite. It was a bitterly cold day and very windy. Anice walked up to each pallbearer just before the rites of final commitment began and told them it was not necessary for them to remove their hats. "I don't want you to catch cold," she said.

The local newspaper, the Pompton Lakes *Bulletin,* gave Terhune's death front-page treatment under the headline: DEATH OF ALBERT PAYSON TERHUNE WIDELY MOURNED BY TOWNSPEOPLE. The story said that, in his honor, the library of the Pompton Lakes High School would be named for him.

His death was reported in newspapers all across America but in those cases it hardly was headline news, for the country was suffering bitter defeats in a new world war and the passing of a retired writer of dog stories was not worth much space. But the few paragraphs reporting his death were carried throughout the world by the news services and almost every paper in this country as well as many in other countries made space for the brief account. Obituary notes appeared in *Time* and *Newsweek,* and in book trade and library publications such as *Publishers Weekly* and the *Wilson Library Bulletin.* His death also rated an editorial eulogy in the New York *Herald-Tribune:* "To his friends he seemed perpetually youthful and full of an unquenchable zest for life. Until his virtual retirement five years ago, he drove himself relentlessly at his task of writing. Just as he believed in discipline for his dogs, so he practiced discipline for himself. Hard work and plenty of it was his fare. He throve on it, spiritually and financially."

Scattered around the United States, a country frightened by the savagery of a new world conflict, there were some thousands of people who read of Terhune's death and went on to other items. Then, with a soft tug of memory, they returned for a moment to the obituary account and remembered why the name had sounded familiar. For a few seconds, the Pacific bloodshed was set aside while faint remembrances of a verdant lakeside place came back to mind, and valiant collies. And . . . wasn't there someone called the Master?

Beyond those casual readers of the news, there were others, a lesser number probably, who needed no reminders about the name. The news startled them, then made them feel deeply sad. For something strangely personal had been extinguished from their own lives and they realized it, although they perhaps could not quite define it.

29

The Visitor drove the rental car slowly through the residential streets of Pompton Lakes, New Jersey. The streets were quiet on this weekday winter's afternoon. People were at work, of course, and the biting cold probably kept many others indoors. He passed the monument to the dead of the Spanish-American War. And the Civil War cannon used in Grant's Wilderness Campaign on display along with the cannonballs captured from the Confederates. And the Freedom Bell honoring the dead of World War II and the Korean War.

He drove past block after block of small, neat homes until he arrived at the intersection of Ringwood Avenue and the Paterson-Hamburg Turnpike and his destination, the final resting place of Albert Payson Terhune.

The Visitor found himself reluctant and somehow apprehensive as he drove up to the Pompton Reformed Church and saw behind it, in the sunlit December coldness, the graveyard that he sought. He didn't like to visit cemeteries. He had never been able to conquer his childhood fear or distaste or anguish at such places. He always preferred to turn away, to keep his car going on down the road.

But he knew that he must see Terhune's grave. He didn't know just why. Terhune, after all, would not know he was there—even if he did he probably would regard him as another of those hated intruders who so disturbed his serenity for years and were the unceasing targets of his hatred and wrath.

The car slowed to a crawl as The Visitor drove along the wide roadway leading to the parking lot at the rear of the church, for the drive was slick with a stubbornly surviving layer of ice. He parked and walked into the door marked Church Office, wondering if he would be received inside as some sort of ghoulish curiosity-seeker, intent on peering at the grave of a long-gone local celebrity.

"Of course," the pleasant, middle-aged church secretary smiled. "If you'll sit and wait for just a few minutes, I'll have one of our caretakers show you the grave." She paused and then, as if sensing his faint discomfort, said quietly, "We have many visitors to Mr. Terhune's grave. They come every now and then, year after year. He certainly has devoted readers, doesn't he?"

The Visitor's feet made a sharp, percussive, crunching sound as he followed the man along a path of the cemetery behind the church. He shivered in the cutting edge of a torrent of winter air off the nearby Ramapo slope and looked with envy at the bulky work clothes and thick mackinaw worn by the workman ahead, who strode apparently impervious to the razor wind.

"Right here," said the man, and pointed to a small enclave over at one side of the graveyard. It was almost a little glen, set aside from the neat rows of headstones that covered the rest of the cemetery by the small trees and shrubs which hovered protectingly around it. "If you won't be needin' me?" he asked politely, then moved back along the lane toward the church building, his thick boots slapping resoundingly on the hard surface.

The Visitor stood still at the edge of the glen, wondering for a moment what was expected of him. What does one do when one comes to pay homage at the grave of a dead writer? What is the proper fashion to salute the resting place of a man you have never met or seen, but who, in some ineffable way, has managed to reach you, guide you, thrill you, and bring you at times to tears. He thought for an instant that perhaps he should bow his head and say some kind of prayer, but the only thing he could think of was the Twenty-third Psalm and he felt instantly foolish, standing shivering, rooted there in the midst of tumbling December wind and sunshine, with automobiles sliding past on the street alongside the cemetery, their drivers looking at him with mild curiosity. So, for want of anything more appropriate, he just stood and stared at the burial place.

It was a large, handsome gravestone there in the midst of the tiny cluster of trees and small shrubs. The stone was in the shape of a big cross. At either side of the base were two smaller stones, marking the graves of Bert and Anice Terhune. Bert's stone, in addition to his name and the dates of birth and death, bore the inscription: I HAVE FOUGHT A GOOD FIGHT. *And on Anice's stone was inscribed:* I HAVE KEPT THE FAITH. *The phrases were apt ones for these graves. They represented the beginning and end of one of the Terhune family's favorite Biblical quotations, from 2nd Timothy: "I have fought a good fight. I have finished my course. I have kept the faith."*

The Visitor silently saluted them for a few minutes, nodded in completion and farewell, and walked back over to the main pathway that bisected the cemetery. He glanced back at the little glen with its imposing cross one more time as if to convince himself that here really rested the fabled Master and Mistress of Sunnybank. From out of a thousand memory-misted days in his childhood, they had come to this, under the frozen ground of a New Jersey churchyard. Even shining memories were mortal. Even people in stories have their rendezvous with earth.

He walked along the path toward the other end of the cemetery. They had told him, in the office, where he would find the large Terhune family plot. There were no glens over here, no sheltering little protective rings of trees and bushes; only the neat squared-off rows of graves with their weathered old stones.

They were all there together, back across the cold grave rows from Bert and Anice, the old family reunited again. The Reverend Edward Payson Terhune, born 1830, died 1907. Mary Virginia Terhune, born 1830, died 1922. Bert Terhune's sisters were buried there too.

And then The Visitor saw the grave of Bert Terhune's daughter. She is buried next to her mother, the young wife who died at twenty-three a few days after giving birth, having tasted less than a year of marriage to a giant young newspaperman who dreamed of writing great books.

The Visitor shivered again in the cold. What was he doing here, he wondered, standing in the pale stillness of a frozen winter's day in the north of New Jersey, a thousand miles from home, looking at the headstones of long-dead strangers? Why was he sad and at the same time curious and more than a little fascinated at the legends of life and death engraved on the stones of people he had only read about, and whose mortality was displayed now before him like a trophy?

And why did there recur in him, again and again, a flooding sensation of loneliness? Not his own. But the loneliness of people who had drifted apart through time and now had all come back together again, when it was too late to smile or wave or gently embrace.

30

Lorraine Virginia Terhune Stevens. Bert Terhune's only child. "The daughter that Terhune refused to acknowledge," as one of her friends described her.

Despite all the hundreds of thousands of words that Terhune wrote about Sunnybank and the people who lived there, he wrote very little, ever, about Lorraine. His autobiography, published in 1930 when Lorraine was almost thirty-two years old, contains only a few passing references to "my daughter." In *The Book of Sunnybank,* published a few years later, one chapter opens with the words, "When my daughter was a child, she spoke of Sunnybank's birds and non-canine animals as 'the little people.' " Nothing more.

Anice Terhune, in her own published reminiscence of her husband's life and their life together, says little of Lorraine. There is a brief anecdote about how Bert kept the wedding party waiting while he got dressed for Lorraine's ceremony, but that's about all.

Why did Terhune, in effect, refuse to acknowledge his daughter? In part perhaps because of his own attitude toward the girl. He never seemed able to love her wholeheartedly—possibly because she was not the son he had wanted so much, possibly because he never could forget his old feeling that her birth had caused her mother's death. But the main reason, most likely, for the shadow in which Lorraine lived was the recognition by Terhune that Anice could not bear to be reminded that her husband had been married before. And he could not bring himself to hurt his wife. Of course they could have treated Lorraine as "their" daughter and proclaimed her to the world (in her father's writings) that way. But Anice apparently just couldn't fully accept the child of another woman as her own. A portrayal of one big happy family just wouldn't wash and Terhune must have known it. Instead, he chose to relegate his daughter to a background position.

After Lorraine grew up and lived away from her parents, Bert and Anice rarely mentioned her when speaking to friends or relatives. Several people who saw the Terhunes frequently said that Lorraine just never came into the conversations. Fritz Van de Water was Terhune's nephew and boon companion and the two families often visited each other at their respective homes in New Jersey and Vermont. Yet, Van de Water's son said recently that he never knew of Lorraine's existence until he was almost a teen-ager and saw her only once—at her father's funeral. His only memory of her is that she had reddish hair and wore a great deal of makeup.

In addition to the omission of Lorraine from Terhune's voluminous writings about Sunnybank, there was another, quite poignant, fact: Terhune invented a fictional son for himself. Just as Terhune and his wife always were referred to in the stories as the Master and the Mistress, the child was called the Boy. He made his first appearance in a story called "One Minute Longer," which was published in 1921 in the collection *Buff: A Collie.* The boy in the story was fifteen years old.

Some students of Terhune's life have speculated that the Boy was modeled after William Friend, the real-life son of Robert Friend, long-time superintendent at Sunnybank, who lived with his family in the gatehouse at the entrance. That may be, but there is no question that the Boy in the several Sunnybank stories in which he appeared was intended to be the son of the Master and the Mistress. He referred to them as "Dad" and "Mother." One can sense the deep hurt Lorraine must have felt to read the stories about life at Sunnybank with a fictitious boy taking her place.

There was one story that might be considered an exception. It is called "Runaway" and appeared in the collection *My Friend the Dog*, published in 1926. Its heroine is a ten-year-old girl who is given the name Fay Denning. She lives with her parents, who breed show collies at an unnamed place that is obviously Sunnybank:

"The morning sun was striking athwart the fire-blue lake. A sluicing rain of the night before had washed the springtime world clean of a week's dust and filled it with a hundred fresh odors. It was hard, on such a morning, to sit primly on the veranda, in one's best clothes, waiting for the car to come around and keeping Ronny from straying into the lake or over the plowed ground of the rose-garden."

It was not one of Terhune's better yarns. Yet the story is significant for its use of a young girl at Sunnybank, whether the Place is called that or not, as its key figure. This was perhaps the only time that Terhune fictionally utilized his daughter in the way that had made his wife and himself so beloved to their legions of fans.

Terhune's old longing for a son never had left him. The boy that he so eagerly hoped for during his first wife's pregnancy was always there to torment him. Among the Terhune papers is an article he wrote for a New York City newspaper in the 1920s in which he used the words, "as I have no living son . . ." And in *The Book of Sunnybank*, he wrote: "I wish I had a living son to carry on. A son who would have inherited our stark Sunnybank complex."

A living son. Was it possible that the use of those words indicated that Bert and Anice Terhune did once have a son, perhaps a child that died in birth or infancy? None of the people who knew them well can recall any mention of such a tragedy. The references in his writings to a living son may have been to distinguish reality from the fictional son about whom Terhune had written. At a deeper level, Terhune may have used this phrase to convince himself, finally, painfully, that the son of whom he had dreamed for so long was gone for good now, no longer even a hope.

Many people have wondered why Bert and Anice Terhune never had children of their own. The reason for their childlessness never was discussed with anyone, not even very close friends and relatives, in an era when proper people kept their own counsel about such matters. It could have been a case of physical incapacity. Bert had proven his ability to sire a child, so if there was a physiological reason why a child could not have been conceived, it likely would have involved Anice.

Some observers of the Terhunes and their lives, especially those who knew of and criticized Lorraine's treatment by her father and stepmother, have suggested that the lack of children could have been a conscious decision unrelated to physical problems, stemming from Anice's obsessive and dominating love of her husband and her unwillingness to abide any competition for his love, even from children to whom she could have given birth.

Such arguments are entirely speculative. It is true that Bert's life was guided to a great extent by Anice's decisions and by his overwhelming desire to keep her happy and content. But it is rather hard to believe that, given his powerful longing for a son, he would accede to a request from Anice that they remain childless for no other reason than that Anice preferred it that way. It is possible, of course, that she deluded him into an acceptance of her decision by telling him that her health would not permit her to go through a pregnancy (which could have been true). The collateral question of their failure to adopt a child also remains unanswered.

There is another line of speculation that comes into discussions of the Terhunes at this point. It is based entirely on hunches and guesswork; there is no evidence for it. Yet it recurs now and then among some of the Terhunes' relatives and those who knew the couple well.

Could the reason for their childlessness have been that Bert and Anice had a marriage blessed with a mutual love of rare intensity, but a marriage entirely without sex? Some who knew Anice Terhune well have described her as "a professional virgin" in terms of her manner, her appearance, her attitudes. Others of a more Freudian bent have pointed to her dress—her lifelong propensity for wearing frilly dresses of white, off-white, or very light pink. Was this an outer manifestation of her feelings about herself as the most virginal of virgins? Did she and her husband have what has been termed a "white marriage," in which they kept their love entirely on what they deemed to be a more spiritual plane?

All this of course is speculation of the rankest sort. Bert Terhune was a big, virile, athletic man with very old-fashioned ideas about masculinity and what it meant to be "a man's man." It is difficult to believe that he did not have a concomitant attitude toward sex. Why would he enter into a sexless marriage; or, if the marriage became so later, why did he remain in it? If there is anything to this thought, perhaps the reason simply was that he loved Anice too much to do otherwise. During his lifetime, vague rumors were heard that Bert Terhune was not averse to an occasional fling with another woman. He had had, the rumors said, more than one affair with show business stars he had come to know. But such stories never got past the idle rumor stage and it is very possible that they deserve no credence at all. There is no evidence to support them and such gossip, after all, is the common heritage of almost every celebrity. If there were any truth to the guessing about a sexless marriage with Anice, however, it could explain a need for an occasional outside escapade in spite of his deep love for his wife.

The only hard evidence on the whole question is that the Terhunes were known to have separate bedrooms on the second floor of the old house at Sunnybank. But this was an arrangement hardly uncommon among people of the Terhune's financial and social status and proves nothing.

The child that Bert Terhune *did* father grew up with a deepening sense of disappointment in him for his lack of real interest in her and with a feeling of separateness from Anice Terhune that gradually turned into an abiding dislike, although the two rivals for Bert's affections remained always on speaking terms and were civil with each other. Anice apparently made it quite obvious to Lorraine from the time she was a small child that she resented her and would not tolerate Lorraine coming between herself and Bert. It is not surprising that Lorraine came to nurture the belief then and always that her father never loved Anice as he had her own mother and that Bert never stopped mourning the loss of the first Lorraine. In adult life, though she rarely discussed her family relationships, Lorraine occasionally made such a comment to her close friends.

Lorraine spent most of the first eight years of her life living happily with her grandmother and grandfather Terhune, as well as some periods of time at the homes of her aunts, Virginia Van de Water and Christine Herrick. Summers and the Christmas holidays were spent at Sunnybank with her parents and they visited her frequently at her grandmother's apartment. At about the age of eight, Lorraine finally came to live with Bert and Anice. She was growing into a bright, attractive child with a quicksilver wit. She was popular with other children and a good student at the Graham School in Manhattan, the respected private school in which she had been enrolled.

Lorraine and her paternal grandmother remained very close until the aged woman's death in 1922. When Lorraine was thirteen, the elder Mrs. Terhune devotedly nursed the child to recovery from a bout with diphtheria; Mrs. Terhune was eighty-one years old at the time.

At Sunnybank, Lorraine developed a fondness for all the animals, but she never displayed her father's intense love for the dogs there. She played with Lad and Wolf and enjoyed them, but much of her time was spent galloping around The Place on one of the horses. As she grew into adolescence, the distance between herself and her parents increased. She grew ever more resentful of Anice and more determined to get out of her parents' household.

Lorraine became a young woman of considerable beauty. She had the determined chin that so dominated her father's face and her grandmother's, but it did not mar her looks. She was of medium height, well built, and had chestnut hair. Her mind had quickly matured and she was showing some signs of the old family inheritance of writing ability. Bert was pleased at this and encouraged her, telling her that he would be glad to open publishing doors for her. Lorraine was gregarious and funny. Her wit was brash, sometimes tinged with acid, and often irreverent, which further antagonized her prim, proper, Victorian stepmother. She loved parties and dancing and good conversation. Her friends called her "Larry."

Lorraine graduated from the Graham School in 1916. The war had begun in Europe and Lorraine and a school friend signed up for a Red Cross course in nursing. She did well in the course and announced to her parents that she was thinking seriously of becoming a nurse or possibly even studying medicine. Bert was angry and upset. He wanted her to be a writer, not a nurse. He just couldn't accept the idea of his daughter not writing when she obviously had ability and perhaps could become a major woman writer as her grandmother had been. He and Anice also held to old notions that it somehow lacked propriety for a young woman of good family to go out into the world and work at a regular job such as nursing. Writing at home seemed much more refined.

The argument was settled with a compromise. Lorraine could begin nursing studies on the condition that she would seriously give writing a try after the war was over.

Lorraine became a nursing student at Columbia-Presbyterian Hospital in New York City and successfully completed the course. After the war, she kept her promise to her parents by making some sporadic efforts to write short stories, none of which was published, but meanwhile she remained on the nursing staff at Columbia-Presbyterian. It was during this time that she met her future husband and also that she first learned she had diabetes.

Franklin Augustus Stevens was a graduate of the State University of Iowa College of Medicine, an internist who had begun practice in New York City and was on the staff at Columbia-Presbyterian. He was thirty-two years old when he and Lorraine, who was twenty-four, were married in June, 1923, at Pompton Lakes.

Dr. Stevens was a small man, not much taller than his bride, quiet and very reserved. Those who could get close to him usually called him "Steve." His personality was radically different from Lorraine's. She was the happy-go-lucky one who constantly kept everybody laughing.

Their life together was short, only about two years. Friends could offer no reason for their separation except that they were such different types of personality. The breakup was an amicable one and they continued to have occasional contact on the telephone, although they rarely saw each other. For unexplained reasons they did not get a divorce. Neither was Catholic, but in those days any divorce was considered a minor sort of scandal and perhaps neither wanted to be the subject of such discussion.

Lorraine continued to work as a nurse for a time, supervising the dispensary at the New York Telephone Company. But her diabetes was becoming a problem and eventually prevented her from further full-time work, so she decided to give writing a more serious try.

Apparently she had no luck in selling her work during the 1920s. Her efforts were entirely on her own since she had refused to take advantage of her father's offers of help. Living alone in Manhattan,

Lorraine still kept as much distance as possible from her parents. She found herself regarding her father more and more as a pompous windbag, full of pious sentiments that had no basis in conviction. She thought his writing mediocre, his success not really deserved. She did not advertise the fact that she was Bert Terhune's daughter in her circle of friends and continued always to use the name of Lorraine Stevens.

She despised Anice. When mentioning her to her friends, she would scathingly refer to her as "Dear Little Anus." She stayed away from Sunnybank as much as she could, except for the visits she felt obligated to make, such as at Christmas. When Bert and Anice returned from one of their many trips, Lorraine was expected to (and usually did) come out to Sunnybank to see them and to hear the compulsory detailed account of their travels. After one such visit she wrote a letter to a good friend in which she described, with a slashing, angry humor, the duty call she had made on Bert and Anice, and the "constipated pink earrings" she had been given as a memento of their trip.

It is likely that Bert and Anice felt they were acting quite properly toward Lorraine, as dutiful parents. They gave her a token gift when they returned from a trip, they presented her with an appropriate Christmas gift, and she was always welcome at Sunnybank. And they gave her financial assistance to enable her to continue her independent life in New York City. Just how much they gave her is not known. Lorraine felt that, in spite of her father's considerable wealth, they were extremely niggardly in their allowance to her. Her friends angrily told each other that the Terhunes supported Lorraine so penuriously the girl sometimes didn't have enough money to buy food. The friends would help her out with money or food on occasion. Once, for Christmas, two of her married friends gave her a meal ticket at a neighborhood restaurant so she could be assured of eating well for a time at least.

In fairness, it isn't clear whether Bert and Anice Terhune were aware of Lorraine's periodic money shortages. They made sure her rent was paid and gave her something extra to live on. Beyond that, they apparently didn't inquire and Lorraine was too proud to come to them for help when she was strapped. She also was not the type to husband her money with any great care.

On one occasion a friend of Lorraine wrote to Anice reprimanding her for her lack of concern for her stepdaughter. The letter warned that Lorraine was not eating properly due to lack of funds. Anice rather wearily replied that Lorraine frequently was sent money by her parents, sometimes as much as $1,000 at a time, and that all she had to do to solve her living problems was to move back to Sunnybank where she would be properly cared for.

Generally, though, Lorraine apparently lived a happy, rather care-free, near-Bohemian sort of existence in the late 1920s and 1930s. Except for an occasional interlude of illness when her diabetes flared up, she spent much of her time going to parties or entertaining friends in her small apartment and, whenever she could scrape up the money, going to the theater, which—like her father—she deeply enjoyed. She ran with a literary set. Mystery writer Dashiell Hammett was one of her good friends; another was Don Blanding, an author, artist, and lecturer who was known as the "Vagabond Poet." Blanding used to refer to Lorraine as "the rowdy duchess."

She dated men, sometimes went with one man for a time, and engaged in occasional sexual relationships. But she always managed to avoid serious romantic entanglements and, so far as is known, never gave any thought to ending her marriage legally to Dr. Stevens or remarrying.

In the early 1930s, Lorraine suddenly achieved some success with her writing. She was living at 318 Lexington Avenue in a narrow five-story building of small apartments. In March, 1933, *Good Housekeeping* published a story of hers called "Friend of the Bride?" and the following year she had another story published in *Good Housekeeping* and two in *McCall's.* She was selling to the country's major magazines, but it was a very limited output by any writer's standards. Her health kept her from any sustained, continuous writing. And even her most loyal friends admitted that Lorraine was very lazy and would turn to her typewriter only when she began getting desperate about money. Her approach to life was casual—she lived as best she could on her small income, depending on the largesse of friends and the allowance from her parents to rescue her when necessary.

She sold seven short stories during the period 1933 to 1937, to *Good Housekeeping* and *McCall's*. Her writing began to attract some attention and she became a client of the literary agent Elsie McKeogh. There were several indications that her fiction was finding a receptive audience. The December, 1934, issue of *Good Housekeeping* carried Lorraine's name on the front cover, along with the more important contributors to that issue, such as mystery writer Mary Roberts Rinehart.

The January, 1936, issue of *McCall's* included this short biographical sketch of her in the front of the magazine:

Lorraine Stevens' wide popularity offers contemporary proof of the adage about building a better mousetrap than your neighbor. The author of only five short stories, she is nonetheless her readers' choice in the field of young love fiction. "For a long time people had urged me to write," she submits. "They insisted that I could. That was their story and I was stuck with it." Happily so for you, as your many letters indicate. Her novelette, *Wherever You are,* should confirm your faith in this brilliant writer. Born in New York, Miss Stevens was educated there. After college she spent three years in training in a large city hospital where she observed life minutely, a circumstance that may explain the appeal of her stories.

Not surprisingly, there was no mention of her famous father; the chances are that the editors of *McCall's* were not aware of the relationship. Terhune went on asking her to let him help advance her writing career, but she always refused. He told a few friends that his daughter was a much better writer than he was. She agreed with him.

Later in 1936, *McCall's* again accorded her the recognition of a brief personal note and a small photo. "New York is her home," the item read, "and the scene of her triumphs which add up to a good many in the light of her years. She is a graduate nurse, a bacteriologist and has worked in industrial medicine. She writes some of the best short stories of the day."

Lorraine's short stories were quite typical of the women's magazine fare of that time—romantic, rather innocuous—but written with an undoubted flair and sophistication. There was nothing in them remotely resembling the work of her father—no dogs, no violence, no melodrama, certainly no Sunnybank. Each story had the obligatory young woman heroine, attractive and bright, usually nearing or just past thirty, with a troubled marriage, or recently divorced or jilted. The description of the heroine in her first *Good Housekeeping* story reads much like a self-portrait: " . . . with her level gray eyes and her sensitive and scornful mouth. With her brittleness and wit, and her recklessness and sweetness. With her arrogance and her capacity for tenderness. With her long thoughts, and her pungent, flippant speech. With her man's sense of humor." Into each story soon came a handsome stranger and the tale wound on to its happy or sad ending. A few of the stories had a medical aspect: one concerns the wife of a surgeon, another is about a woman who works in a bacteriology lab.

Though none of the stories is about fathers or stepmothers or dogs, there are one or two tantalizing little finds in them that seem unmistakably related to Lorraine's own life. In her first published story, for example, she writes of the man loved by the heroine: "And that one year in his life that he never talked about—that young marriage twelve years ago, when he had been twenty-three, that had terminated with the death of Marie Louise, the one woman he ever completely loved, and whose bewildered little wraith never quite left him."

It may be straining coincidence only slightly to note that in the passage just quoted the name of the dead wife, which is not at all relevant to the story itself and does not appear again, is given as Marie Louise. The initials M.L. are a reversal of L.M., the initials of Lorraine Marguerite Terhune, the author's mother.

In one of her later *Good Housekeeping* stories, there is a minor character named Bert. The use of her father's name for him was hardly accidental. Bert Selby is the cousin of the story's heroine and is a fatuous social climber; he makes a habit of inviting artists, writers, and actors to dinner. The heroine is puzzled by these affairs: "She never quite knew what bait lured them there, but she had a darkening suspicion that their presence was due to a combination of lowered resistance, curiosity, and an earthly weakness for terrapin." (As it happened, terrapin was one of the specialties of Pauline Andrasse, the cook at Sunnybank, and frequently was served to guests there.) The heroine of the story goes unenthusiastically to her cousin's current dinner party and listens resignedly as Bert tells "one of his interminable stories."

Lorraine's brief foray into the literary world of major magazines ended late in 1937. Possibly the reason was her lack of interest in writing any more than she had to, perhaps it was her physical condition, or perhaps the creative well simply ran dry. Nothing more by her ever appeared in *Good Housekeeping* or *McCall's,* the two publications in which her short fiction had been published intermittently over a period of almost five years.

She still needed money to supplant her allowance from Bert and Anice. Her agent managed to get her an assignment from a movie magazine and then secured more work from similar publications. Most of it involved adapting the screenplays of Hollywood movies of the day into fictional prose form for publication in fan magazines. The adaptations—not too far removed from the sort of work her father had done early in his career—fed the hunger of the magazines' readers for romance and also served as good promotion for the films. The writing was easy for Lorraine and the money welcome. At times she would have three separate stories in one issue of a magazine, each under a different pseudonym. The movie magazine writing continued for a number of years and represented the only published writing that Lorraine did for the rest of her life.

As the 1930s ended, Lorraine was more than forty. Her father's condition, the obvious fact that he was mortally ill, seemed to have little effect on Lorraine's relationship either with him or with Anice. The wounds were too old and deep for there to be any sudden, sentimental healing. Lorraine's ever-ready wit always turned sardonic, and just a bit sneering, when the subject was her father. "Our Father Which Art in Pompton," she sometimes called him.

Once some old friends from Pompton Lakes called on her at her apartment. Lorraine was in another room as they entered and she yelled to them, "Take a look at the book on the coffee table. It's my father's new autobiography." They picked up the book. It was Bert Terhune's recently published story of Christ, *The Son of God.*

After her father's death, the two rivals for the love of Albert Payson Terhune, victor and vanquished, were left with only each other. There was no real change in the situation. Anice stayed on at Sunnybank, Lorraine in New York City. They got together on occasion; Lorraine still made the duty visit to The Place at Christmas, Anice would stop briefly at Lorraine's apartment when she came into

Manhattan for the theater or opera. Anice continued to send Lorraine an allowance, although Lorraine told her friends that the money was barely enough to cover her rent, with nothing left over on which to live.

Other than Christmas, special days were ignored by both of them. Anice once told a friend, a rather wistful tone in her voice, "I never get anything from Lorraine on Mother's Day." Then she lifted her chin and said firmly, "We just don't believe in that sort of thing."

One strangely contradictory bit of evidence about the relationship between Anice and Lorraine exists among the Terhune papers at the Library of Congress. In a neat scrapbook are congratulatory letters received by Anice from friends after the publication of her novel *The White Mouse,* in 1929. Among them, addressed to "Dear Mother," is a note from Lorraine, who had just read the book. The letter is brimming with praise for the novel; it appears to have been written with great warmth and love. Perhaps its significance was that the feeling of Lorraine for her stepmother varied from time to time. Or possibly Lorraine happened to be in particularly good spirits the day she wrote the letter and felt charitable toward Anice. In any case it represents a tiny oasis of warmth amidst years of hard feelings.

In 1950 Lorraine moved to an apartment in a dingy, narrow, four-story brownstone building at 25 East 39th Street. She remained there until her death. Her last home was only a few minutes' walk from the main New York Public Library where her father's eager fans kept his books in constant circulation, though he had been dead by then for almost a decade.

Her life continued much as it had before, but as the years passed Lorraine stayed more at home. She no longer was the party goer she once had been and the laughing groups of friends didn't come storming into her apartment as they used to. But the good friends, the closest ones, stayed loyal to her. They took her to lunch or dinner now and then, or to the theater, and sometimes turned over some used but still good clothing to her. Once they bought her a new typewriter after hers had broken down and she had nothing on which to do her writing.

Much of Lorraine's time during the last years of her life was spent at home reading. Books overflowed the tiny rooms of her apartment.

She still wrote occasionally for the movie magazines and sometimes took on an odd job, such as working as an election official at a polling place. The only constant companion of the daughter of the great apostle of dogs was a cat: she had one living with her all the time and was very devoted to it. She told her friends that she wasn't particularly fond of dogs and especially had no use for collies.

Always fascinated by the world around her, she kept up with politics and world events and read her favorite newspaper, the New York *Herald-Tribune,* almost from front page to back every day. Shortly before his death, Bert Terhune had asked his agent and business adviser Bruce Chapman to meet with him. He had a special favor to ask, he told Chapman: "When I die, will you be sure to notify my daughter? She never reads the newspaper, doesn't know what's going on. Will you please see her in person and make sure she knows of my death?" Chapman assured Terhune he would do so. But a few weeks later, Terhune contacted Chapman again and told him to forget the whole thing. No one knows why Terhune made the request (did he believe that Anice would deliberately fail to notify Lorraine?) or why he mistakenly thought that Lorraine did not read the newspaper and keep up with events.

Terhune's comment about his daughter caused Chapman to believe that perhaps Lorraine was an alcoholic. Others who knew Terhune had heard similar rumors and among Terhune fans such stories have persisted to the present day. But two of her closest friends have said that such stories were totally false. Lorraine was only a social drinker, they said. Her favorite drink was sherry and she never drank to excess.

During the 1950s Lorraine's health grew worse. The diabetes brought her low from time to time although she kept it under some control with insulin, which she took by self-injection. She was a heavy smoker, but was forced to stop for periods of time when she was stricken with a respiratory disease, possibly asthma, possibly emphysema. When she needed medication, she would telephone Dr. Stevens and he would send the necessary prescription to her.

Through all this, Lorraine remained unruffled and reasonably content with her lot, though she did get very concerned at times when her financial situation grew desperate. She would contact one friend or another and say quietly, "Could I borrow fifteen dollars? I'm in a spot." During such periods she would resort to sleeping pills to get some rest.

Toward the end of her life Lorraine told friends that she had begun work on a book. The way she referred to it made them think that it was an autobiographical novel, but after her death, no trace of the manuscript was found. Possibly she never actually had started it—or perhaps she thought better of it and destroyed what she had written.

On the night of January 13, 1956, a neighbor who hadn't seen Lorraine in a couple of days got a passkey from the building superintendent and checked her apartment. She was lying unconscious on the floor. An ambulance rushed Lorraine to the city emergency hospital, Bellevue, where she was found to be in a diabetic coma. She died there shortly before midnight. She was fifty-seven years old.

Some time before her death, Lorraine had instructed a close friend, "If anything should happen to me, do not—under any circumstances—give them my stepmother's name." But officials at Bellevue did somehow learn that Anice Terhune was Lorraine's closest living relative and notified her of the death. Anice arranged to have Lorraine brought back to Pompton Lakes for burial.

Lorraine's small funeral was held at Sunnybank. The casket was placed in front of the famous fireplace in the famous living room. Only those who had been invited were present, about twenty or thirty friends of Lorraine and of the family. Dr. Stevens did not attend.

Anice Terhune was then eighty-three years old and almost deaf. She spoke in an unintentional shout. Just before the service began, she walked up to one of Lorraine's best friends and loudly demanded to know the whereabouts of a ring she had given to Lorraine years before. It had been an engagement present to her, Anice declared, and now she wanted it back. Another friend, overhearing the exchange, smiled and whispered that the ring had been in and out of pawnshops for years. He was so right. The ring had been Lorraine's only valuable possession and she had willed it to a married couple from Pompton Lakes, two of her oldest and dearest friends. They later found it in a Manhattan pawnshop where Lorraine had pawned it for $75.

Anice was confused and uncertain about where Lorraine should be buried. The place alongside Bert was of course reserved for herself and there were only two gravesites in that small plot. The question was resolved when Bert's nephew, Edward Terhune Van de Water, offered to give up his own plot in the Terhune section of the old church graveyard so that Lorraine could be laid to rest there, next to the mother she never had known.

Just six months after Lorraine's death, the man she had married in 1923, Dr. Stevens, died in New York City at the age of sixty-five. In a manner strangely synchronous with the lonely death of his long-estranged wife, private funeral services were held for the doctor, whose short newspaper obituary did not list any survivors.

31

The Visitor was preparing to leave Sunnybank, to drive slowly through the unfamiliar expressways back to the frozen metropolis, and then to the airport to begin the trip back home.

He stood at the edge of the lake and looked up the hill at the brooding, solitary old house, and then on up through the cold, empty trees to the gate and the road beyond.

The afternoon was fading and the lessening light only made the empty grounds seem more lonely, more dismal, and now even forbidding and unfriendly. The Visitor stood and looked up the hill in order to see one more perspective, one more view as they had seen it, back in the golden time.

He decided to examine one far corner of the estate that he had not yet seen. So, slowly, he walked along a lakeside path that went northward beyond the old barn, past the ruins of what must have been the little boathouse that Terhune used to mention.

As he gingerly made his way over the rough ground, The Visitor thought to himself with a shudder that he likely would freeze to death before anyone found him here, if he fell and broke a leg or kneecap. The Place was enveloped in the stillness of a late winter afternoon. Only the hum of passing cars from the road on the hill or the intermittent grunt of a tractor-trailer shifting gears on the grade broke the silence. The house above him was boarded up, dark and still. A furlong above, as Terhune used to phrase it, was the house at the gate, still occupied by a caretaker. But that house, too, was dark today and no one had answered his knock earlier when The Visitor sought to ask permission to walk into The Place. Off to the south, he could see the lights of the next house over, but it was far enough away that no one would ever hear a cry for rescue. And to the north, in the direction he was walking, were only scrub woods and underbrush.

He was, he realized, a fool to risk death by exposure in this doomed old estate in the middle of the New Jersey winter. But he kept walking, his strides short and anxious, along the bumpy path, his desire to see another part of Sunnybank overcoming his usual abundantly cautious approach to danger to life or limb.

The path took him past a few more dog graves, the earliest ones at Sunnybank, the ones where the pets of Terhune's parents were buried back in the late decades of the nineteenth century. A few more feet through the darkening woods and he came to a jumbled strand of barbed wire which obviously marked the northern limits of the property. The original Sunnybank must have extended a considerable distance further north, he knew, but this was the furthest limit of the smaller place that still survived. He looked around him at the trees and knew that this, too, was country redolent of Terhune, that these hillside undergrowths were the scenes of rescues of lost puppies by Lad or Bruce or Gray Dawn, or collies digging up grisly trophies they had buried here and proudly flinging them into the laps of the Terhunes or their horrified guests after seeing the pleased response to other gifts brought to the veranda. Whether such incidents had actually, historically happened didn't really matter to The Visitor, for they had come alive in the stories and now were buried deeply in the memories of those who had read about them; so they did enjoy a life still, and this was where they were born, on this frigid, sacred, silent ground.

The Visitor knew that his time was running out. He walked carefully back along the lake shore and then, having crossed the open point on which Terhune used to sit and write, worked his way slowly back up to the house.

He looked up at the boarded windows on the second and third floors of the

crumbling building and wondered what had happened to all the joy. He
wondered about time's ability to waste as well as to build, and the disappear-
ance of love and laughter, leaving only blasts of cold air, fragmenting stucco,
and knifelike wistaria that jabs unceasingly at unprotesting, breaking walls.

The Visitor walked to the edge of the famed old veranda. He put one foot
up on its edge and waited. Around him was only silence. He waited to hear
something—perhaps the distant sound of barking or a deep voice of greeting.
Only the angry, muted wind assailed his ears.

The Visitor spoke aloud, feeling all at the same time ridiculous, awed, and
expectant. "Bert, if you're here, won't you let me know?" he said softly. "I
feel your presence. Won't you speak to me and let me know?"

He stood there, one foot on the veranda, the other balanced on the ground
below, and waited for the voice as the darkness slowly closed down around him.

32

There was a curious epilogue to the life and death of Albert Payson
Terhune. His widow came to believe that she had established communication with the spirit of her deceased husband and that he had given
her a mandate to tell all the world of the "Life Continuous." She did
so in a little book, published in 1945 and called *Across the Line,* which
has had a surprising popularity and durability.

That book, and the entire affair, will strike some as miraculous or
"remarkable" (the adjective used by *Newsweek*). To others of a more
skeptical bent, it will be questionable; while those who are firm in
their conviction that such things just cannot be true will regard it as
pathetic, the deluded imaginings of a lonely old woman.

Whatever its veracity, it must be reported here as an episode of
significance in the lives of the Terhunes and Sunnybank.

It should first be made clear that Bert and Anice Terhune were not known to be connected in any way during their lifetimes with spiritist, occult, or psychical research organizations. They were, however, people of a deep religious faith and an integral part of that faith was belief in an afterlife.

There is, in addition, some evidence from his writings that Bert Terhune was interested in the question of possible continued existence after death. He did considerable reading on the subject and there are some indications that he had vague plans to write a book about it. Like many writers, he was intrigued and tantalized by situations and happenings in which a supernatural influence was implied, if not explicitly stated.

For instance, in a story called "Something," Terhune wrote of a collie which had always seemed to sense when his master was in danger of some kind. Then the master went to war in Europe, leaving the collie, Jock, with his wife and child. One night, as Jock went for a walk with his mistress:

of a sudden, the silences were shattered by a sound that wailed forth in hideous cadences from hill to hill; re-echoing until the placid night fairly screamed with it. Klyda gasped aloud at the horror of the plangent din, and she spun about to locate its cause.

There in the moonlight twenty feet from her stood Jock. The dog's every muscle was tense, as if with torture. His head was flung back. From his cavernous throat was issuing a series of long-drawn howls, slow, earsplitting, raucous,—howls of mortal anguish.

At that same moment, the woman later learned, her husband had died at an Army hospital in France.

But moments after the dog's horrible howling ceased, the woman felt a strange sense of her husband's nearness. She spoke her husband's name wonderingly. Here is how Terhune concluded the eerie story:

As she spoke, the collie raised his head, as in joyous greeting. He came swiftly over to where his mistress stood.

But it was not towards her he was moving. Nor was it at her that his rapturously welcoming gaze was turned.

The dog was hurrying, with eyes aglint and plumy tail waving toward a

spot directly beside her. Thus had he advanced, many a time, to greet his
master, when Dick had returned from brief absences and when Jock had seen
him standing there with his arm thrown protectingly about his wife and his
eyes smiling down into hers.

To humans, the tensely waiting woman would have seemed to be standing there in the moonlight, alone. But it was not into empty space that the
advancing dog gazed so eagerly.

No one, seeing the collie then, could have doubted for an instant that
Jock was looking at—*Something!*

There was a strange real-life parallel to this incident. On the night
after Bert Terhune's funeral, Fritz Van de Water was sitting with
Anice in the living room at Sunnybank. One of the dogs was lying on
the rug in front of the roaring fireplace. Suddenly the dog jumped to
its feet, fully alert. It walked over to the door, looked at it, and then
watched across the width of the big room with its eyes, as if something
was moving directly across its field of vision. Van de Water was and
remained a complete skeptic about life after death. Yet he admitted
that the incident left him shaken.

Terhune also was fond of relating several stories of unusual happenings at Sunnybank that might be labeled coincidence, but might
also be taken in other ways. One involved a Sunnybank dog, a mongrel named Rex who was devoted to Terhune and who, not being
allowed in the dining room, made it a practice at mealtimes to stand
just outside the dining room window, watching his master. Rex also
would often lie at Terhune's feet, in front of the living room fireplace.

Rex died in March, 1916. About eighteen months later, an old
friend of Terhune who had known Rex well came to visit Sunnybank.
Just before leaving that night, he commented to Terhune on Rex's
adoration, saying that he had watched him for a long time that evening
as the dog devotedly stared at Terhune, who sat before the fireplace.
Reminded that Rex had been dead for a year and a half, the friend
stubbornly insisted, "I saw him lying on the floor beside you, all this
evening."

The following summer, another visitor came to Sunnybank—an
old college friend of Terhune's, a clergyman who had never seen Rex.
He and Terhune sat in the dining room one afternoon, enjoying some
cold beer. When they got up to leave, the guest asked Terhune the

name of the dog that had been standing out on the veranda, looking in through the dining room window. It was not a collie, he insisted. And then he proceeded to give a detailed description of the dead Rex, including a crooked scar across his nose.

At some indeterminate time before his death, Terhune had written the rough draft for an essay titled "Across the Line." It was an argument for the reality of life after death.

"The real Self—not the physical Shell—is unrottable." The real Self journeys forth in dreams, he argued, so "what is to prevent the same Element from going on; after permanent Slumber has stilled the Shell that holds it?"

He concluded his draft: "The wisest of men, of all ages, from Solomon down, have affirmed a positive life after death. Not mere wild-eyed visionaries and cranks, but men of proven wisdom and practicality. . . . It is not ridiculous to believe—to KNOW —there is something very definite, Across The Line. It is ridiculous to believe there is not."

The book that was published in 1945, three years after Terhune's death, is listed as "By Albert Payson Terhune, With Notes and Comments by Anice Terhune." Apparently Anice insisted that it be credited in this way, but in fact only the first ten pages of the book are given over to the rough notes made by Terhune. The remaining 103 pages consist of an account of Anice's supposed conversations with her dead husband.

The slim book is, according to Mrs. Terhune, "the record of an amazing, thrillingly happy miracle. . . . You will wonder how you could ever have doubted that the Future Life is an actuality! . . . Since my husband . . . left the earth, he has urged me to let his many friends know that he is 'not dead.' 'If you love me,' he insists, 'tell the fact of my *actual living* to everyone we know.' "

Mrs. Terhune began the account by telling of the utter sense of emptiness that overcame her after her husband's death. He seemed completely, finally gone. Then, she wrote, she began to feel a sense of his nearness once again.

Two strange incidents occurred. She was desperately searching for the pedigrees of the remaining Sunnybank collies, which were needed for legal reasons, and she had repeatedly gone through her husband's papers without success. Then, giving up in exhaustion and discouragement, she was sitting in depression at his desk when she suddenly heard Bert's voice giving her clear, distinct instructions on where to find the missing papers. She turned to the place indicated and quickly found the pedigrees, stuck in the midst of other papers through which she previously had sifted several times.

Later, on Maundy Thursday evening, she went to church services with a friend. Thinking of her husband buried in the cold cemetery outside the church, she pulled down her veil and sat, quietly weeping, as the service proceeded. Suddenly she looked up and saw two lights moving about near the church ceiling. She was certain that they could not be reflections of anything inside or outside the church. One of the lights disappeared, but the other came nearer and nearer to her. Then, she wrote,

. . . as it descended and drew nearer to me, it became, almost miraculously, the form of my husband! There Bert was! Not something frightening, something abnormal, but just Bert, my husband! The radiance was still about him; and he wore a sort of gown or surplice. He remained perhaps twelve feet above me; but there he was, the Bert who had been my husband for over forty years! His eyes looked into mine eagerly, but with such a lovely beaming radiance that I cannot convey it to you. The compelling message that came to me from those eyes was this: "I'm not out there in the churchyard. I'm right here! With you! You must realize it! I'm right here inside this building with you, not out there, don't you see? I'm not dead. I'm alive."

A few days later, Mrs. Terhune asked the minister whether he had noticed anything unusual during the service. "No, Mrs. Terhune," he said. "I saw nothing. But I saw your face—and I knew you had seen a vision!"

About that time, as she thought about her childhood introduction to Bert and their life together, Mrs. Terhune decided to write a brief, tender reminiscence of her husband. She set to work on it, calling it *The Bert Terhune I Knew*.

Shortly after she had begun writing, Mrs. Terhune received a letter from a woman who declared that she had enjoyed some success with automatic writing and would like to offer her help. She gave the name of a mutual friend as a reference.

Automatic writing is the process by which some persons who believe that they have psychic ability receive written material from sources unknown, but which the psychic usually believes to be the spirits of the dead. It has been practiced for hundreds of years. The medium may receive the automatic writings via a pen or a typewriter or through that ancient occult device, the Ouija Board. The honest medium is quite certain that he or she is not consciously originating the communications; they seem to be coming from some other source.

Mrs. Terhune admitted that she felt some apprehension about engaging in such activity. But after checking with the mutual friend and getting an excellent report on the character and honesty of the letter writer, she invited her to come out to Sunnybank.

The new acquaintance was identified by Mrs. Terhune in the book only as Mrs. S. She came to Sunnybank and after the two women had chatted for a while on the famed old veranda, Mrs. S. took up paper and pencil and waited. Within a few minutes, the pencil began to move and the following message appeared on the paper:

I, Bert Terhune. Cure of our ills is instantaneous. I never felt stronger than now. Comes one thrilling experience after another. Someone called to me, "You will be permitted to write a letter to your wife!" I could not believe it! I am here upon the porch, with the writer and those who are as I am, in the spirit. Of our thoughts there is a curious embodiment of electric force which gives the soundless impulses of the radio; but of vastly finer power for effecting a human instrument. It is positive, powerful electric force.

Our love will endure forever. You are the poor one left behind. Let us stay as close as we can. I fondly hope we shall not be separated long.

The message continued in this vein, with Terhune telling his wife that he would eventually be able to communicate directly with her mind, and that he was somewhat disturbed and confused by the lack of privacy, as others were aware of his words.

Mrs. Terhune was overwhelmed by the communication purporting to come from her husband's spirit. In her account of the incident, she made much of her feeling that the language was very much that of her husband and not Mrs. S. Her new acquaintance had never met Terhune or heard him speak and said that she had never read any of his writings.

Tremendously excited by the apparent message from Bert, Mrs. Terhune asked Mrs. S. if she would return periodically to Sunnybank and attempt further communications. The woman agreed and made several additional visits. Each one brought more of the automatic communications. In one of them, Terhune stated that they would not be dependent on the help of Mrs. S. for much longer: "There will be a better connection between us later. There are some positive forces to acquire before I am able to put through of my own volition."

In the early conversations and in many others included in the book, Anice asks about relatives and friends who have died. In most cases, she is told that Bert has seen them: "I have seen many friends of whom *you* speak as dead. . . . They are as well and strong as ever. Is it impossible to accept the fact of Life Continuous, when we always glibly acknowledged our faith in that life?"

Terhune constantly expresses his longing for Anice and his overwhelming desire to have her with him "in actual living." His expressions of loneliness frequently bring her to tears and he urges her to remember that they must submit their own wills to God. He begs her not to weep, telling her that her sadness and grief tear him apart.

There were even flashes of the old Terhune ego in the messages:

(To Mrs. S.) "I am teaching Annie writing."

"Mrs. S. said, 'She's my pupil.'

"At which Bert came right back with, '*I'm* the guy who writes!' "

During this period, Anice had completed the manuscript of *The Bert Terhune I Knew* and had sent it to Harper and Brothers, publisher of many of her husband's books. Shortly after, the ghostly voice of her husband assured her that Harper would accept the book for publication (which they did) and that she must not worry any more about it.

In further conversations through the mediumship of Mrs. S., Terhune declared that he was kept busy learning things in his new existence, that he was living with his parents, and that they, too, would communicate in time with Anice.

She wondered whether he approved of the book she had just written and he told her emphatically that he did, then added, typically, ". . . I think it will add to your income."

A few days later, as promised, Anice did receive a message that apparently came from the Rev. Edward Terhune, her late father-in-law. He told her that he had brought Bert to the church to console her at the Maundy Thursday service and that he had been the second light she had seen.

On August 5, 1942, slightly less than six months after Bert Terhune's death, Anice Terhune herself received an automatic communication; from that time on, she no longer needed the assistance of Mrs. S. When she felt a message coming through, she simply picked up a pencil and paper. Soon the pencil would begin to move and, to her inexpressible delight, the words of her husband would appear on the paper.

Anice constantly asked Bert for more information about the afterlife and she faithfully recorded everything written by the moving pencil. She asked if there were any birds there, for example, and he answered, "The birds are more beautiful than I ever imagined birds could be! I walk about and am taken to see the wonders of this place. They cannot be described; at least, I am not capable of describing them."

He spends his time studying "Spiritual Sending," according to the messages, and in a later communication he told her: "My work is to learn to teach others to help themselves. I go down to a lower plane and show the poor ones there what their mistakes are. It is a beautiful and satisfying duty to be able to give a helping hand to those who wish to be helped."

Asked once again to describe his world, the pencil wrote: "It is impossible to describe. One must experience it for oneself. It is a great expansion of Power, A great expansion of Love. A great expansion of Beauty in all directions. A quickening. An increased intensity of thought, of mind, of perception. An all-encompassing beauty!"

One day, Anice asked him the inevitable question—were there dogs where he was? He answered: "Laddie and Wolf knew me at once. It was so good to have them bounding around me again!" He commented in a later message that the other dogs were sometimes with him.

As the weeks went on and the communications continued, Anice got the hoped-for letter from the publisher, telling her that *The Bert Terhune I Knew* had been accepted for publication. In her next session of automatic writing, Anice received congratulations from Bert on the acceptance that he had repeatedly predicted. Then he added, in another characteristic comment: "Your book will have marked success, and you will add very much to your income, more than you dream of. It will help you to pay your silly and iniquitous inheritance tax. Remember that I tell you that."

Also inevitable were questions by Anice as to whether Bert had encountered the spirits of well-known people. "Browning's here!" he exulted one day. "And Elizabeth, his wife. They are delightful. I see them often. I could not tell you of all the congenial spirits I have met . . . but gradually I will let you in on our 'Criticism Club,' so to speak." In another conversation, he told her that the spirit of St. Peter was just as he had imagined him, that the Apostle John preaches in the "Great Assembly Hall" and that John the Baptist tells the Eternal Truths in a "droning, resounding voice." It was droning, he responded to his wife's question, because John the Baptist is the same soul as he was on earth.

One day Anice asked, ". . . have you seen The Christ?"

The answer came: "Yes, Christ has stooped to bless me. He is gentleness personified."

"Does He look like the paintings of Him we have seen?"

"No painting could portray the beauty of His countenance."

In some of these fragmented, diverse, random bits of dialogue, there are moments of great poignancy. Whether one believes or not, it is difficult not to be moved by the wistful loneliness of these words, written by Anice on a late September morning as she sat in her husband's old study and attributed by her to the spirit of her dead husband:

I am writing at my old desk, where I have written so many thousand words. It is very strange, indeed. I love to see you sitting in my old chair that you gave me so very many years ago. I long to touch you. I do it, but you do not know—though I feel sure that you *do* know, often!

It is the best we can do, Annie, till you come here to stay. It is hard to wait; but we must be patient. It will come.

Keep close to me, Annie. We must never give up the writing. I will talk more to your mind. I will try always to make it better. Now, Annie, I must stop writing at my old desk; with the little boxing glove on it, and the old typewriter and the little red soldier; and all the dear things you have given me!

It all seems very familiar. And it hurts a little. The old life came back with a rush for a moment. But we will be happy, happy, happy together again, never fear.

The communications continued. Bert kept urging his wife to take the rough notes for his essay on life after death and the written record of the conversations with him after his own death and have them published as a book. "If you love me, give written proof of my living to everyone you know."

The final communication is dated October 17, 1942. But the book concludes with a brief epilogue stemming from a further message from Bert in September, 1944. In it, he tells Anice that he is with an ancestress of hers named Phebe Barlow, who is centuries old. Anice declares firmly that she had no such ancestress, but Bert insists he is correct.

A few weeks later, wrote Mrs. Terhune, she was asked by an editor of *Colonial Families of America* to look over an updated sketch of the Stockton family. It included the history of the Olmstead family, into which her maternal grandmother had married. Mrs. Terhune asserted that she never had seen an Olmstead family history and knew nothing of that family. With only cursory interest, she read quickly through it until she saw:

"Capt. James Olmstead married, on May 1st, 1673, Phebe Barlow, daughter of Thomas Barlow of Fairfield, Connecticut."

Regarding this discovery as overwhelming evidence that she had indeed been communicating with her dead husband, Mrs. Terhune ended her book: "I am more than thrilled to be able to close this precious book on such a triumphant note."

Across the Line, Anice Terhune's faithful recounting of the conversations with her husband's spirit, was published in 1945. She obviously had difficulty in finding a publisher for it. It was turned down by Harper and Brothers, her husband's long-time publisher, and presumably also by E. P. Dutton, the publisher of *Lad: A Dog.* There undoubtedly were other rejections as well, which account for its eventual publication by the Dryden Press, a small company known primarily for its textbooks.

The slim book attracted little attention in the literary world. It was ignored by most reviewers, although *Newsweek* carried a major story on the book on its religion page. While describing the book as "remarkable" and quoting a number of excerpts from the spirit conversations, the *Newsweek* story also quoted an unnamed editor from one of Terhune's long-time publishers as saying: "That doesn't sound like big, robust Bert—one of the boys—who didn't think much about after life." The article mentioned that Mrs. Terhune had signed over all royalties from the book to charity.

The royalties during the first year or two of publication apparently were pretty skimpy. The Dryden Press gave *Across the Line* little advertising or promotion and it was not finding an audience. Anice Terhune was desperate to make some sort of new arrangement for the book that would give it the readership she felt it was destined to have.

Such an arrangement finally was worked out with E. P. Dutton, but the publishing company drove a hard bargain. They agreed to take over further publication of *Across the Line* and promised to keep it perpetually in print. In return, however, Anice must agree to give up any further royalties from three Terhune dog books originally issued by Dutton: *Lad: A Dog, Bruce,* and *His Dog.* It was a high price to pay, particularly in the case of the now-classic *Lad: A Dog,* but Anice agreed to the stipulation because she believed her husband's spirit felt that the message of *Across the Line* was the most important thing Bert Terhune ever had communicated and that it was essential the book find a sizable audience. The agreement was signed. About two years after the book's original publication, Dutton began issuing *Across the Line* under its own imprint and took over ownership of all rights to the three dog books.

The agreement was negotiated with one of the members of the Macrae family that controlled the Dutton firm. To his credit, Macrae later went to see Anice Terhune and told her he felt the original agreement had been unfair to her. Although Dutton would retain ownership of the three books as agreed, it would also pay Anice an allowance (the payment is quoted as being $100 a month) for the rest of her life. The new agreement was not ungenerous; as the years went on, the allowance to Anice probably exceeded the revenues received by Dutton from the three books in question.

By 1970, *Across the Line* had gone through eight printings. In 1975, it was still in print, thirty years after original publication. There is some evidence that *Across the Line,* with the improved distribution provided by E. P. Dutton, has found a considerable audience over the years. Anice told friends that the book had brought her letters from readers all over the United States, from Canada, England, and South Africa. She claimed that a number of people had been saved from suicide by reading the book. She personally answered each fan letter, sometimes staying up until 3:00 A.M. to do so. There are still waiting lists at public libraries for the book.

Among the communications allegedly from Bert Terhune's spirit in *Across the Line* was a promise that another book concerning the afterlife would be dictated to Anice. By 1952, Anice told some of her friends that she had received two more books from Bert, one of them titled *That You May Know.* She said that Bert would not yet permit her to send the manuscripts to the publisher because *Across the Line* was still doing its great work in preparation for the next two books. She had provided that all royalties from the additional books, when published, would go to the same three charities that had benefited from *Across the Line.* From time to time, Anice would read portions of the manuscripts to her friends; the new books were similar in nature to *Across the Line,* with detailed descriptions of the life after death and of the processes involved in it. She never permitted others to read the manuscripts themselves, and it is not known what became of them after Anice's death. No one who was involved with her estate remembers seeing them or being told of their whereabouts.

What does one make of all this? Can it be believed? Is it true?

The argument over automatic writing rages as hotly today as it did in 1945 and indeed in 1845. True believers in the occult need no convincing. Communication with the dead is possible, they contend, and the products of automatic writing provide evidence for it. Others are just as firm in their disbelief and scorn. One such person was Bert's nephew, Fritz Van de Water. After hearing from Anice that Bert's spirit had sent some messages for Fritz, Van de Water decided to work up a test. He sent some questions to Anice and asked her to put them to the spirit voice—the answers were known only to Bert and his nephew. Anice provided answers to the questions that Van de Water felt could not possibly have come from Bert.

Of Mrs. Terhune's honesty and sincerity, there is no reasonable doubt. In the first part of *Across the Line,* she wrote:

I'm not a fanciful person nor in the least neurotic. Instead, I'm just an ordinary, everyday, busy, practical woman; and my imagination does not run away with me. So when I say that what I am about to disclose is God's own truth, every word of it, please believe me unquestioningly and read the record through to the very end. What I shall tell you is not something that happened to someone else; it is what actually happened to me.

Her belief in the utter reality of her husband's continuing existence after his death was apparent in many things she did and wrote. In October, 1945, after the book's first publication, she wrote to a newspaperman thanking him for a favorable review of *Across the Line* and said: "I know Bert will read it and be glad his old friend is *still* his friend and mine!"

33

The composure that Anice Terhune had displayed at her husband's funeral did not last very long. Overcome by grief, she refused to eat and said that she wanted to die, she must be with Bert. She became so weak that nourishment had to be given to her intravenously. Friends and relatives could not comfort her—she could not stand life without Bert. Finally she completely broke down and had to be hospitalized for a time.

When she returned to Sunnybank, Anice was more composed and more able to face the thought of going on alone. Then came the beginning of the communications with what she was convinced was Bert's spirit and she knew she was not alone, after all. She was able to resume a fairly normal life, content in the belief that Bert still was looking after her. The house was kept exactly as it had been when he lived. The papers and books in Bert's study remained in their places, as if waiting for him to return and get back to work on a new yarn. In the dining room, no one was allowed to sit in Bert's chair.

A friend has told of paying a call on Mrs. Terhune at Sunnybank, several years after Bert's death. She wanted to ask whether the grounds of the famous estate could be used for a day by a local dog club. The widow of the famed writer received her graciously and agreed to permit the small dog show at Sunnybank. The conversation was carried on in the living room. Not far from them, on the wall, was a large portrait of Bert Terhune; a light shone on the face and gave it a sort of eerie life. But even more eerie was the way in which Anice included her husband in the conversation. She frequently would ask him if he didn't agree with her and then look expectantly at his face in the painting as if awaiting an answer. She regarded him as there, with them in the room, and taking part in the discussion. (Lest this seem totally ludicrous, it should be mentioned that the painting had been referred to in *Across the Line* and Bert's spirit had told Anice that he sometimes watched her from the painting.) Similar experiences were reported by Hal and Ruth LeRoy. When they walked into the house to visit Anice, she would turn to the painting and say, "Bert, Hal and Ruth have come to see us." She told other friends that Bert communicated with her every evening and apparently continued steadfastly to believe this until her own death, almost twenty-three years after that of her husband.

A lonely old woman, sick, growing senile? Imagining . . . remembering . . . losing touch with reality? Or a woman no longer lonely? Convinced, absolutely certain, that her dead husband had come back and was there, at Sunnybank, with her . . . just as he had vowed. Who knows?

The last will and testament of Albert Payson Terhune had been written in 1934, eight years before his death. The will left everything except Sunnybank to Anice, with the stipulation that if she died before her husband, the entire estate would go to Bert's daughter, Lorraine. The will asked Anice in turn to leave everything to Lorraine, but typically specified that this merely represented Bert's wish and was not required of Anice. It also provided that certain other unspecified income (from rents, etc.) would go to Lorraine; but this apparently did not mean much money for her and she was known to be bitter that her father had not left Sunnybank to her. The will specified a rather strange arrangement for Sunnybank. The estate was left to Fritz Van de Water, but only on the proviso that he and his family make Sunnybank their permanent home and reside there at least nine months a year. This quite obviously was an attempt to ensure that Anice would be properly cared for after Bert died, for the intent was that she would live on at Sunnybank with the Van de Water family to look after her. Whether Bert had discussed this with his nephew when he wrote the will is not known, but Van de Water—when the will was read—declined the offer. He had his own beautiful spread of almost 200 acres in Windham County, Vermont, and did not want to leave it. The Terhune will indicated that, if Van de Water refused to live at Sunnybank, ownership of the estate was to revert to Lorraine (possibly a last effort on Bert's part to bring the two women together after his death). But it continued to be Anice's property. The only logical explanation is that Anice bought it from Lorraine; certainly Lorraine had no desire to live there and that would have been the easiest way to resolve the matter.

The Terhune will also included a bequest of $1,000 to superintendent Robert Friend (who had died two years before his old boss) and $5,000 each to the Andrasse sisters. Not surprisingly, it made detailed provisions for the remaining dogs at Sunnybank: "The executors shall sell the younger dogs and see that they are given good homes in the country. They are not to be given to persons living in large cities. I . . . have more regard for securing a home for them than the price to be received. As to my house dogs and older dogs, I ask that my wife let such of them as she may desire to keep continue to remain at Sunnybank with her and that the others be put to death painlessly. I desire that this be done especially for those dogs I have been keeping in their old age because of their past value to me. It will be the kindest fate for them as no one else will want them."

The ample estate left by Bert Terhune enabled Anice to live the quiet, gracious, orderly life of a well-to-do widow. Her personal needs always were filled by the loyal retainers from Martinique. A caretaker kept the grounds in reasonably good condition, although signs of decay were beginning to appear now that Bert was not there to keep his steely watch over every plant and tree.

Anice kept up with her music, dutifully practicing the piano and organ, and continuing to compose songs for children. Friends visited her often at Sunnybank and every few days a family of Bert's loyal readers would come to the gate, asking permission to enter and see that marvelous place so often read about. Whenever possible, they were given leave to come in. Sometimes Anice would greet them personally, show them the few remaining collies, and even lead them about the house, taking great pride especially in the study where the Master used to write.

Letters from Bert's readers continued to pour into Sunnybank. Anice wrote to a former business associate of her husband: "My fan mail is tremendous: It comes from people everywhere who cannot feel that he is dead! They still love him; still want his stories; feel that somehow I ought to go on writing his stories. That I could never do, of course."

Anice read a great deal, listened to classical music on the radio, and, as the 1950s started, became fond of television. She regularly attended services at the church in Pompton Lakes and arranged with the minister to continue the anonymous Christmas charity which her husband had supported for so many years. She volunteered to visit members of the congregation who were confined to their homes by illness. At least once a month she would stop in to see an invalid and spend an hour or two, talking and playing the piano. She also accompanied her minister on his pastoral calls to a home for the aged poor. She was a familiar figure around town, still wearing the long white flowing dresses she always had worn, although as age and poor eyesight began to overtake her, there were sometimes stains or spots on her clothing. Those who had known her to be always immaculate simply shook their heads sadly.

She visited her husband's grave regularly, no matter what the weather. On occasions when a heavy snow had just fallen, she would give the cemetery caretaker a tip to shovel a path through the deep snow so that she could get to the grave. At Christmas and on the anniversaries of Bert's death, she would bring a bouquet of flowers to lay at the foot of the big stone cross. Rather typically, local flowers were not good enough—the bouquet always was ordered from a New York florist.

She maintained always a strong, almost aggressive, pride in being the wife of Albert Payson Terhune. When she received a letter from a friend addressed to Mrs. Anice Terhune, she wrote back and asked the friend to address her as Mrs. Albert Payson Terhune and added, "I am still proud to bear my husband's name." In 1962, twenty years after Bert's death, she refused the gift of a colored handkerchief, telling the friend involved that she still was in deep mourning and would wear only white as a sign of that mourning.

Through all the years with Bert and without him, Anice remained ever the Victorian grande dame, the very proper lady of strong opinion and refined taste. Once two friends had offered her a gift of tea, but Anice was not at all reluctant to decline politely but firmly:

I want to thank you for your kindness in sending me the tea but it seems all has not gone well. You asked me to choose my variety of tea and I promptly chose the Chinese Tea and I thought all was well, but from your next letter you told me that you had a little trouble in locating the Chinese Tea and you suggest instead of that an English Breakfast Tea. There is all the difference in the world in the lovely Chinese Tea. I am familiar with English Breakfast Tea and to be perfectly honest, it is so very insipid that I never under any circumstances, dearly as I love you both, I couldn't bring myself to take any. I absolutely loathe it. I suggest we forget all about tea forever. I never liked it anyway. Your friendship is absolutely priceless to me, so please keep coming to see me and know that you will always be more than welcome. Lovingly, Anice.

Anice continued to make frequent trips into New York City to shop, to attend the opera, to visit the old friends she and Bert had so loved to be with. The ranks began to diminish, however. In some cases, the friends had been primarily Bert's and his death greatly weakened the ties. A few others were increasingly dismayed by Anice's new interest in spiritualism and the people that she had begun to associate with after the publication of *Across the Line.* There were "just too many swamis hanging around," said one woman, who allowed her old friendship with Anice to fade away.

One of her closest friends continued to be Ethel Vreeland, the widow of the Pompton Lakes physician who had cared for Bert Terhune for many years. During Bert's last illness, when Anice had felt she could bear no more, she would telephone Mrs. Vreeland—sometimes in the middle of the night—and her loyal friend would come over to Sunnybank to offer comfort and solace. After Bert was gone, it was a long-standing custom for Mrs. Vreeland to come to Sunnybank on Saturday and spend the day with Anice while the two maids were given the time off to go into town and see a movie. The two elderly ladies would sit and listen to music and play cards, or just reminisce about the years when their husbands were alive. Later, when Anice was confined to bed, Mrs. Vreeland would go into New York, see an opera, and then hurry to Sunnybank to give her fellow music lover a detailed report on the production.

Over the years Sunnybank had begun to wither and shrink. It had for many years totaled 44 acres after Terhune had bought some small adjacent parcels in the 1920s. There was the most famous portion of the estate, along the lake and extending northward almost to the Schuyler Bridge and also the area of woods and meadows further up the hill, across Terhune Drive. The land across the road was always considered a part of Sunnybank although the ownership of a considerable part of it was held by Terhune's sisters. In 1939 a local osteopath bought 18 acres of the tract and built a palatial seventeen-room home there. Later another 14 acres was added to the property; this changed hands again and then was sold in 1963 to American Cyanamid, which used the house and land to entertain customers and company executives. (The property and home went back on the market again in 1972 at an asking price of $535,000.) Meanwhile, probably because the care of her land was an ever-increasing concern, Anice began gradually to sell off parts of the lakeside property, a few acres here and there.

Gradually most of The Place passed into other hands until finally, in the late 1950s, all that was left was the heart of Sunnybank—the slightly more than 9 acres along the lake and surrounding the house. It was to be Anice's last refuge as she waited for death. This she never would part with, for she was determined all along that she would die at Sunnybank and would never give up The Place.

Bert Terhune had expressed the hope that, after he and Anice were gone, Sunnybank might serve somehow as a home for children or perhaps a school for the training of guide dogs for the blind. Anice knew that these dreams probably were not possible, but she told friends she prayed that somehow Sunnybank might be kept always as they had known it, to serve as a memorial to Bert and a haven for literary people.

Other than expressing such vague hopes, Anice either didn't care or was not well enough to make more specific plans for the fate of Sunnybank after she was gone. Her will called for the establishment of an Albert Payson Terhune Foundation that would take control of the estate and its assets after her death. With the assistance of two attorneys, the foundation was organized while she was alive and she and the lawyers chose a group of prominent people in the area to serve as its first trustees. Thereafter the trustees would be self-perpetuating, choosing their own successors as the years went on.

Early in 1957, Anice excitedly told her friends that her husband's name and works soon would become familiar to millions of additional people through the mighty medium of television. Newspapers reported that a Hollywood television film producer had acquired television rights to the Albert Payson Terhune stories and syndicated features. He planned to use them as the basis for a syndicated television series to be called "Dogs Courageous." Each program in the anthology series would feature a different breed of dog, and production would get under way immediately. The producer said he had negotiated a combined cash, royalty, and profit participation deal with Mrs. Terhune and her agent, Bruce Chapman.

To Anice's great disappointment, the series never became a reality. A pilot film was shot, but it aroused little interest and the series did not go into syndication. The pilot was used in a couple of other TV anthology series, but Terhune's name could not, by terms of the contract negotiated by Chapman, be utilized for this.

In 1960, when she was eighty-seven years old, Mrs. Terhune fell and suffered a broken hip. She was confined to bed for the remainder of her life. Some reports had it that the accident occurred when Anice stumbled over the head of a bearskin rug that had stretched for years across the living room floor. But Anice herself blamed it all on the composer Jean Sibelius and her reverence for his music. She had been thinking about Sibelius, she told friends later, and decided to play his *Finlandia* on the organ. She was stretching her foot to reach a bass pedal when she heard a loud crack, presumably the breaking bone in her hip. As she tried to get off the bench, she fell heavily to the floor.

The two elderly servants now had to be augmented by nurses who provided round-the-clock care for their aged patient. Pauline Andrasse had become a near-invalid herself prior to Mrs. Terhune's injury and she died in 1963. Her sister Josephine, the ever-faithful "Fifine," was left to cook and care for the woman who had been her mistress for fifty years.

Even though confined to her bed in her large pink bedroom, Anice Terhune—despite failing sight and hearing—remained clear-minded. After Bert's death, she had resumed sending the traditional Christmas card with an original carol on it and she carried on this practice until just two years before her own death. She continued to be fastidious about her grooming—a friend who saw her just a few months before the end remembers that she was very concerned about how she looked—and she kept up with world news with the help of her radio. Her friends loyally continued to call on her, although in steadily diminishing numbers as age inexorably took its toll.

Her beloved music now could come to her only through the radio; playing the piano and organ was no longer possible. Once a friend walked into her bedroom and found her gently pressing the keys of a child's toy piano that belonged to the daughter of one of her nurses.

Outside that sparkling pink bedroom with its vases of freshly picked flowers, however, Sunnybank was slowly going to ruin. The old house urgently needed repair, but there was no one to order it done. The grounds began to spoil, weeds were winning the eternal battle, the flowers and plants of the "Garden from Everywhere" were dying.

Anice could no longer see what was happening and the truth was kept from her. Every so often she would ask Fifine to tell her what it was like outside, today at Sunnybank, and Fifine would patiently give her a glorious description of the estate in its bygone days of magnificence. The dying old woman would listen, a smile of bliss on her face as she remembered the sun-filled days with Bert.

A friend told of visiting Mrs. Terhune in her bedroom a few months before she died. The bedfast woman knew Sunnybank only as a place of lush, glowing beauty. She was able to see only a small piece of ground through the window and someone had freshly planted flowers there so that those few feet of earth at least were radiant with blooms. Mrs. Terhune looked through the window at the bright summer sky and said to her visitor, "I know the rose arbor is gorgeous today. It always was so lovely at this time of year." The visitor nodded in agreement, though the rose bushes had long since died and the old arbor now was only a narrowing corridor through the underbrush and weeds.

Loyal readers of the stories and books still came to see Sunnybank, though not so many as before. Some were lucky and were admitted by the caretaker, who gave them a brief tour of the grounds, climaxed by the homage at Lad's grave, always the most-visited spot. The house, of course, was now closed to all. The summer of 1964 brought a sharp influx of would-be visitors. They were coming to New York City from all over the country for the World's Fair and made a stop at Sunnybank to visit the fabulous place of their childhood's imagination. But they were stopped at the entrance by the caretaker, who mournfully told them that visitors no longer were permitted because Mrs. Terhune was gravely ill. So they drove back out of the driveway, passing the neat little sign proclaiming that this was indeed Sunnybank. For many it would be the only chance ever to see The Place. All they really got to see was the entrance gate, the caretaker's house alongside and, down there almost hidden by the hillside forest, the barest outlines of the house that they had known so well and longed to see. Then they drove away.

As her own death approached, Anice was prepared and unafraid. She remained convinced that her beloved Bert awaited her there . . . just "across the line." She looked toward their reunion with great joy.

On November 9, 1964, at ninety-one, Anice Terhune died. As she had wished, funeral services were held for her at Sunnybank and she was laid to rest beside her husband in the church graveyard at Pompton Lakes.

There is no immediate family left to watch over the graves of Bert and Anice Terhune, but they are not forgotten. Several times a year, Terhune fans come to the graves and clean them. And they bring with them holly and violets from Sunnybank to lay in front of the stones in gentle tribute.

After the death of her mistress, Josephine Andrasse left Sunnybank, her home for over a half century. She moved to a nearby town where she took up residence with one of the nurses who had cared for Mrs. Terhune during her final illness. More recently she has gone to live in a nursing home in the area.

After she left, the crumbling old house at Sunnybank was empty of life. The Place was desolately silent, except for an elderly caretaker, who had come to work for Mrs. Terhune in 1957, and his wife. They continued to live in the gatehouse, retained by the executor of Mrs. Terhune's estate to stay on and try to keep The Place from being overrun by vandals and thieves.

They only partially succeeded. One of the first casualties was the small sign at the gate, which identified the estate as Sunnybank. It was soon stolen.

34

By the early 1960s, Bert Terhune had been dead for two decades. Yet he remained manifestly alive through his work. Some seventeen of his books were still in print and selling steadily. In 1958 alone, his books had sold over 125,000 copies.

And in 1962, Hollywood finally discovered *Lad: A Dog,* the Terhune classic originally published forty-three years before. In June of that year, Warner Brothers released the first cinematic version of the great Terhune book.

The movie project began when producer Max J. Rosenberg bought the film rights to *Lad: A Dog* from E. P. Dutton for his Vanguard Productions. Rosenberg later sold the rights to Warners. The big Hollywood studio became concerned when its executives learned that there were three books of Lad stories and that Dutton had owned and sold the movie rights to only the first of them, the original collection of stories. Warner Brothers was hoping the film would be successful enough to merit a sequel and possibly could be spun off into a television series and they felt they must have the rights to the other Lad books as well, which remained the property of Anice Terhune. Bruce Chapman negotiated the sale for Mrs. Terhune. He has said he believes the movie studio paid about $25,000 for the film rights to all three of the Lad books, with most of the money going to Dutton. The publisher and Mrs. Terhune set up Terhune Lad Stories, Inc. for the purpose of the deal with Warner Brothers.

The beloved story was adapted for the screen by Lillie Hayward, a veteran of many screenplays—westerns, comedies, and children's stories—and a lesser-known writer, Roberta Hodes. The project got into trouble right from the start with the assignment by Warner Brothers of a most unlikely director, a talented, aggressive young ex-film editor named Aram Avakian. He was described later by a magazine as "the quintessence of a newly successful breed of maverick, dropout film maker to whom Hollywood means handcuffs."

Avakian, with his avant-garde tendencies, was an incredibly bad choice for the sentimental old dog story. He wrote about it later: "I wanted to make a kind of pop, camp thing that wouldn't be a complete ordeal for parents. And nobody—the assistant director, the actors— wanted anything but Dick, Jane and Doggie. They zapped me all the way." The biggest zap came from studio boss Jack Warner, who demanded that Avakian play the film straight. When the director refused, he was summarily fired. Another, more conventional director took over and finished the film.

Peter Breck played Terhune and Peggy McKay was his wife, although they were called Stephen and Elizabeth Tremayne in the film. The part of the obnoxious newly rich neighbor, Hamilcar Q. Glure, was played by none other than Archie Bunker himself, veteran character actor Carroll O'Connor. The character of Glure is one of Terhune's sillier ones, overdrawn and exaggerated; it was a tribute to O'Connor's talent that he made the man seem human and, particularly in a scene where he has to tell his small daughter that her cherished collie puppy has been killed in a fire, a person of dignity and love. The child was portrayed by Angela Cartwright, who was well known to television audiences as the daughter on the popular Danny Thomas Show in the late 1950s and early 1960s.

The cinema Sunnybank was a typical Hollywood overstatement— a giant expanse of lawn stretching into the distance, a waterfall, a rustic wooden bridge crossing a stream, a placid river floating past instead of the famous Pompton Lake, a huge dock area complete with potted plants and tables with beach umbrellas. There was even a family of geese floating around on the water.

The Tremaynes' house was mildly reminiscent of the real Sunnybank house (the small stone lions on the veranda bestriding the front steps were duplicated) although it was much too large, with a veranda about three times the size of the real one and bordered by white columns that looked like something left over from *Gone with the Wind.* The interior scenes took place mostly in the living room and it too had something of the flavor of the real-life room as described so often in the books, but again was far larger.

The script tied together several of the separate stories in *Lad: A Dog* and made them a single narrative by changing some of the characters. For instance the crippled child who miraculously walks again while trying to defend Lad against undeserved punishment is, in the film, Glure's daughter.

There had to be a villain to break into the house and permit Lad to display his watchdog bravery and punishing savagery. In a perhaps unintentional bit of humor, the writers of the film—taking note of Terhune's oft-stated disdain for the mountain people known as Jackson Whites—invented an all-purpose villain who attempted to hunt deer on Sunnybank land only to be thrashed by Lad . . . set fire to the barn, nearly killing Lad, Lady, and Mrs. Tremayne-Terhune . . . and broke into the house attempting to steal a valuable gold cup, only to be apprehended and almost fragmented by the ever-alert Lad. The screen writers gave the villain the name of "Jackson White."

Terhune's sentimental writing does not translate well into a film in the second half of the twentieth century; the motion picture often was cloying. And yet devoted Terhune fans viewing the film found themselves totally absorbed in it, as if they were renewing acquaintance with a very dear, long-lost friend. Perhaps it was the handsome collie who was winningly cast as Lad (pre-release publicity for the film declared that "an enormous canine talent hunt preceded shooting" before the right collie was found in the San Fernando Valley). Perhaps it was hearing voices up there on the screen actually pronouncing the sacred words—Sunnybank, Lad, Lady, Wolf.

Whatever, there was something about the film. Something. It was a cheaply made, Grade B picture (the complete text of *The New York Times* review ran: "A bucolic drama of no discernible merit"). Yet to a loyal, unwavering Terhune fan, it somehow was an *event*. There, again, was that peculiar, enigmatic magic of Terhune, filtering through the stickiness of a minor, unsung film and coming stubbornly across the void to us.

Besides the film, there were other ways in which the long-dead Bert Terhune apparently entered finally into American folklore, or perhaps one should be satisfied just to say American trivia.

For example:

Then Levine issued his challenge. "Bogart."
"Bogart," affirmed Weiner.
At Nostrand Avenue Weiner had named fourteen movies wherein Bogart had been featured but not starred.
By the intersection of Nostrand and Church Avenues he had named the horses of Tom Tyler, Bob Steele, George O'Brien, Hoot Gibson, Ken Maynard, and Buck Jones; nine books by Albert Payson Terhune; the four Boy Allies; the three Battle Aces of G-8; and five more movies wherein Bogart had been featured but not starred.
—Wallace Markfield, *To an Early Grave* (1964)

The first dog I remember well was a large black and white mutt that was part German shepherd, part English sheep dog, and part collie—the wrong part in each case. With what strikes me now as unforgivable whimsey, we called him Ladadog from the title by Albert Payson Terhune. He was a splendid dog in many respects, but, in the last analysis, I'm afraid he was a bit of a social climber.
—Jean Kerr, *Please Don't Eat the Daisies* (1957)

A man is strolling down the street, puffing contentedly on his pipe. He wears a sweatshirt emblazoned with the face and name of Beethoven. Alongside him, on a leash, strolls—equally contentedly—his dog. The dog wears a doggie blanket bearing the name and visage of Albert Payson Terhune.
—Cartoon, *The New Yorker* (December 19, 1970)

Her eight dogs "leap on her in a scene that would have Albert Payson Terhune down on his knees sobbing."
—Article on Jane Fonda, *Life* Magazine, March 29, 1968

The passing comment about Terhune in the *Life* article, by the way, brought a rejoinder letter to the magazine from a loyal APT admirer: "That's a rather cruel comment about a man who can't answer back. Mr. Terhune was a wonderful writer, loved dogs, but he was not a maudlin dog lover, and there is a difference."

35

The death of Anice Terhune left the fate of Sunnybank very much in doubt. She had made no specific provision for The Place, which was left in the hands of the Albert Payson Terhune Foundation. Her own will left most of her personal possessions and household valuables to a nephew and two nieces in New England.

Mrs. Terhune was generous with cash bequests. A friend was left $5,000, a secretary was bequeathed $2,500. She left $2,500 to her church, $2,000 to her sister and brother, and $1,000 to each of three long-time Sunnybank employees. And for the faithful Andrasse sisters, only one of whom survived Anice, the will set up a $20,000 trust fund. A small sum of money also was left for the erection of a tablet at Sunnybank that would memorialize the names of Sunnybank and Bert and Anice Terhune. The remainder of the estate was left to the Albert Payson Terhune Foundation.

A short time after Anice Terhune's death, the executor of her estate opened the house to the public for a day and the remaining possessions were sold on the spot to those who bid highest for them.

Now the old house, so familiar and dear to Terhune's thousands of readers, stood quiet and empty awaiting its own death. Its windows were dark. The only sounds around it were the occasional cracks from the rotting roof as the ever-insistent wisteria poked at it in a loving dance of death, or the muted breaking of glass as vandals wreaked their destruction on an aged, defenseless structure.

Bert Terhune often had worried about the fate of Sunnybank after he and his wife would die. He knew that his daughter had no interest in living there. In his book about Sunnybank, published in 1934, Terhune had poignantly expressed his fears:

> When she and I shall be dead, there is nobody who will care to carry on. Nobody with our fanatic adoration for our home and for every inch of our land. There is nobody who will have our foolish love of The Place and our desire to keep it up and to plant for the future.
>
> Alien hands will hew down the mighty trees which mean so ineffably much to us. The Place will be cut up into dinky bungalow development lots —"attractive lake shore residence sites"—or it will be sold at a bargain for a hot dog Pleasure Park or for an inn.
>
> Or with the sign, "Tourists Accomodated" on its ancient stone gateposts, this house which was built into a shrine by my gentle mother and then by my gentler wife, will be turned over to the motor tourist.
>
> Again calling sanity to my aid, I realize it cannot matter either to the Mistress or to myself what may happen to Sunnybank after we fall asleep. Yet—
>
> I wish I had a living son to carry on. A son who would have inherited our stark Sunnybank complex. I wish with all my soul there were someone who might feel as the Mistress and I feel about the loved old homestead and carry on our manner of life here.

The trustees of the APT Foundation had no idea what to do with Sunnybank. But it became increasingly clear that something must be done; they could not afford simply to let it stand vacant.

For a long time the story among Terhune fans was that Anice Terhune had died in debt, that her illness and long life had exhausted her resources, and that the estate eventually had to be sold to settle those debts. Even Bert's nephew, Fritz Van de Water, believed this to be the case. In a 1968 letter he said: "The long illness of my uncle's widow seems to have left the estate in an egregious mess, physically and financially."

In fact, Anice Terhune left a substantial estate over and above the personal possessions that were bequeathed to friends and relatives. After all bequests, debts, and taxes were paid, about $150,000 in stocks, bonds, and cash was turned over to the Foundation.

At the time the Foundation was established, Mrs. Terhune and her lawyers set up a companion corporation, Albert Payson Terhune, Inc. Ownership of 45 per cent rested with Mrs. Terhune (her share went to the Foundation upon her death); 45 per cent is owned by Bruce Chapman, the Terhunes' long-time business adviser and agent; and the remaining 10 per cent was owned by Mrs. Terhune's attorney and now belongs to his widow. The copyrights to all of Bert Terhune's writings (except for those otherwise disposed of, as in the case of the three books that reverted to E. P. Dutton) belong to APT, Inc. Whatever royalties are earned by these writings go to that corporation, which in turn passes them on to the APT Foundation.

As long as they remained in print, the Terhune books produced steady, if unspectacular royalties for the Foundation. For many years some fifteen titles were published as children's books by Grosset & Dunlap under licensing arrangements with the original publishers. The figures show that by the end of 1970, the Grosset & Dunlap editions had sold a total of more than 650,000 copies. (For the curious, the best-selling title, by far, was *Buff: A Collie* with just under 150,000 copies sold at that time. A distant second on the list was *Faith of a Collie* with just over 90,000 copies. The list does not, of course, include *Lad: A Dog* which always has been published exclusively by E. P. Dutton and Company.)

The sales gradually began to taper off, however, and within the last few years, Grosset & Dunlap has allowed the books to go out of print. In 1975, only four Terhune titles remained in print: Grosset & Dunlap's *The Faith of a Collie* (hard cover, part of their Famous Dog Stories series) and *Lad of Sunnybank* (part of their Tempo paperback series); and E. P. Dutton's *Lad: A Dog* and *Across the Line.*

In recent years, as the sales of the books have slowed down, the APT Foundation has received only a small amount of money in royalties from the publishers. Most of its income was produced by the investments made with the balance of Anice Terhune's estate. An informed source says that the Foundation has been disbursing about

$9,000 annually, with the money going to educational and charitable causes: three hospitals in the Pompton Lakes area, the Y.M.-Y.W.C.A.; Boy and Girl Scouts, and a New York animal hospital, among others. Between ten and fifteen such agencies receive contributions from the Foundation each year.

After Anice Terhune's death, with the fate of Sunnybank hanging in the balance, considerable pressure was brought on the Foundation trustees by Terhune fans to put the resources of the Foundation into saving The Place, somehow, as a perpetual Terhune memorial. The trustees carefully considered the problem, but soon came to the conclusion that it was impossible to heed the requests. For one thing, to do so would have quickly used all the resources of the Foundation and put it out of existence. This, they felt, would have violated the explicit instructions of Anice Terhune, who had set up the Foundation with the primary purpose of dispensing money for charitable and educational causes.

The trustees sounded out local governmental agencies as to their interest in taking over Sunnybank as a Terhune memorial, but there was no perceptible interest. So they had no alternative. In the summer of 1965, it became known in the Pompton Lakes-Wayne area that Sunnybank was for sale.

A proposal began to circulate among some members of the Wayne Township Council to purchase The Place and establish it as a Terhune museum and tourist attraction. But, as was always the case with Terhune, there was immediate controversy over the proposal. Some residents of Wayne expressed their opposition to using public funds to celebrate the memory of a man who always had provided fame to a neighboring borough rather than his own community and, indeed, who still was remembered by some as a person of prodigious temper and inhospitable nature.

The Wayne Council debated and temporized on the proposed purchase. More months went by. Opposition to the purchase crystallized and grew stronger. It began to appear increasingly unlikely that approval for the purchase would be forthcoming.

The lawyer handling Mrs. Terhune's estate decided that he could wait no longer. On December 1, 1965, Sunnybank's remaining 9.6 acres were sold to a Pompton Lakes real estate developer who soon announced that he would divide the property into ten lakeside lots. On one of them he would construct a home for himself; he would sell the other lots with the proviso that the homes erected on them must fall into the price range of $75,000 to $100,000. It would be, he promised, one of the most beautiful residential areas in New Jersey.

And what of the Terhunes and their memories? The developer stated that somewhere on the site he would install a marker to inform posterity that this once had been Sunnybank. His plans for the disposition of Lad's grave and the burial places of the other collies were not announced, but it was assumed by local residents that the remains of the dogs would be exhumed, since their presence was not exactly conducive to a luxurious lakeside residential development.

The announcement of the plans to divide Sunnybank was almost a precise confirmation of Terhune's sad prophecy thirty years before that his beloved home would someday be cut up into "attractive lake shore residential sites." It now would fade into an all-encompassing suburbia and would cease to exist, except in the descriptive passages left by its long-dead owner and in the memories of those who loved his stories.

But what had not been taken into account by the developer and by many others who had given up The Place for lost was the passionate feeling for this small tract of land inculcated by Terhune in his many loyal readers. Now, in a dramatic fashion that the old collie man would have relished, they went into action.

Terhune admirers in the Wayne-Pompton Lakes area spread the word about the threat to Sunnybank. Dog magazines and collie club publications passed on the warning. Then the response began coming in. It was not a torrential flood of protest or anything quite so spectacular, but rather a steady flow of anguished pleas to officials of Wayne Township to "Save Sunnybank!"

Local newspapers took up the fight. One of the leading campaigners was Mrs. Evelin Armstrong Struble who, under the pen name of Susan Royal, wrote many articles about Terhune and Sunnybank for a weekly newspaper in the area. "The problem of what to do with Sunnybank," Mrs. Struble wrote in May, 1966, "is no longer a local matter. Its fate concerns all of Bert's readers from near and far. Readers who want to see the estate preserved in his memory. School children write their pleas for its preservation. They take polls to obtain public opinion. They offer their help in cleaning up the grounds."

Spurred on by the newspaper stories, other Terhune admirers began joining the campaign to save Sunnybank. Local people formed a group called "Citizens for Sunnybank Restoration." The State of New Jersey was persuaded to list Sunnybank officially as a historical site with the hope that this might encourage financial aid from large foundations.

A devoted Terhune admirer in nearby Paramus, New Jersey, Mrs. Claire Leishman, began trying to drum up national support. She concentrated on collie people, urging them through dog publications to rally to the cause.

Letters from Terhune admirers throughout the country were coming in, begging, pleading that Sunnybank not be abandoned. Many letters came from children born years after Terhune's death and decades after his stories were written. The emotional letters showed that the magic of Terhune's writing had not faded with the years.

Wrote one teen-age girl in Oklahoma: "I love Sunnybank as I love no other place in the world. Although I have never seen it with my own eyes, I have seen it a billion times with my heart."

The campaign finally began to have some effect on Wayne officials, one of whom was Mayor Edward Sisco who, years before, had been playing hookey from school to roam Sunnybank, was caught by a furious Terhune, and then invited to stay to dinner and meet the collies. The Wayne councilman whose district included Sunnybank, Edward Feddema, was so moved by the renewed outpouring of interest that he resolved to make a new attempt to see if the township could purchase the old estate. He decided that the most feasible approach was a plan to transform Sunnybank into a park. That way it could be of current use to the citizens of the township and hopefully also would serve as a continuing memorial to the author who had lived there.

The Wayne Council began new discussion of the possibilities and soon the tide turned in favor of the new proposal. The real estate developer made strong protest over the move to deprive him of his acquisition. Despite his opposition, however, Wayne Township began condemnation proceedings with the purpose of designating Sunnybank as a township park. A court battle was threatened, but eventually an agreement was reached with the developer; with the assistance of state park development funds, which paid half the cost, Wayne Township purchased Sunnybank from him. The final vote by the council came on April 19, 1967, with six of the nine members voting in favor of the proposal to buy the estate for $145,240.93. Since then, federal funds also have been made available for the project which, when added to money provided by the State of New Jersey, required Wayne Township to pay only about $9,000 of the total price.

In October, 1967, the estate was dedicated by Wayne Township as the Terhune-Sunnybank Memorial Park. The problem now was what to do with it. Some disgruntled citizens who had steadfastly opposed purchase of the land now bitterly fought any attempt to appropriate more public funds for improvement and repair of the property.

Township maintenance men, assisted by volunteers, cut the grass and began removing the weeds and underbrush. The little collie graveyard behind the house was tidied up. The quiet old estate was the scene of an art show, a concert, a dog show and exhibit.

Meanwhile the loyal Terhune fans turned their thoughts to the fate of the famous house. Their hope was that it could become a Terhune museum, with at least a few rooms restored and much of the Terhune memorabilia on display. The building was by now in deplorable shape and, along with the other structures at Sunnybank, had been condemned and sealed shut. There were no public funds available for restoration.

Again the Terhune followers went into action. Claire Leishman set up the Terhune Sunnybank Memorial Fund to raise money on a national scale, while the Citizens for Sunnybank Restoration canvassed the local area. The New Jersey state architect inspected the tottering house and said that it could be saved, but the cost would be $250,000; Wayne officials estimated it at $350,000. Frantic efforts began to seek the funds.

At this point, the almost fairytale-like story of the saving of Sunnybank by Terhune's passionate admirers begins to sag back into the hard confines of reality. The national fund-raising campaign, hampered by a lack of publicity outside collie circles, did not go terribly well. Some of the collie people gave very generously. A well-known collie breeder in California quickly pledged $1,000 to the drive. But most of the gifts were small ones. And there were still, as with the Midwest collie club mentioned previously, pockets of resistance to giving anything at all to honor so controversial a man. A national collie magazine, *Collie Cues,* devoted a great deal of space to the campaign and other canine publications helped, but the total amount of money received rose very slowly. In all, over the years, something over $8,000 was contributed to the campaign, far short of the amount needed to save the building.

Meanwhile, Wayne officials grew more and more alarmed at the perilous condition of the building, which was becoming ever more fragile and decayed. Neighborhood kids could not resist exploring it and intruders occasionally lived in the house until they were discovered, having broken away the plywood covering doors and windows. Plaster walls and ceilings were ripped apart. Stair rails and fireplace mantles were torn away. On a wall of the famous living room, one of the invaders had written: "This place is almost dead already!"

Charles W. Kelly, head of Wayne's Department of Parks and Recreation, knew that he could not much longer forestall the destruction of the house, though he, too, had hoped it could somehow be saved as a museum. But township officials were convinced that Wayne would become the target of a large damage suit as soon as someone was seriously injured in the old building and that it was only a matter of time. Knowing the house's demolition was imminent, Kelly began carefully photographing and measuring the rooms of the house with the hope that some sort of limited replica might be built in the future, to serve as the museum everyone wanted at Sunnybank.

Finally the decision to destroy the house could be delayed no longer. Once made, it was quickly put into effect. On April 29, 1969, a dreary, overcast day, the 100-year-old house was bulldozed into oblivion. The tools of modern housewrecking found much of their work already accomplished for them by nature's wreckers—piercing wistaria vines and wind and winter's ravages. The house crumbled easily; there seemed no more point to resistance. The will to live was gone. The staunch old house was destroyed in just fifteen minutes.

By a piece of consummate irony, the demolition of the loved house had an unexpected audience. A troop of Brownies from Hohokus,

New Jersey, had come that day to visit the Sunnybank they had heard so much about. The children watched with a mixture of horror and fascination as the house crumbled into dust.

Also torn down the same day were the barn and the flimsy old gazebo. The barn had no foundation and inspectors had found its bottom to be completely rotted away. The gatehouse was allowed to remain for the time being and the old caretaker and his wife stayed on as employees of the township. A year later, the caretaker died, his wife left, and the gatehouse also was destroyed.

The loss of the famous house deeply saddened the Terhune fans who had fought to save it, but they immediately turned their thoughts to the future of Sunnybank itself. The Citizens for Sunnybank group appropriated $1,500 for the development of a master plan for the park. The ambitious plan called for woodland conservation areas, the reinstating of the Garden from Everywhere and the lush rose walk, a bird sanctuary, bandstand, boat basin and ramp, and—perhaps most important—the building of a park center that would offer a meeting room for local groups and also would include a faithful restoration of the two most famous rooms in Sunnybank House: the L-shaped living room and the music room. The plan, which would cost an estimated $210,000, was accepted by Wayne Township and renewed efforts began to raise funds to implement it. The efforts, with some help from the APT Foundation, still continue.

During 1971, the money provided by contributors helped pay for a series of improvements at The Place: stonecutters recarved and reset the headstones of the dog graves, making the original letters deeper and also washing the stones to restore their original color. The federally funded Green Thumb Project of the New Jersey Farmers Union supplied men to work on landscaping projects. The Pines Lake Women's Club paid for the rebuilding of the masonry around the lily pond and also built a new gazebo, in a slightly different location from the old one. The old puppy yard was restored by the Terhune Sunnybank Memorial Fund, and Mrs. Leishman also began accumulating any available Terhune memorabilia that might be saved for the day when the park center would serve as an APT museum. Among the acquisitions were most of Terhune's old dog trophies.

On October 8, 1972, a little more than two months before the one hundredth anniversary of Albert Payson Terhune's birth, several hundred persons gathered at Sunnybank to celebrate his centennial and to dedicate a monument to Terhune erected by the Terhune Sunnybank Memorial Fund.

Visitors from all over the country still stop at Sunnybank. Not, of course, the tremendous numbers that came during Terhune's prime, but a steady stream of still-loyal readers, particularly in the summers. A friend who visits The Place often says that she usually finds some fresh flowers on Lad's grave.

The rest of Sunnybank, the land across the road and up the hill, is going the way of civilization. Until very recently, under its succession of owners since the late 1930s, the land across the road had remained very much as Bert Terhune had described it—woods and meadows. But in 1974 a sign was erected, proclaiming that two-third acre building sites were available. By the summer of 1975, streets circled through the tract and many of the big trees had been removed.

Albert Payson Terhune has been dead for more than three decades. It has been about forty years since the last of his dog stories was written. Yet he remains a figure of controversy—the recipient still of abuse and love, as when he was alive.

The November 7, 1971, *The New York Times Book Review* carried a scathing attack on Terhune, in which Professor Gaddis Smith of Yale University accused Terhune of bigotry, snobbery, economic royalism, hatred for the disadvantaged, and numerous other crimes. The article was based on a superficial knowledge of Terhune's writings. A few of the charges had some basis in fact—such as the accusation that Terhune relied much too heavily on gory violence in his tales—but most of them were exaggerated and many could be directly refuted.

Terhune hardly was a paragon. He shared the patronizing attitude toward Blacks held by almost all of white America in those times and his feelings sometimes crept into his writings. But there is no evidence that he was a person of violent prejudice as alleged by the Yale historian. His behavior was inconsistent: in 1927 a newspaper article written by Terhune contained a comment that could be considered mildly anti-Semitic. Yet Jewish residents of Pompton Lakes liked and admired him and never considered him to be prejudiced. One of his closest friends was Henry Grah Hershfield, a Jewish real estate man and one-time mayor of the village. A local newspaperman described Terhune as "a man of forceful character and a liberal during days when the area was emerging from bigotry, prejudice and provincialism." The evidence indicates that he was no bigot, but he was a man of strange contradictions.

In 1932 Terhune received an award from the Mussolini government in Italy for articles he had written about that country. It was a time when many Americans looked upon the Mussolini régime with benign approval. Hitler had not yet come to power and the horrors of fascism were not readily apparent to most Americans. There is no evidence of which I am aware that Terhune wrote further about Italy or that he ever wrote anything approvingly of Hitler.

The criticism of Terhune, though it still surfaces from time to time, is rare now. Much more apparent are the gentle messages of approval and love that still come to him from today's children. ·

The letters no longer come in the torrents of old, but they do come steadily, a few each month. They are carefully answered by Barbara Backer, the wife of a Pompton Lakes postal worker, or by Claire Leishman of the Terhune Sunnybank Memorial Fund.

Most of the children have only recently discovered the Terhune stories and they are not aware he is dead. They write to praise his work and to ask questions about his collies and sometimes to ask if a puppy can be purchased. They write with a child's honesty and passion: "I have just finished your book. It is the best book I have ever read

. . . even though Lad is dead I love him he truly was the greatest dog on this earth! If you get this letter I have a longing that if you find time PLEASE write to me!"

Some of them understand that Terhune is gone, yet still they write, addressing their letters "Dear Sirs" and saying things like: "I thank him for sharing with me his Great novels. This letter is not written with all the neatness and punkuation and spelling but it comes deep from my heart and expresses something a proper written letter could never. Mr. Terhune will always be idolized by me and the dogs in his novels will always hold a spot in my heart."

The letters prove that so long as the words of Bert Terhune are there to be read, the enchantment will be there too. And once a child reads those words, they will be remembered always with joy and love. Any writer would be proud to leave behind such a gift.

37

The Visitor walked slowly through the gathering night up the driveway of Sunnybank. The winter sun was gone now, down behind the Ramapo hills across the lake. The fading of the light caused the coldness to move stealthily across the blurred line from bearable to unbearable. The absence of the sun took the starch out of the will: to combat the freezing air was no longer a worthy battle. Winter is the inexorable winner in darkness. Now was the time to flee the cold.

The night seemed to set in upon Sunnybank with a finality, a sense of triumph. The Visitor realized that the dark seemed all-victorious because it was unopposed. The Place was shrouded in the thickening gloom—it bore not a single light. The houses to north and south were too far off among the trees to be more than distant pinpoints of lighted windows. Behind him, to the west, was only the ice-pocked lake, threatening in its silent blackness.

Only the trail of headlights and red brake lights moving silently over the streets on the other side of the lake afforded a sense of life and movement and warmth. But they were so far away that they seemed the tracings of creatures on a distant, dark planet. Now and again the diesel roar of a heavy truck broke the freezing silence, from the distant village or from the road up above. The sounds never seemed to impinge on the heavy-hanging silence here in the deadness of Sunnybank.

The Visitor paused on the unused driveway and looked about him. For one last time he studied this sylvan tomb of trees and grass and rotting wood that once had been a paradise for one man and one woman and a few animals. The night wind off the lake shivered the oaks once more and the trees seemed almost to cry out with grief. The old house now was just a dark shape against the clear western sky as it turned from pale blue to the last weak whiteness that momentarily holds off the night.

This place of life and raucous dog voices had become only an empty place among the oaks, beside the water of the lake. The day had permitted memories and fantasies of miraculous returns, but now, The Visitor saw, came the truth of night. The sunlight had allowed illusion; the darkness revealed. And what it revealed was absence. This was the saddest of all places, The Visitor knew. For it had known love and now, without it, no longer had life but merely continued to exist.

The Visitor gathered his coat about his neck as he shivered. His feet were solid blocks of unfeeling. He found himself, as he climbed the last yards of the hill, thinking more and more about his own warm, bright home and the family that awaited him there. Sunnybank's hold on him was ebbing once again and he was returning to the world. The spell of The Place was dimming, suffocated by the truths of the night.

For the thousandth time since he had arrived here, in the morning of this now-fading day, The Visitor tried to understand why. Why had he come, what had drawn him here? Why did others feel the same draw? Why was an unimportant writer, as measured by almost any literary standard, able to take the emotions of so many readers and hold them in a grasp that defied time and the grave? Why did mature people, busy with the activities of their own lives, allow themselves to be lured here to this place of aching loneliness in order to remember a long-dead writer and his dogs?

There seemed almost a mystical quality to this return to Sunnybank. Was *there a divine joke in all this—a laughing God toying with simple-minded people? Or was there some transcendent message involved, a song of reassurance and hope? Was Sunnybank a metaphor for the world: a sanctuary of tranquility, virtue, and innocence in the midst of our time's corrupting complexity of technology, noise, violence, and cold indifference?*

Perhaps it is all a debate in aesthetics. Who are the great writers, The Visitor wondered, as he climbed the final slants of the turning driveway underneath the dark hillside oaks. Our intellectual mentors—the critics and the scholars—proclaim that certain names be worshipped. And most readers dutifully pay homage to those anointed monarchs of the printed word, obediently accepting their claims to greatness. Yet so often these readers struggle in bewilderment—seeking in vain for a noble theme, an epic narrative, or even one or two moments of coherence, in the opaque, almost impassable volumes that seem more and more often to be celebrated and honored.

And then there are the writers like Terhune. The "popular" writers—the word often is said in a tone that is both scornful and patronizing. The scholars ignore him and he is not to be found in histories of American literature. He never claimed greatness, nor did others claim it for him. Yet thousands upon thousands of readers were thrilled by him, moved by him, and remember him. Most of all, remember him. Year after year passes, decade after decade. Yet his words still live. And the people who read those words so long ago still come here to walk among the oaks and remember.

But what if somewhere there is The Ultimate Literary Critic and he (or she) decrees that Terhune's work is the real *literature of our time—these simple animal stories that delight the childlike mind. Ah, what a wild, nasty, delicious joke it would be!*

The Visitor ached with cold and loneliness as he climbed to his car. Perhaps he was only a tasteless Philistine, but he knew that Herzog never could have brought him to this dark hillside, nor Gatsby, nor the other giants of literary propriety. Only a big, tousled man with a loud voice who uttered some kind of muted incantation amidst the pages of his production-line books. It was that magic that had drawn him here, to walk for a freezing day among the ghosts at Pompton Lake.

What was this strange quality that had kept Sunnybank alive for him and had brought him here, after so long, on this day? The Visitor had no answer. But he wished, fervently, that somewhere there might be new children who would carry on this unexplainable love for Sunnybank that he had known since his own childhood. So that there always would be someone to remember the old glories here and the stories written about them.

The Visitor's journey was over now. It was time to leave.

He stood at the gate, then turned back toward the lake to take a last long look down the hillside. Sunnybank was all purple and black—even the towering oaks were merging into the night. The Place had returned once again to the custody of its spirits.

The Visitor, his hands painful with the cold, opened the door of the car, got in, and started the engine. He knew he would have to come back again some day. There was a part of him in this place. There always would be.

Then, with no further glances back, he drove slowly out the stone gate and down the sloping highway toward the faraway lights.

Index